Bakery Food Manufacture and Quality

Water Control and Effects

Bakery Food Manufacture and Quality

Water Control and Effects

STANLEY P. CAUVAIN
and
LINDA S. YOUNG

Campden & Chorleywood Food Research Association
Chipping Campden
Gloucester, UK

**Blackwell
Science**

© 2000 by
Blackwell Science Ltd
Editorial Offices:
Osney Mead, Oxford OX2 0EL
25 John Street, London WC1N 2BL
23 Ainslie Place, Edinburgh EH3 6AJ
350 Main Street, Malden
 MA 02148 5018, USA
54 University Street, Carlton
 Victoria 3053, Australia
10, rue Casimir Delavigne
 75006 Paris, France

Other Editorial Offices:

Blackwell Wissenschafts-Verlag GmbH
Kurfürstendamm 57
10707 Berlin, Germany

Blackwell Science KK
MG Kodenmacho Building
7–10 Kodenmacho Nihombashi
Chuo-ku, Tokyo 104, Japan

First published 2000

Set in 10/12pt Times
by DP Photosetting, Aylesbury, Bucks
Printed and bound in Great Britain by
MPG Books Ltd, Bodmin, Cornwall

The Blackwell Science logo is a trade mark of
Blackwell Science Ltd, registered at the United
Kingdom Trade Marks Registry

DISTRIBUTORS

Marston Book Services Ltd
PO Box 269
Abingdon
Oxon OX14 4YN
(*Orders:* Tel: 01235 465500
          Fax: 01235 465555)

USA
Blackwell Science, Inc.
Commerce Place
350 Main Street
Malden, MA 02148 5018
(*Orders:* Tel: 800 759 6102
              781 388 8250
          Fax: 781 388 8255)

Canada
Login Brothers Book Company
324 Saulteaux Crescent
Winnipeg, Manitoba R3J 3T2
(*Orders:* Tel: 204 837-2987
          Fax: 204 837-3116)

Australia
Blackwell Science Pty Ltd
54 University Street
Carlton, Victoria 3053
(*Orders:* Tel: 03 9347 0300
          Fax: 03 9347 5001)

A catalogue record for this title is available from
the British Library

ISBN 0-632-05327-5

Library of Congress
Cataloging-in-Publication Data

Cauvain, Stanley P.
    Bakery food manufacture and quality: water
  control and effects/Stanley P. Cauvain and
  Linda S. Young.
       p. cm.
    Includes bibliographical references and index.
    ISBN 0-632-05327-5
    1. Baked products. 2. Baking—Quality
  control. I. Young, Linda S. II. Title.
  TX552.15.C38 2000
  664'.752—dc21   99-049521

For further information on
Blackwell Science, visit our website:
www.blackwell-science.com

Contents

Preface

Water is an essential component of almost all of the foods that we consume, yet its presence may pass largely unnoticed. We derive considerable quantities of the water that we need to sustain our lives from this 'hidden' water in foods.

The original idea for this book came from the running of seminars on water activity in bakery products. Much is known about the contribution of water to food spoilage and how microbial shelf-life can be influenced by restricting water availability. After all, just like us, microorganisms need water to grow and flourish: restrict the availability of the water and you can restrict microbial spoilage.

The contribution of water to organoleptic and other bakery food qualities has also been studied and is largely appreciated. As with microbial growth, the availability of water can be used to explain some of the quality changes that were observed during product storage. The role of water as a plasticiser is becoming established and is being used to help explain product structure formation and quality changes during storage.

Despite the quantity of knowledge available on water in foods there seemed to be two problems: there is too little understanding or appreciation of the basic and unique properties of water; and while scientific texts on water in foods exist, there are no practical or technical treaties on the role of water in bakery foods. While the safety and quality of water for human consumption is a very important subject, it is not directly addressed in this book.

As with many books, the original idea was only part of the story. In putting together an outline for this book we realised that we too had failed to appreciate the underpinning role that water plays in the manufacture of bakery foods. Here was an ingredient that was essential to the quality of the baked product, but its level had undergone a radical change during the baking process. We knew that a higher level of water at the start of baking processes was important in achieving the required final product quality but it was only when we began thinking about this book that we realised just how important the relationship between starting and finishing water levels are.

After introducing water, its unique properties and the relevant basic concepts, the next few chapters of this book consider the role that water plays in the transition from ingredient formulation to baked product. In some ways, Chapters 2 to 4 might be described as 'baking from the point of view of the water', while the importance of water in the context of food safety, quality and shelf-life are considered in detail in Chapters 5 to 9.

In many ways water may called the 'neglected ingredient' in baking. There have been many books on the technology of baking in which the role of water has been relegated to what might be described as a 'supporting role'. But water has a much bigger part to play in baking than can be described in a few lines and we hope that this book will go some way to redressing the balance in favour of water so that it can take its rightful place as an 'essential' ingredient in baking as in life.

Stanley P. Cauvain
Linda S. Young

1 Water and its roles in baked products

Water is the most abundant compound on the earth. Over 60% of the surface of our planet is covered by the waters of the oceans and seas, and over large areas of the land we encounter water as precipitation (rain and snow) and in streams, rivers and lakes. Water is also found combined in rocks and minerals as water of hydration and crystallisation.

The essential role that water plays in supporting life, both plant and animal, is well appreciated (Hegarty, 1995). Without water, plants and animals cannot survive or grow. Even the senses of sight, smell, taste, hearing and balance all depend on water or wet surfaces. Almost all of the chemical, physical and biochemical reactions that are part of the thread of life depend on the presence of water, but often because we cannot 'see' water we do not fully appreciate its role. This is because the water is combined or bound in various forms with other compounds, for example about 75% of the total mass of the human body is water held within the matrix of the body structure; higher proportions of water are held within the structures of many plants.

This 'hidden' water together with added and 'visible' water is present in the many ingredients we use in the preparation of manufactured foods. After combining the various ingredients during food preparation the water that is present in the food formulation may be redistributed between components and again later during processing, especially the various forms of thermal processing that are part of baking. Such changes in the location of water and its availability for other physical, chemical and biochemical reactions make important contributions to the palatability of many bakery foods because of its contribution to structure formation, as shown for example by gluten formation in breadmaking (discussed in detail in Chapter 2).

THE COMPOSITION AND HEAT-RELATED PROPERTIES OF WATER

Perhaps because of its abundance in nature and its relative availability the special properties of water are often overlooked. Chemically water comprises two atoms of hydrogen combined with one atom of oxygen to give the compound formula familiar to us all, H_2O. Even though pure water is a compound of two gases at temperatures between 0°C and 100°C at standard pressure, it exists as a liquid. When the temperature falls below 0°C, pure water turns to the solid we call ice; when the temperature rises above 100°C it turns to the vapour we call steam. These transitions from one form to another are very important in the manufacture of baked products since we may use temperatures below 0°C to preserve foods or as an aid to delay processing, and we need to raise the temperature above 100°C in order to heat-set (bake) the majority of bakery foods.

Many compounds of a similar molecular size to that of water are gases rather than liquids at 20°C, and therein lies a clue to the special properties of water. It is not within the scope of this book to detail the nature of the bonding which may occur between the atoms in water, but we must recognise that because of its structure the electrostatic charges within the water molecule are not equally distributed. The oxygen nucleus has a positive charge of eight while the hydrogen nuclei each have positive charges of one, so that in the water molecule there is migration of the negative charge from the hydrogen nuclei in the direction of the oxygen nucleus. The uneven electronic charge causes the water molecule to behave as a weak dipole or 'molecular magnet' which attracts other water molecules. A three-dimensional structure forms in water because of these electrostatic charges based on *hydrogen bonding*, the existence of which contributes significantly to the ability of water to take part in many of the chemical reactions that are important in baking.

Each individual water molecule will have four nearest neighbours and such a distribution of water molecules leads to the formation of a tetrahedral structure. This systematic structure in water produces an X-ray diffraction pattern akin to that of crystalline structures, although the full crystalline structure is not completed until water turns to ice. In the case of ice, water molecules bond to form hexagonal rings which build up to give a 'cage-like' or 'porous' layered structure. When sufficient energy is applied to ice, for example by heating, it first melts to form water; with continued heating, the bonding between molecules is weakened and water changes to steam.

Water has a number of special properties which arise from its particular structure. It is only in water that the maximum potential for hydrogen bonding can be realised because of its equal and opposite pairs of positive and negative charges. As a consequence water has a much higher *specific heat capacity* (*see* Table 1.1) in comparison with other substances that are liquids at normal temperatures. This means that water can absorb large amounts of heat by comparison with other liquids for the same rise in temperature. The large quantities of heat required to raise the temperature of water make a significant contribution to the design of the heating and cooling processes commonly used in the manufacture of bakery products. These will be considered in more detail in Chapters 2 to 4. It also means that water plays a

Table 1.1   Specific heat capacities at 15°C.

Substance	Specific heat capacity at 15°C (kJ/g/°C)
water	4.19
acetic acid	1.96
ethyl alcohol	2.43
glycerol	2.36
propionic acid	2.34
invert syrup	1.98

significant role in temperature control during the preparation of batters and doughs (*see* Chapters 2 and 3).

Because of the presence of hydrogen bonding in water, part of any heat transmitted to water is used to break intermolecular bonds, leaving the remainder to increase the temperature by increasing the molecular kinetic energy. If we begin to heat pure water its molecular kinetic energy continues to increase and the temperature rises to 100°C. At this temperature a large supply of energy is required to break the mass of hydrogen bonds present in the water in order to vaporise it and turn it to steam. The transition from water to steam at 100°C requires considerable energy for no change in temperature and the heat required is described as *latent heat*. At 100°C we are considering the *latent heat of vaporisation*. The energy required for this transition from liquid to water vapour is much greater than would be needed for the same change to take place in the same mass of other liquids.

At the other end of the temperature scale, when cooling water we encounter another point at which the phenomenon of latent heat is observed: in this case it is at 0°C when water changes to ice and *latent heat of fusion* is involved.

It is possible for molecules in a solid to gain sufficient energy to make the direct transition from the solid to the vapour phase. This change is often referred to as *latent heat of sublimation*. It is encountered with wrapped products held in deep frozen storage where the water sublimes from the frozen product during storage to become a vapour which is then cooled and forms as 'snow' in the pack. Loss of water (ice) through sublimation is part of the process in frozen bakery products known as 'freezer burn' (*see* Chapter 4).

Generally, as a liquid cools to become a solid its density gradually increases as the temperature falls. However if we were to measure the density of water as it cools we would find that the density increases to reach a maximum at 4°C before falling slightly (i.e. becomes less dense) as the temperature of the water approaches 0°C. This property of water means that as its temperature falls below 4°C and approaches 0°C it expands to occupy a greater volume (*see* Fig. 1.1). The volume increase is about 9% for this change in temperature. This anomalous expansion is the reason why frozen pipes burst in winter when they are thawing and contributes to the cracking of rocks and other mineral based materials. It also accounts for why we can see water underneath the frozen surface of many ponds and why icebergs float. The effects of water expansion on freezing (cooling) and thawing (warming) also influences the quality of bakery products, for example in the production of frozen unbaked pies and bread doughs (*see* Chapter 4).

VAPOUR PRESSURE AND RELATIVE HUMIDITY

The molecules of a mass of water standing with its surface exposed in a closed container at a given temperature are in constant motion, and a number of them will have sufficient energy to escape into the atmosphere above the liquid surface. In the still conditions of a closed container, a similar number of molecules to those that have escaped return to the surface to rejoin the liquid and an equilibrium is reached (*see* Fig. 1.2). If the layer of water vapour molecules above the water is disturbed for any reason, such as by opening the container and exposing it to the atmosphere,

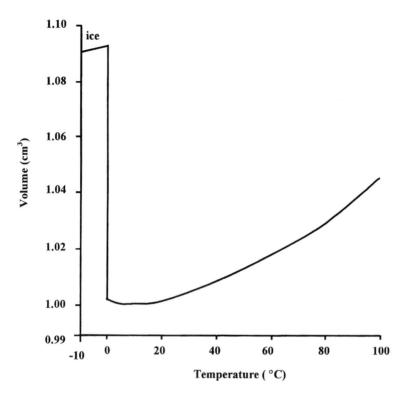

Fig. 1.1   Effect of temperature on water volume.

those vapour molecules that have sufficient energy to escape from the water mass may be swept away and the equilibrium of the system is disturbed. In such circumstances more water will evaporate from the liquid surface in order to try to restore the previous state of equilibrium; if this process continues for long enough, all of the water in the container will evaporate. Such dehydration processes can play a significant role in the manufacture of bakery products, e.g. proving and retarding (*see* Chapter 4), and can lead to unwanted losses in product quality.

The rate at which molecules escape from the water mass depends on a number of factors, including the temperature of the liquid and the movement of air across the

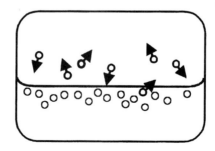

Fig. 1.2   Liquid and vapour equilibrium.

surface of the liquid. The higher the temperature of the liquid, the greater the energy of the molecules and the faster will be the rate of evaporation. The importance of air movement in controlling evaporation and dehydration processes can be readily appreciated by considering the example of wet washing hung on a line in the open air. If there is a breeze blowing, the washing will dry more readily than if the air is still, for a given temperature. In the bakery context, dehydration from air movement (exacerbated by other factors) is most commonly seen in the practice of retarding (holding doughs at refrigerated temperatures) when dehydration of dough pieces leads to the formation of a tough, dry skin on their surfaces (*see* Chapter 4). In order for water molecules to evaporate and try to restore equilibrium in an open container they must obtain heat (energy). The only source of heat is from within the remaining mass of water, and consequently as water molecules evaporate from the surface the temperature of liquid mass of water falls. It has been estimated that less than 2 g evaporating from 1 litre of water will reduce the temperature of the mass by 1°C.

Within a closed vessel containing water (or other liquids) in equilibrium with its vapour, that part of the pressure that may be attributed to bombardment by the vapour molecules is known as the *saturated vapour pressure* (SVP). SVP varies as the temperature changes, rising as the temperature increases (see Fig. 1.3). The abrupt end to the curve in Fig. 1.3 corresponds to critical conditions of temperature and pressure, and above this point there can be no liquid and no vapour pressure; in the case of pure water this temperature is 100°C – its boiling point. The sublimation of water from frozen products discussed above can occur because ice (like many other solids) at temperatures below 0°C has a vapour pressure, so that the curve does not end at zero.

Reference has been made to the potential adverse effects of evaporation of water from doughs at various stages of their processing. One of the driving forces for evaporation was identified as air movement across the surface of a liquid, or a dough or batter. This was the case where the liquid surface was exposed and the vapour

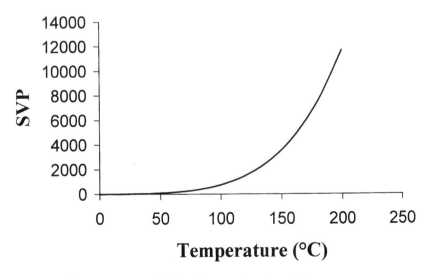

Fig. 1.3 Saturated vapour pressure (SVP) and temperature for water.

molecules could be carried away by the air movement. If the air is now held within a closed container so that it does not escape then full dehydration cannot occur. In baking there are many examples where we deliberately control the rate of evaporation from products in order to preserve product quality; for example, in proof where doughs are held in a closed box (*see* Chapter 4), and in packaging where the permeability of the film may be used to adjust product shelf-life (*see* Chapter 9).

For any given set of conditions we can measure the water vapour content of the air. This measurement is commonly referred to as the *humidity*, or *absolute humidity*, of the air and is given as a mass per unit volume, e.g. g per m³. Under a given set of conditions, a given volume of air can hold only a given mass of water vapour and the air is said to be *saturated*. If the temperature of the given volume of air is raised then it will be able to hold more water vapour; if it is lowered it will be able to hold a smaller mass and condensation can occur.

In the baking industry, the concept of *relative humidity* is commonly encountered. This may be defined as the ratio of a mass of water vapour present in a given volume of air to the mass which would be present if the sample were saturated, if the temperature and total pressure remain the same. Relative humidity (RH) is usually expressed as a percentage. An alternative definition of RH is the ratio of the *partial pressure* of the vapour present to the saturation vapour pressure at the same temperature, again expressed as a percentage.

Water is present in large quantities in many bakery intermediates and final products, and it is therefore possible to consider that they too have a relative humidity. If no evaporation occurred from any exposed surfaces, the RH would be uniform throughout the product. However, some surface evaporation does occur and the surface usually has a slightly lower RH than the centre. This RH gradient throughout the product means that water will gradually migrate from the centre to the outside of the product in order to try and restore equilibrium with the product atmosphere. If equilibrium cannot be achieved the products will continue to dry out, but only until the surrounding atmosphere becomes saturated. Thus in an enclosed system equilibrium is eventually reached, but if the volume of the enclosed space is large by comparison with the mass of available water then considerable dehydration of a product can occur. To minimise such moisture losses from products, it is necessary to increase the humidity of the air surrounding the products; in proving this will usually be done through the introduction of water vapour so that the difference in product RH and air RH is minimised (*see* Chapter 4).

Since the rate at which moisture will evaporate from a product is affected by the difference in RH between products and the surrounding atmosphere there are two ways in which moisture losses can be minimised in bakery products. The first is to raise the humidity of the atmosphere surrounding the product and has been commented on above in the context of proving. For baked and wrapped products, we are not usually in a position to raise the atmospheric humidity through the introduction of water vapour so we must turn to the potential of matching the product RH with that of the atmosphere. Usually the atmospheric humidity is lower than that within many bakery products so the action we must take is to lower product RH. To do this we may adjust the product formulation either by lowering added water or final moisture content, or adding materials that will lower the vapour pressure within the product. The principles that apply, and the techniques that can be used, are discussed in more detail in Chapters 5 to 8; at this stage it is sufficient to say that the quantity of a given material, its structure and its affinity for water, principally its solubility, are all important in establishing its ability to limit evaporation. The bakery technologist has not only to establish the effect of a material on evaporation rates in baked products, but must also appreciate the other functional properties that the material will contribute to the character of the final product. Examples of such challenges are discussed in some detail with respect to extension of product shelf-life in Chapter 9.

The measurement of RH is known as *hygrometry* and the instruments for measuring it are called *hygrometers*. The instruments used to make RH measurements take a number of different forms; those encountered frequently in the bakery context are the wet-and-dry bulb hygrometer and the hair hygrometer. These instruments are useful for establishing the RH in the atmosphere but would not be suitable for measuring the RH within a bakery product. In such cases specialised techniques must be used, and because of the importance of RH to bakery products appropriate techniques are described fully in Chapter 6.

WATER HARDNESS

Rainwater from the more remote parts of the earth is normally the purest form of water readily available. It contains in solution oxygen, nitrogen and carbon dioxide absorbed from the atmosphere, along with traces of ammonium nitrate which is formed by electrical discharges in the atmosphere. Other dissolved gases may be present, for example oxides of sulphur, which are derived from the combustion products of fossil fuels at levels that depend on geographical location (they will be higher around industrial areas and cities and lower in country areas). Particles of dust are suspended in rainwater droplets.

Rainwater as such is not commonly used in baking. More usually water is drawn from reservoirs and wells. Desalinated seawater may be used in some parts of the world. Rainwater falling on the ground will dissolve soluble rocks such as chalk (calcium carbonate); the resulting dissolved carbon dioxide forms a weak solution of carbonic acid, causing the pH to fall below 7.0. Water runs off the land into reservoirs, and percolates through the soil and rock layers to collect at the aquifer levels which supply wells. During its passage it continues to dissolve minerals, the quantity and type of which depend mainly on the geographical location.

The dissolved minerals confer special properties to the water, usually recognised by its ability to form (or not) a lather when agitated with soap (Brownsell *et al.*, 1989). Water that readily forms a lather is classified as *soft*, and that which does not as *hard*. The relative hardness of water is expressed in *degrees of hardness*, one degree of hardness being the equivalent of 10 ppm calcium carbonate in water. Hardness in water is due mainly to calcium and magnesium bicarbonates and sulphates. Hardness caused by bicarbonates can be removed by boiling and is usually referred to as *temporary*, while that arising from the sulphates cannot be removed by boiling and is therefore considered *permanent*.

Boiling hard water results in the thermal decomposition of the soluble bicarbonates with the resulting release of a water molecule and one of carbon dioxide, and the precipitation of the insoluble carbonates. This precipitation is most often seen as the 'furring' of heating elements in kettles and radiators in heating systems, which eventually leads to a loss of their efficiency. In the bakery hard water can lead to problems with water heaters in the steam generators used in provers and ovens where, along with the furring problem, there is a potential for spray nozzles to become blocked.

To avoid problems such as those described above, hard water can be softened without having to resort to boiling. The methods employed in water-softening lower the levels of calcium and magnesium salts but can result in an increase in the levels of soluble sodium salts, depending on the softening method used. One method is to add sodium carbonate, which results in the formation of insoluble calcium and magnesium salts which then precipitate out of solution. An alternative and common method is to use the principle of *ion exchange*. In this method the hard water passes down a column or through a cylinder filled with an ion exchange resin where the soluble calcium and magnesium ions are adsorbed on to the resin and 'exchanged' for soluble sodium ions, which then pass into the water.

IONISATION AND SOLUTIONS

As discussed above, the basic composition of pure water is two hydrogen atoms combined with one oxygen atom to form a neutral molecule. However, in the liquid state a few molecules are dissociated into ions, i.e. submolecular components that carry an electrical charge. It is generally considered that hydrogen ions (H^+) do not exist in the 'free' state but are attached to water molecules forming hydroxonium ions, H_3O^+. This situation can be described using the following equation:

$$2H_2O \rightleftharpoons H_3O^+ + OH^-$$

The equation is reversible, so that in water the number of molecules that dissociate equals the number re-associating, and so pure water remains neutral. Some hydrogen ions (H^+) can exist in water and at a given moment if we measure their concentration in pure water we would find that it would be in the order of 10^{-7} moles/litre, which equates to a pH of 7.0. (A *mole* is defined as the amount of a substance that contains as many elementary units as there are atoms in 0.012 kg (12 g) of carbon-12 – the most common isotope of carbon.)

The hydroxonium ion is able to form in water because of its dipolar character described above. If an ionic solid such as common salt – sodium chloride, NaCl (Na^+, Cl^-) – is placed in water, because of the dipolar character of water molecules they orient around the ions on the surface of the solid. There will be an attraction between ions with dissimilar charges greater than the attraction between the molecules in the crystal lattice of the solid and progressively ions become detached from the crystal matrix. Eventually the solid becomes dispersed throughout the water mass: it has dissolved. Many substances dissolve in water to form solutions, that is mixtures of water and other molecules. In many cases the dissociation of other molecules in water may be considered to lead to solutions containing given concentrations of hydrogen ions (H^+). The true situation is somewhat more complex than this simple model but is outside the scope of this book since we are not concerned with the intricate details of the chemical reactions in baking, rather in their influence on the technology of bakery products.

We can calculate the hydrogen ion concentration in a given solution based on a knowledge of the chemistry of its components, and relate this to the hydrogen concentration in water. The scale we use to compare hydrogen ion concentrations ranges from 1 to 14 and is commonly referred as the pH scale; water being neutral, as described above, is at the centre of the scale with a pH of 7.0. Values lower than pH 7.0 indicate solutions that are acidic; higher values indicate solutions that are alkaline (or basic). The pH scale is logarithmic, that is organised on a base of ten, so that differences of one pH unit indicate significant differences in hydrogen ion concentration (see Table 1.2).

Table 1.2 The pH scale.

Concentration of H^+ ions	pH
1 g per litre	0
1 g per 10 litres	1
1 g per 100 litres	2
	3
acid increasing in steps of 10	4
	5
	6
1 g per 10 million litres	7
	8
alkali increasing in steps of 10	9
	10
	11
	12
	13
17 g OH^- per litre	14

A true solution occurs when both the solvent and the solute break down into individual molecules, or ionise. They may be mixtures of one liquid with another, a liquid and a solid, or even a liquid and a gas. All three types of solution are encountered in the manufacture of baked products and often all three occur in the same baked product at the same time. Examples of solutions in baked products are discussed in detail in later chapters.

The dissociation of the two components of a solution into molecules or ions provides a means of differentiation between solutions and other forms of mixtures commonly encountered in baking. There are three main forms of mixture (each is discussed in more detail below:

- *Suspensions*, in which particles never ionise in the solvent. They are little affected by the pH of the solvent.

- *Colloids*, in which the particles are so finely divided and dispersed in the solvent that they are invisible to the naked eye. They are very sensitive to the pH of the solvent.
- *Emulsions*, in which materials are held as small droplets. They may be affected by pH.

Water is also a good solvent for substances that do not ionise but have a marked hydrogen bonding potential. Such substances are said to be *polar compounds* and include those which contain hydroxyl (OH), carboxyl (COOH), carbonyl (C=O) and amino (NH_2) groups. All of these groups occur in the ingredients that are commonly used in the manufacture of bakery products, and many play key roles in the formation of product structures and textures.

THE SOLUBILITY OF SOLIDS AND THEIR RECRYSTALLISATION

While many substances dissolve in water they cannot do so *ad infinitum*, that is as we add more and more of the substance a point is eventually reached when we will be able to see undissolved solid in the bottom of the container. At this point the solution is said to be *saturated*. The *solubility* of a substance is usually expressed in grams dissolved in the presence of excess solid in one litre of water. The solubilities of some typical bakery ingredients are given in Table 1.3. The solubility of a substance increases as the temperature of the water increases. A *supersaturated* solution is one that contains more of the dissolved substance than a saturated solution and is formed when a saturated solution cools or when the solvent evaporates.

Table 1.3   Solubility of bakery ingredients in water at 20°C.

Ingredient	Solubility (g/L)
salt	357
sugar (sucrose)	1790
dextrose	830
sodium bicarbonate	69

Crystalline substances, such as salt and sugar, have regular ordered structures. In the case of pure salt this structure takes the form of a cube. When crystalline substances dissolve in water they lose their ordered structure but may regain it if the solution is cooled or if some of the solvent evaporates. In such cases the dissolved substance may recrystallise. Many substances, for example sugar (Jones *et al.*, 1997), are manufactured and purified using processes which involve recrystallisation. Slow cooling favours the formation of large crystals of the dissolved substance and rapid cooling the formation of small ones. Even the formation of ice crystals, which occurs during the freezing of foods, will follow this pattern of events (*see* Chapter 4).

In the manufacture of bakery products, we are dealing with complex mixtures of many substances, so that we cannot expect the solubility processes to be as straightforward as those described above. Indeed if we add a simple mixture of only two soluble substances to water we will affect the amount of both that can now dissolve in the given quantity of water. The solubility of a given substance in a given solvent is reduced in the presence of other substances that are soluble in the same solvent. While the mass of the individual substances in the mixture does affect how much of each goes into solution, other factors come into play, not least being the molecular weight and ionic character of the substances concerned. In some cases, depending on the masses of solute and solvent, one substance is more likely to go into solution at the expense of the other and this may effectively lead to a displacement of the second substance which is then seen as a reduction in its solubility. Recrystallisation of the second substance may occur if the water level is further reduced, for example during baking.

Solution and recrystallisation are important processes in several stages of bakery product manufacture and make major contributions to final product quality. One important example, which will be discussed in more detail in all the chapters that follow, is sugar (sucrose), a common ingredient in cakes and other sweet bakery products. Some of the many functions of sugar which occur because it is soluble in water are:

- Contributes to product sweetness
- Dissolves in water to yield a sucrose solution, which affects starch swelling and gelatinisation during baking (*see* Chapter 3)
- Raises the boiling and lowers the freezing points of solutions (*see* Chapter 4)
- Affects product shelf-life after baking and reduces product spoilage (*see* Chapter 6)
- Helps control moisture movement during storage (*see* Chapter 7)

Should recrystallisation of sucrose occur in baked products it can lead to surface blemishes on cakes (*see* Fig. 1.4) or to 'gritty' eating qualities in creams and fillings. In the complex mixtures that characterise bakery products, sucrose solubility may be reduced by the presence of other soluble substances (*see* Chapters 6 and 7).

WATER OF CRYSTALLISATION

When hydrated ions crystallise from solution, they may carry with them *water of crystallisation*, that is water molecules that will be held within the crystalline matrix of the material. The water molecules are held within the crystalline matrix by forces that usually require a significant input of energy to release the water, for example, the blue crystals of copper sulphate actually consist of five molecules of water bound to one molecule of copper sulphate as shown by the formula $CuSO_4.5H_2O$. Following the application of heat to copper sulphate, four of the water molecules are released when the temperature reaches 100°C, while the last one is not lost until the temperature reaches 250°C.

An interesting example of recrystallisation associated with water in bakery

Fig. 1.4 Sucrose recrystallisation on the surface of a cake.

products is the formation of sucrose hydrate crystals seen as crystalline 'growths', 'craters' (Robb, 1983) or 'eruptions' on the surface of icings and other sucrose-based toppings, especially those which are frozen. Sucrose hydrates take the general form of 'needle-like' crystals, collections of which appear to grow in size during storage. At first the sucrose hydrate crystals appear as dull, grey spots on the surface but as the water content falls through evaporation the spots increase in size and appear to erupt from the surface. Young *et al.* (1951) studied such formations and showed that sucrose hydrate growth was inhibited as the storage temperature approached –34°C (–30°F) or when a portion of the sucrose was replaced by corn syrup, invert sugar or maltose. They considered that dextrose would not make a suitable hydrate inhibitor because of its potential for spontaneous crystallisation.

VAPOUR PRESSURE OF SOLUTIONS

Water boils when its saturated vapour pressure is equal to the prevailing vapour pressure. At any given pressure, the presence of a dissolved substance (solute) in pure water raises its boiling point above 100°C, as represented in Fig. 1.5. The temperature of the steam evolved from the solution, however, is still the temperature of the saturated steam at the prevailing atmospheric pressure. A simple explanation for the effect of a solute on boiling point is that those molecules at the surface of the solution are themselves unable to evaporate but hinder the escape of the water molecules from the solution.

The presence of a solute in water also affects the freezing point of the solution and depresses the freezing point of pure water below 0°C. The actual temperature at which the solution will freeze depends on the concentration of the solute. Practical evidence for the depression of the freezing point of water is provided by the action of spreading 'salt' on the roads in winter to prevent the formation of ice on their surfaces when the atmospheric temperature falls below 0°C. In baking, the depression of freezing point has a major impact on the quality of many intermediate and final baked products (*see* Chapter 4).

In a solution that undergoes cooling when the freezing point is reached, some of the water molecules form ice crystals and separate from the liquid. Thereafter during cooling the solute concentration in the solution increases until all of the water molecules have turned to ice and the ice crystals already formed become embedded in a matrix of much smaller crystals. At high concentrations the solute

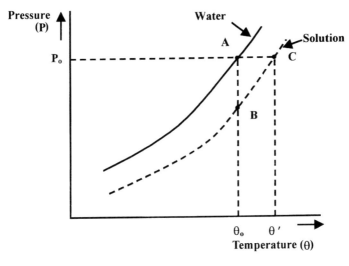

Fig. 1.5 **Effect of solute on boiling point.**

may crystallise first; in this case the residual liquid becomes less concentrated and the temperature at which the solution finally becomes solid (its freezing point) will change. The size of the ice crystals, the rate at which they form and their subsequent rate of thawing all play a role in determining the changes that may occur in frozen bakery products.

The attractive forces which exist between ionic and polar compounds play their part in lowering the saturated vapour pressure in a solution. The reduction in vapour pressure should depend on the proportion of water to solute, i.e. the concentration of solute per unit volume of water. This is provided that the solute remains in its molecular form in the water. As discussed above, many substances when they dissolve in water dissociate, i.e. the molecular bonds in the structure are weakened and broken, and this means that their effects on the saturated vapour pressure of a solution are greater than would be predicted solely from their concentration effect. Several ingredients used in baking, for example salt, fall into this category, and have significant effects on manufacturing processes and the quality of baked products. The effects of solute concentration and differences in their nature on the saturated vapour pressure within a baked product play a key in determining the shelf-life of that product, and are discussed in more detail in Chapter 6.

OSMOTIC PRESSURE

If a solute is added to water held in a container from one end of the container, the solute will gradually diffuse throughout the water; conversely, water will diffuse throughout the solute so that in time the two become intimately mixed, even if they are not shaken or stirred. The existence of life depends on the controlled movement of solutes, whether in true solution or suspension, and the segregation and organisation of solutes. In plant and animal cells the movement of water and solutes in and out of the cells is essential to processes of life.

The cell walls of plant and animal cells consist of a porous membrane that surrounds and contains all of the essential components for its particular function in life. The cells are many and varied in form but all require water to some degree to remain viable (alive); they obtain the necessary water through the porous membrane. The process by which water moves in and out of plant and animal cells is known as *osmosis*. It may be defined as 'the process of diffusion of a solvent (e.g. water) through a semi-permeable membrane from a solution of low concentration to one of a higher concentration'.

When a cell is immersed in a solution which has a different composition to that within the cell, a pressure gradient is set up across the membrane, known as the *osmotic pressure*. This effect can be observed by fixing a sheet of cellulose film tightly across one end of a thistle-shaped funnel attached to a long glass tube. A quantity of sugar solution is placed in the funnel part of the arrangement, inverted and placed in a container of water, as shown in Fig. 1.6. After a short while the pressure gradient across the film causes the sugar solution to move up the glass tube. In this example the cellulose film acts like a cell membrane, and while it is sufficiently impermeable to prevent the sugar solution being lost (in this case from the funnel) it is not sufficiently impermeable to prevent the movement of water. This is because the movement of water molecules is much greater than that of the dissolved sugar and they therefore have a much greater chance of finding and passing though a pore in the membrane. The faster the molecules move the more likely they are to pass through the membrane; in practice we can increase the rate of movement by raising the temperature of both solution and cell.

The most common example of osmosis in the bakery environment is the use of bakers' yeast in fermented products. A key role for bakers' yeast, *Saccharomyces cerevisiae*, is the conversion of simple sugars to yield ethyl alcohol and carbon

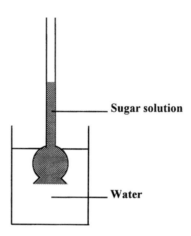

Fig. 1.6 Principles of osmotic pressure.

dioxide, the latter being required for the aeration of bread doughs (Cauvain, 1998). It is the selective permeability of the membrane with regard to solutions that controls the movement of nutrients into and the release of carbon dioxide out of the cell. The different forms of yeast and descriptions of their functionality and applications in baking can be obtained elsewhere (Williams & Pullen, 1998).

GASES IN SOLUTION

Gases are only partially miscible with liquids, and the mass of a gas that will dissolve in water depends on the nature of the gas, the temperature and the pressure of the gas in contact with water.

In baking we are interested in the so-called 'neutral' gases, that is those gases which do not dissociate to form ions in solution, including nitrogen and oxygen. Such gases are only slightly soluble in water. Strictly speaking, the liquid in doughs and batters is a complex mixture of at least salt and sugar solutions but this has only a limited effect on the solubility of neutral gases. Thus these gases tend to be present in water more in suspension than solution, but nevertheless they play a significant role in determining the quality of baked products. For example, nitrogen gas bubbles provide the gas bubble nuclei that are essential to expansion of fermented doughs in the prover and during the early stages of baking (Cauvain, 1998), and oxygen provides a necessary component for the oxidation processes involved with ascorbic acid (Williams and Pullen, 1998).

An essential gas in the formation of the structure of baked products is carbon dioxide derived from fermentation by yeast or evolved from the action of a suitable food acid on sodium bicarbonate (Thacker, 1997). Unlike nitrogen or oxygen, carbon dioxide is readily soluble in water (shown in Table 1.4). The solubility of gases in water increases as the temperature falls, but the solubility increase for carbon dioxide is far greater than for nitrogen or oxygen, a fact which has significant implications for the production of retarded and frozen fermented doughs (*see* Chapter 4).

In baking processes the carbon dioxide gas that is evolved continues to go into solution until that solution is saturated and thereafter any further carbon dioxide produced comes out of solution to inflate any other gas bubbles that are present in the dough or batter matrix (*see* Chapters 2 and 3). As the temperature of the matrix is raised during baking, the release of carbon dioxide from solution accelerates. Increases in atmospheric pressure increase the amount of carbon dioxide that will

Table 1.4 Solubility of gases in water.

Gas	Solubity (cm^3/L)	
	at 28°C	at 0°C
nitrogen	14	23
hydrogen	17	22
oxygen	27	49
carbon dioxide	650	1650

dissolve in water. Aerated waters and other drinks contain carbon dioxide gas held in solution at pressure above atmospheric so that when the pressure is released by opening the bottle bubbles of gas are seen to rise to the surface as continuous streams.

SUSPENSIONS

When a finely ground solid is shaken with a liquid in which it is insoluble in a container, the solid particles will remain floating, or suspended for a while before settling. Whether the particles float or sink depends mainly on their density. Those less dense than the liquid they are mixed with will float, while those that are more dense will sink. Particles that are more dense than the liquid settle at different rates with variations in particle size, the larger ones sinking faster than the small ones. Small particles take longer to sink because they have a large surface area compared with their weight and have to 'brush past' the liquid molecules to reach the bottom of the container. The greater surface area of the small particles increases the friction between the particle and liquid molecules, and thus slows down the descent of the particles.

The separation of insoluble materials from suspensions also depends on there being no interaction between the particles and the suspending liquid. Some materials may not truly go into solution in water but may form weak bonds with water molecules, which will increase considerably the length of time for which the material will remain suspended. This can be observed when flour and water are shaken together: the mixture will retain its 'milky' appearance for many hours because of hydration of the proteins and starch. When the size of particles of many materials is made very small it possible to produce a *colloidal suspension* (*see below*).

The rate at which and degree to which materials come out of suspension depend not only on the density of the particles but also on the density of the liquid. When materials go into solution in water the density of that solution will be different from that of water alone. This change will also affect the rates of separation from a suspension. For example, dissolving salt in water increases its density. In some seas, e.g. the Dead Sea, the concentration of salt increases the density to such an extent that the human body, which would normally sink in pure water, can float without the need for swimming motions.

COLLOIDAL SUSPENSIONS

The forces that lead to a material dissolving in water can also operate on large molecules or molecular aggregates which would be too large to form a true solution. Such materials are known as *colloids*. Many of the substances that are part of living organisms are colloids, and there are many examples associated with the manufacture of bakery products. For example, colloids are part of the coagulation, dispersion and stabilising processes associated with the egg albumen proteins in the manufacture of meringues, cakes and some confectionery fillings.

In a simple two-phase colloidal system, one of the components is dispersed throughout the other in the form of small particles or droplets. The substance forming the small particles is said to be in the *dispersed phase* while the other component of the system is known as the *dispersing medium*. In order to have a colloidal solution, the dispersed phase must be insoluble in the dispersing medium.

There are two classes of colloidal systems that are of particular interest in the study of bakery products: lyophobic (solvent-fearing) and lyophilic (solvent-loving). When water is the dispersing medium it is more common to refer to the solvent-fearing system as 'hydrophobic' (water-fearing) and to the solvent-loving system as 'hydrophilic' (water-loving). There are a number of potential dispersing media used in the manufacture of bakery products, but water is the main one encountered and the one of concern in this book.

The colloidal particles in a lyophobic colloidal system show no tendency to combine chemically with the dispersing medium, or to absorb it, but they may carry positive or negative electrical charges. When water is the dispersing medium the electrical charge originates from the adsorption of hydrogen ions (H^+), or may be attributed to hydroxyl ions (OH^-) adsorbing on to the colloidal particles. Which of these two ions is adsorbed depends on the nature of the substance of which the colloidal particles are composed, and in complex mixtures more than one component may become charged and not always with the same charge sign. Without electrical charges a lyophobic colloidal system cannot exist.

Adsorption plays an important part in determining the properties of a colloidal system. If a solute is introduced into a mixture of two solvents which themselves do not mix (e.g. oil and water), the concentration of the solute at the interface between the two solvents will affect the energy relationship between the two solvents and the stability of the total system. In lyophobic systems adsorption is responsible for the adherence of ions to the solid colloidal particles.

HYDRATION

Lyophilic colloidal systems are characterised by the fact that the dispersed phase shows an affinity for the dispersing medium. In the case of water the colloidal particles are hydrated. The colloidal particles of a lyophilic colloid may carry electrical charges, although some pure lyophilic colloids are stable even when uncharged. The sign of a charge on a lyophilic colloid depends more on the environment than the nature of the colloid. Where the media has an excess of hydrogen ions (H^+) and is therefore acidic in nature, lyophilic colloids are often positively charged; in alkaline environments (excess of OH^- ions), they are often negatively charged. The most important factor in the stability of a lyophilic colloid is the layer of the dispersion medium adhering to each particle.

Many hydrophilic colloidal systems occur naturally. Egg albumen has already been mentioned; another which occurs in bakery environments arises from the use of gelatine as a stabiliser. The hydration of wheat proteins and starch (and other cereal starches) during dough and batter mixing is a very important example and essential to the manufacture of some classes of baked goods (e.g. bread and cakes); it will be considered in more detail in Chapters 2 and 3.

WATER AS A PLASTICISER

The principles of water dynamics, such as water activity (*see* Chapter 6), have been used alone for many years to explain the role of water in determining the quality of baked products, but in the last two decades considerable progress has been made in the understanding of the dynamic behaviour of foods with the realisation that many undergo a 'glass-like' dynamic transition. The terms now commonly used to describe the physical state of a polymer are *'rubbery'* and *'glassy'*. The polymer is more mobile in the rubbery state than in the glassy state, where the viscosity of the system is much higher and the mobility of all molecules is severely restricted.

In the transition from a rubbery to a glassy state, the mobility of water in foods is significantly reduced, i.e. the water becomes more 'bound' in the food matrix. Now it is more common to refer to *glass transitions* in foods and to describe many of the changes in the textural properties of foods at different temperatures in terms of their *glass transition temperatures* (T_g). However, it is important to recognise that the descriptors 'rubbery' and 'glassy' refer to the physical state of the system rather than the texture or eating quality of the foods.

The concept of water as a plasticiser in bakery foods has been borrowed from polymer science. Sears and Darby (1982) defined a plasticiser as "a material incorporated in a polymer to increase the polymer's workability, flexibility, or extensibility", clearly a definition consistent with the role of water in the manufacture of baked goods. For example, in the mixing and manipulation of fermented doughs as discussed in Chapter 2.

The manufacture and qualities of baked goods owe much to the special properties of the proteins and starch that are present in wheat flour. Details of these special properties can be found elsewhere (Bent, 1997; Stauffer, 1998), but in summary they are the ability of a substantial portion of the proteins present to form a gas-retaining protein matrix in fermented goods, known as gluten (Cauvain, 1998), and the changes in the crystalline structure of the starch granules that occur during baking, known as gelatinisation (Street, 1991). In the transformations which are key to the formation of the different structures we encounter in baked products, the plasticising and solvent roles of water are essential. It is not only as a plasticiser and solvent in the formation of baked products that water plays a key role, but also as a plasticiser in baked product changes that occur post-baking. The qualities of all baked products change during storage, and many of the changes result in a loss of product quality commonly embraced in the general term *'staling'*. Such changes are discussed in detail in Chapter 5.

Gregory (1998), commenting on the increased understanding of the dynamic behaviour of proteins, considered that "The impact of this new understanding of proteins as plasticised polymers in the food sciences has been little short of revolutionary...". Undoubtedly there has been considerable progress in showing how the underlying properties of bakery foods are influenced by their rubbery or glassy state, as shown by Levine and Slade (1990), but the application of such fundamental ideas has yet to reach the practical level of the bakery floor. In part this is because bakery foods are complex and non-equilibrium systems subject to fluctuating process and storage temperatures, so that there are many transitions taking place in the matrix throughout the product life, and this may be difficult to define from model systems.

SURFACE TENSION AND CAPILLARY ACTION

The surface of a liquid like water is in a state of tension and appears to have an elastic skin covering it. This simplistic statement goes some way to explaining why it is possible to float a needle on the surface of water, why some insects are able to walk across a water surface, and why drops of water remain suspended from taps for a short period of time. These are all examples of a property commonly referred to as *surface tension*. The surface tension of water is higher than that of all common liquids; only metals in the liquid state have a higher surface tension than water.

For any given water molecule beneath the surface of the liquid there are equal numbers of other water molecules surrounding it. This is shown diagrammatically in Fig. 1.7 where the sphere shown about point A represents the location of other water molecules. In this position the net force will be zero with any attractive forces being perfectly balanced by repulsive forces. In the case of any molecules at the surface of the liquid there are very few vapour molecules above the surface compared with the numbers below. If the molecule labelled B is displaced slightly upward, there will be net attractive force working in the opposite direction. To break this downward force and allow the molecule B to leave the surface requires an input of energy greater than the attractive forces.

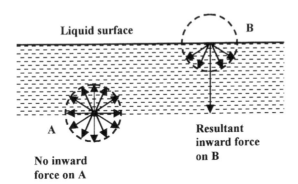

Fig. 1.7 Molecular forces in water.

If a narrow glass tube is immersed vertically in water, the liquid will rise up the tube. The narrower the tube the higher the liquid will rise. The movement of the water up the tube arises from *capillary action*, due to the forces of adhesion between the glass and water molecules being greater than the cohesion forces between the water molecules themselves. Capillary action takes place in many contexts, although it is not always as obvious as the effect of blotting paper soaking up ink.

Many materials affect the surface tension and capillary forces which act in water. Some can lower surface tension forces and cause a change in the flow properties of water; such substances are often referred to as *surfactants*. If we carefully place a drop of water on to a solid surface it will come to a position of equilibrium determined by surface tension and interfacial forces (for example, the adhesion between forces between water and glass discussed above). This delicate balance can be destroyed by physical actions or the careful introduction of a surfactant, and the water flows across the solid surface. In simple terms we could say that the surfactant had helped the water to 'wet' the surface. The reduction in surface tension which occurs with the many substances that might be classed as surfactants plays an important role in the uptake and mobility of water in many different natural processes.

GELS AND EMULSIONS

When a colloid sets to a semi-solid with no visible liquid present the product is often referred to as a *gel*. A simple explanation is that the solid particles of the colloid join together to form a three-dimensional network that traps water in the spaces of the net, much as water is held in a sponge. Proteins are capable of forming such gels as shown by the setting of table jellies, the principal component of which is the protein gelatin. Labuzza (1977) found that the greatest bonding for this particular protein–water gel was due to hydrogen bonds between the CO and NH groups, and not electrostatic bonds.

Protein–water interactions in foods were reviewed by Schnepf (1989), who described the formation of protein gels. A three-dimensional network is formed in protein gels based on protein–protein (*aggregation*) and protein–solvent interactions. Large quantities of water can be held in the gel by as little as 1% solids, even though the distance between the individual macromolecules can be very large. The type of gel depends on the temperature at which the gel forms, the pH of the system and the presence of any salts in solution. When protein gels are heated, water is lost from the gel and the protein undergoes random aggregation, commonly referred to as *coagulation*. This particular process plays a major role in the formation of the (relatively) rigid structures that are formed during baking.

Gels are also formed when water and starch are mixed together and heated. After some initial swelling a paste is formed as the starch *gelatinises*, a process involving the disruption of the crystalline structure of the starch (Street, 1991). The temperature at which starch gelatinisation occurs depends in part on the source of the starch, the ratio of water to starch and the presence of soluble materials. An example of the role played by soluble materials in changing the pattern of wheat starch gelatinisation is the presence of sucrose in solution in cake batters (*see* Chapter 3).

Emulsions are two-phased systems in which one (the *disperse*) phase is suspended as small droplets in the second (*continuous*) phase. The size of the suspended particles is usually too small to be seen with the naked eye, but they are not always small enough to be considered as colloids. Following the act of dispersion there is a very large increase in the surface area between the two components of the system, and for the emulsion to be stable there must be a reduction in interfacial tension and an increase in adhesion. Substances that promote stability in emulsions are known as *emulsifiers* and they work by forming a 'bridge' between the two phases; in effect they form a double surface, one for each component.

The common example given to show the principles of emulsification are the liquids oil and water, a situation which can occur in cake batters (although more correctly, in cake batters the two main liquid phases would be oil and a sucrose solution in water). After being mixed together, oil and water soon separate on standing, but the addition of a suitable emulsifier and its double surface effect confers stability to the mixture. In an oil-in-water emulsion the oil droplets, by virtue of an adsorbed emulsifier layer, present a hydrophilic surface to the water, which itself, through the emulsifier effect, presents a hydrophobic surface to the oil; the strong adhesive forces so formed help to maintain emulsion stability. Varying the ratios of oil and water will influence whether there is an oil-in-water or a water-in-oil emulsion. Both occur in bakery products; for example dairy cream is an example of oil-in-water while buttercream is an example of water-in-oil. Such differences have significant implications for the emulsion systems that are required to maintain cream stability.

Another example of a bakery emulsion which requires comment is the incorporation and stabilisation of air bubbles in liquid phases, such as seen in cake batters and creams. The stability of such emulsions has a major impact on the quality of bakery foods but they are mostly outside the scope of this book. One of the key emulsifiers, glycerol monostearate (GMS), a fatty solid, is at its most effective when it has first been mixed with water under optimised conditions of concentration and temperature. Krog and Larsen (1968) studied the phase diagram for mono- and diglycerides (the main components of GMS) in water and showed there were eight different forms, the most important of which for conferring batter stability are the *lamellar* and the *alpha gel*. In these forms the GMS emulsion is able to confer stability to foams, such as cake batters (Cauvain & Cyster, 1996) and creams, and to complex with wheat starch to delay product staling (Kamel & Ponte, 1993).

WATER IN BAKERY INGREDIENTS

Water is a major constituent of foodstuffs and as such it is present to some extent in almost all of the raw materials that are used in the manufacture of baked products (the exception being naturally occurring oils). In many cases the natural moisture level in many ingredients is high enough to provide a suitable environment for the proliferation of microorganisms (*see* Chapter 6) and the moisture content of many ingredients has to be lowered in order to avoid spoilage during storage. The moisture contents of some typical ingredients used by the baking industry are given in Table 1.5.

In the manufacture of bakery foods, achieving the optimum water level in the formulation during processing is essential to the formation of the appropriate structure in the baked product (*see* Chapters 2 and 3). The water required for this purpose may be added as water or may be derived from a number of the other ingredients that might be used. For example, cake batters commonly contain whole egg at levels too low to fully hydrate all of the other ingredients, so that more water may be added as milk or simply as water according to taste. In some baked products, e.g. carrot cake, so much water comes from the ingredients used that there is no need to make additions of extra water.

Table 1.5 Ingredient moisture content.

Ingredient	Moisture content (%)
flour	12.0–14.5
whole liquid hen's egg	approx. 75
cows' milk	approx. 87
sugar (refined, white)	0
glucose syrups	18.0–20.0
carrot	approx. 95
butter and margarine	14.0–16.0
apple (fresh)	approx. 85
bakers' yeast	approx. 70
salt	0

All ingredients and foodstuffs try to achieve a moisture equilibrium with their surroundings so that moisture may be lost or gained with time. The loss or gain of moisture by a particular ingredient during processing has significant effects on product qualities (*see* Chapters 2 and 3). The effects of water movement in the final products are discussed in Chapter 7.

CONCLUSIONS

The special properties of water are not only essential to life but play a key role in the manufacture of bakery foods, whether we are considering the solid (ice), liquid (water) or gaseous (vapour) forms. In the formation of doughs and batters, water plays a major role as a plasticiser of polymers and as a solvent for other recipe components. The properties of the solutions formed during mixing strongly influence the rheological behaviour of doughs and batters during processing and contribute directly to the formation of the final product structure. The evaporation of water, especially during baking, causes many changes in the properties of the other materials in the product matrix and is an essential part of structure formation. The formation of ice affects product shelf-life and texture.

Water plays a part in almost all of the chemical and physical changes that occur in the production of bakery foods and the processes that control their qualities during storage. The ubiquitous and far-reaching roles of water are discussed in detail in the chapters that follow.

REFERENCES

Bent, A.J. (1997) Flour specification, in *The Technology of Cakemaking*, 6th edn (ed. A.J. Bent), Blackie Academic & Professional, London, UK, pp. 5–17.

Brownsell, V.L., Griffith, C.J. & Jones, E. (1989) *Applied Science for Food Studies*, Longman Scientific & Technical, Harlow, UK.

Cauvain, S.P. (1998) Bread – the product, in *Technology of Breadmaking* (ed. S.P. Cauvain & L.S. Young), Blackie Academic & Professional, London, UK, pp. 1–17.

Cauvain, S.P. (1998) Breadmaking processes, in *Technology of Breadmaking* (ed. S.P. Cauvain & L.S. Young), Blackie Academic & Professional, London, UK, pp. 18–43.

Cauvain, S.P. & Cyster, J.A. (1996) Sponge cake technology. *CCFRA Review No. 2*, CCFRA, Chipping Campden, UK.

Gregory, R.B. (1998) Protein hydration and glass transitions, in *The properties of water in foods ISOPOW 6* (ed. D.S. Reid), Blackie Academic & Professional, London, UK, pp. 57–100.

Hegarty, V. (1995) *Nutrition, Food and the Environment*, Eagan Press, St Paul, USA.

Jones, G., McAughtrie, J. & Cunningham, K. (1997) Sugars, in *The Technology of Cakemaking*, 6th edn (ed. A.J. Bent), Blackie Academic & Professional, London, UK, pp. 84–99.

Kamel, B.S. & Ponte, Jr, J.G. (1993) Emulsifiers in baking, in *Advances in Baking Technology* (ed. B.S. Kamel & C.E. Stauffer), Blackie Academic & Professional, London, UK, pp. 179–222.

Krog, N. & Larsen, K. (1968) Phase behaviour and rheological properties of aqueous systems of industrial distilled monoglycerides. *Chemistry and Physics of Lipids*, **2**, 129–35.

Labuzza, T. (1977) The properties of water in relationship to binding in foods, a review. *Journal of Food Processing and Preservation*, **1**(2), 167–90.

Levine, H. & Slade, L. (1990) Influences of the glassy and rubbery states on the thermal, mechanical and structural properties of baked products, in *Dough Rheology and Baked Product Texture* (ed. H. Faridi & J.M. Faubion), Van Nostrand Reinhold, New York, USA, pp. 157–330.

Robb, J. (1983) Craters on frozen doughnut icing. *FMBRA Bulletin*, **3**, 145–7. CCFRA Chipping Campden, UK.

Schnepf, M. (1989) Protein–water interactions, in *Water and Food Quality* (ed. T.M. Hardman), Elsevier Applied Science, New York, USA, pp. 135–68.

Sears, J.K. & Darby, J.R. (1982) *The Technology of Plasticizers*. Wiley Interscience, New York, USA.

Stauffer, C.E. (1998) Principles of dough formation, in *Technology of Breadmaking* (ed. S.P. Cauvain & L.S. Young), Blackie Academic & Professional, London, UK, pp. 262–95.

Street, C.A. (1991) *Flour Confectionery Manufacture*. Blackie Academic & Professional, London, UK.

Thacker, D. (1997) Chemical aeration, in *The Technology of Cakemaking*, 6th edn (ed. A.J. Bent), Blackie Academic & Professional, London, UK, pp. 100–6.

Williams, A. & Pullen, G. (1998) Functional ingredients, in *Technology of Breadmaking* (ed. S.P. Cauvain & L.S. Young), Blackie Academic & Professional, London, UK, pp. 45–80.

Young, F.E., Jones, F.T. & Lewis, H.J. (1951) Prevention of the growth of sucrose hydrates in sucrose sirups. *Food Research*, **16**, 20–9.

2 The role of water in the formation and processing of bread doughs

The formation of a dough is the first step in the manufacture of fermented bakery foods and owes as much to the special properties of water discussed in Chapter 1 as it does to the unique properties of wheat and the flour milled from it. Edible seeds, including the forerunners of modern wheats, have formed a significant part of the human diet for many thousands of years. To make the seeds more suitable for human digestion, they had to be removed from the seed coat with some form of threshing process. Crushing the wheat seeds to release the inner starchy endosperm would have made them easier to consume, especially if they were mixed with water to form a thick porridge-like mass. It is not known when the gluten-forming properties of wheat proteins with their ability to trap the gases of fermentation were first discovered, but once appreciated the bases of breadmaking and other forms of baking were established. The synergistic relationship of water and wheat flour in the manufacture of fermented baked products is explored in this chapter.

WHEAT FLOUR PROPERTIES

Since wheat flour and its hydration plays a key role in the formation of all baked product structures it is appropriate to consider briefly some of the key properties concerned. A description of the processes used to convert wheat to flour can be obtained elsewhere (Catterall, 1998). Many different types of flour can be obtained from the milling process according to the requirements of the baker and consumer; some of the more common types are listed in Table 2.1.

In deciding which type of flour to use for fermented products, the baker must match the flour's properties with the requirements of the baking process and the essential characteristics of the product under manufacture. Most baking processes and product characteristics require very specific flour properties, and millers and bakers have evolved a range of chemical and physical tests that help identify whether the flour being produced is suitable for its end purpose (Catterall, 1998). These analytical tests vary in their ability to predict baking performance and end product quality, but most have been used for a sufficient length of time to have become established and accepted in the flour milling and baking industries.

Since it is outside the scope of this book to consider the relevance or otherwise of the analytical testing of wheat flours, discussion will be restricted to those in common use. They are, in no particular order:

Table 2.1 Wheat flour types.

Flour type	Description
wholemeal (wholewheat)	100% of the wheat grain converted to flour
white	around 75% of the wheat grain, mainly the starchy endosperm
patent	30 to 50% of the wheat grain, mostly starchy endosperm
brown	85 to 90% of the wheat grain, a mixture of starchy endosperm and bran
wheatgerm	white flour enriched with wheatgerm

- *Moisture content* – a measure of the water content present. Its level affects the water absorption capacity of the flour.
- *Protein content* – a measure of protein, commonly based on the determination of nitrogen. The level present affects the water absorption capacity of the flour and the optimum level of water addition in doughmaking.
- *Protein quality* – an assessment of the rheological properties of the proteins present. A number of different techniques are in common use (Catterall, 1998).
- *Flour grade colour* – a measure of the level of bran present, especially in white flours. Bran absorbs water and so its level will affect the overall water addition required.
- *Ash content* – an alternative to grade colour figure.
- *Hagberg Falling Number* – a measure of the cereal *alpha*-amylase level present in the flour. Higher levels may affect the level of dough water addition through dough softening.
- *Water soluble proteins (pentosans)* – their level has a significant affect on the water absorption capacity of flour even though the overall percentage present in flour is low (Stauffer, 1998).
- *Damaged starch* – a measure of the proportion of starch granules that have been damaged during the milling process. They have a significant effect on water absorption capacity because damaged starch granules absorb more water than undamaged ones.
- *Water absorption capacity* – usually determined as the level of water addition required to provide an optimum bread dough for processing (*see below*). The level required will vary with the breadmaking process and the type of equipment being used.
- *Particle size* – a measure of the distribution of the size of the wheat grain fragments. This measurement is of particular concern in cakemaking (*see* Chapter 3).

THE FORMATION OF BREAD DOUGHS

The proteins present in wheat comprise the albumins, globulins, glutelins (glutenins) and the prolamines (gliadins). Glutenins and gliadins are commonly referred to as the *gluten storage* proteins because they combine with water to form the gluten protein network that is critical for the retention of air and carbon dioxide gas in the dough during breadmaking. As well as undergoing hydration, it is necessary to impart energy to a flour–water mix in order to develop a gluten structure.

The transition from (relatively) dry flour proteins to a dough in which gluten has been formed is best appreciated by undertaking mixing of bread dough components by hand. The stages of the process are illustrated in Fig. 2.1 and may be described as follows:

(1)   Place the flour on a flat table and spread it out so that a round, empty 'bay' is formed in the centre.
(2)   Pour the required amount of water into the bay, add the salt and mix to dissolve it. Disperse the yeast in the salt solution.
(3)   Starting on the inside of the bay gradually draw flour into the dough water and mix together.
(4)   Continue this process until all the flour has been brought into contact with the dough water. At this stage there will be some dry and some wetter patches but we have not yet formed a dough.
(5)   The loose mixture (known as the 'flock' stage) now requires the input of energy through the process of *kneading*. The dough mass requires progressive working backwards and forwards on the table top, folding in any dry or wet patches until a smooth and homogeneous mass has been formed. This may take 15 or 20 minutes by hand, but is considerably quicker with a machine.

By the end of the process a dough will have been formed, but it will still be necessary to modify its rheological character in order to optimise its gas-retaining properties. A number of different processes may be used to achieve the required modification, and these form the basis of the different breadmaking processes that are in use around the world (Cauvain, 1998a).

The gluten proteins present in wheat flour are embedded in the flour particles along with the other flour components, mainly starch granules. When an excess of water comes into contact with the flour particles there is a gradual uptake of water. The precise nature of the gluten protein–water interactions is complex and still unclear. Bernadin and Kasarda (1973) observed that flour particles under the microscope 'exploded' when brought into contact with excess water, and strands of protein were rapidly expelled into the aqueous phase. If subjected to linear stresses (e.g. by moving the coverslip on the microscope slide) the protein strands stretched. The rate of hydration of the protein strands depends on the ratio of water to protein and proceeds more rapidly when there is an excess of water. In breadmaking, the added water level does not usually exceed the flour weight and so it is unlikely that the features observed by Bernadin and Kasarda are the sole mechanisms by which protein and water come into contact with one another.

Stauffer (1998), in reviewing the principles of dough formation in breadmaking, described the protein in flour as existing "as a flinty material" which softened during hydration. This description is consistent with the observations of Hoseney *et al.* (1986), who considered that as water is taken up by the wheat gluten proteins they pass through a glass transition stage changing from a hard glassy material to a

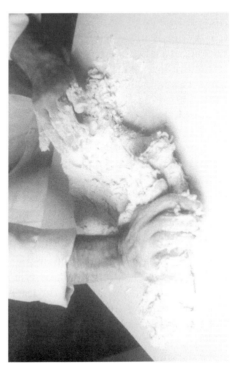

Fig. 2.1   Stages of handmixing bread doughs.

soft rubbery one. Hoseney and Rogers (1990) suggested that for both handwashed and commercial glutens this occurs at about 16% moisture content at room temperature (20°C). It is worth noting that flour and water temperatures at the start of mixing in many breadmaking processes may well be somewhat lower than room temperature, so that the T_g for gluten will occur at moisture contents above 16% but in most cases probably still within the 'typical' water-to-flour ratios that we see in breadmaking.

Starch granules are also embedded in the flour particles and during mixing they may become detached. This effect is seen when handwashing gluten from flour in an excess of water and a milky-white liquid comes out from the dough matrix. This liquid comprises mainly starch granules suspended in water. In normal dough-making, the water content is not in excess of the flour weight and the process is carried out in some form of container so that any starch granules lost from the softened flour particles will soon be swept up again as mixing continues. In the end, the developed dough matrix essentially comprises a gluten protein network on to which are attached starch granules and hydrated flour particles. Also distributed throughout the dough are the flour lipids, fibre and soluble materials (e.g. any naturally occurring sugars).

As discussed earlier, a proportion of the starch granules present in flour have experienced some mechanical damage as a result of the milling process. The ability of these damaged granules to absorb water is increased fivefold. In addition the damaged granules will absorb water faster than those that are undamaged. The absorption of water by starch is necessary for it to undergo the *gelatinisation* process that occurs on heating (this is discussed more fully in Chapters 3 and 4). The uptake of water by starch granules provides an element of competition for the available water with the flour proteins, although the effect of this on the rate and degree of gluten development is small. Nevertheless, high levels of damaged starch are known to have adverse effects on bread quality, such as a greying of the crumb and loss of cell structure fineness. Farrand (1969) suggested that there was an optimum relationship between flour protein content and damaged starch level, and considered that the latter should not exceed the quantity of protein squared and divided by six. This mathematical relationship is no longer considered completely valid, but there is no doubt that flours with higher protein contents are more able to cope with higher starch damage levels and produce better bread quality, especially with no-time doughmaking processes.

The damaged starch granules found in flour are susceptible to attack from *alpha*-amylase enzymes, which may be naturally present in the flour (cereal) or added by the miller or baker (fungal, maltogenic or bacterial). Breakdown products from this enzymic action are dextrins, which may lead to problems with stickiness and collapse in bread; maltose, which provides a substrate for the yeast; and water. The degree to which *alpha*-amylase activity occurs in bread doughs depends on the level of initial activity present, the availability of substrate (i.e. the damaged starch level), the temperature of the dough and the time available for the reaction. In general the timescale of mixing is too short for significant *alpha*-amylase action to occur, even with the higher dough temperatures that are encountered with no-time dough-making processes. When longer timescales are involved in breadmaking, for example during bulk fermentation (floortime) or proof, or where temperatures are raised, i.e. during proof and baking, then the effects of amylase activity on dough viscosity are more pronounced. Such effects are considered later in this chapter and again in Chapter 4.

Approximately 2 to 3% of the weight of flours comprises a mixture of water soluble proteins and pentosans. Their roles in breadmaking are unclear and complex. The water soluble pentosans have a significant water-absorbing capacity, which Stauffer (1998) estimated to be around seven times their own weight, and are able to form viscous solutions. This latter effect is of particular value in formation of rye bread structures, where the gluten-forming potential of the flour is limited (*see below*).

The fibrous components of the wheat grain, which derive from the bran skins, also absorb water during mixing but more slowly than other flour components. This slower hydration is evident when wholemeal flour doughs are taken from the mixer and are then processed. Initially such doughs have a surface which is sticky to the touch, but this stickiness is gradually lost as the character of the dough changes with time after mixing. A practical consequence of this change is that the doughs become more viscous, or 'stiffer', as though the doughs are lacking sufficient water. This adverse effect on dough rheology can lead to sub-optimal bread quality following the interaction of the dough with any handling or moulding equipment (*see below*).

Marsh (1998) summarised the requirements of mixing as:

- To disperse uniformly the recipe ingredients;
- To encourage the dissolution and hydration of those ingredients;
- To contribute energy to the development of a gluten structure in the dough;
- To incorporate air bubbles within the dough;
- To provide a dough suitable for processing.

Water addition has an impact on all of these aspects of mixing, but most importantly on the first, second and last requirements of those listed. Dispersion, dissolution and hydration have already been discussed when considering the handmixing process, and the formation of a suitable dough for processing is discussed in subsequent sections of this chapter.

The direct role that water plays in energy contributions and air incorporation is limited. Most of the energy associated with the dough mixing process comes from the mechanical interactions with ingredients. The rate of transfer of energy to the dough is to some extent related to the viscosity (consistency of the dough). Within limits, energy is transferred to the dough faster when the viscosity is higher, that is when less water has been added. Such changes are recognised as an increase in temperature rise during mixing, especially when doughs are mixed to a fixed time, e.g. with a spiral mixer. When doughs are mixed to a fixed energy expenditure, as is the case with the Chorleywood breadmaking process (CBP) (Cauvain, 1998a), the faster transfer of energy with stiff doughs is seen as a shortening of the mixing time, though only by a few seconds. In most breadmaking processes, using stiffer doughs to shorten mixing times or increase the rate of energy transfer has little practical value because dough development depends to a significant extent on optimum water additions (*see below*). The more viscous doughs that are obtained with sub-optimal water additions are less suited to subsequent processing and may yield impaired final product qualities.

The incorporation of air and the creation of small gas bubbles are critical to the development of bread cell structures; a detailed discussion of the processes involved is outside the scope of this book, but can be obtained elsewhere (Cauvain, 1998a). The role that water plays in these aspects of the mixing process is largely that of facilitating the development of a suitable gluten network in the dough. In summary the processes involved are:

- The entrapment of air as small bubbles by the developing gluten structure, 5–300 µm in size;
- The loss of oxygen from the air bubbles mainly because of the action of the yeast;
- The retention of the nitrogen gas bubbles in the gluten matrix;
- The release of carbon dioxide from solution in the dough water to expand the remaining nitrogen gas bubbles (*see* Fig. 2.2).
- The expansion of the nitrogen gas bubbles.

Much of the expansion of the gas bubble structures in bread doughs occurs post-mixing, especially in the proof and baking stages, and depends on the gas retention properties of the dough (Cauvain, 1998a), which in turn depends on the dough development that has been achieved. A gluten structure with the 'correct' rheological properties is a critical element in the retention of gas and the expansion of fermented doughs (*see below*).

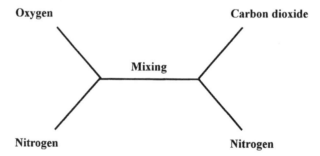

Fig. 2.2   Changes in gas composition with mixing.

OPTIMUM DOUGH WATER LEVELS

It is apparent from the comments above that there is an optimum water level for each of the flours used in bread doughmaking. This optimum water level is usually set according to the required viscosity and other dough rheological characters that will result in the 'right' product qualities. Optimum dough water levels are somewhat arbitrary and set by bakers according to their ability to process the dough into its required sizes and shapes with a minimum of effort and damage to dough properties (*see below*). If the dough has too little water, it will have a high viscosity and be 'stiff', and it will be difficult to change the shape of the dough during dividing,

Fig. 2.3   Bread from a dough with less than the optimum water level.

handling and moulding. An example of a loaf made with a dough lacking sufficient water is given in Fig. 2.3. In contrast, if the added water level is too high in the dough it will have a low viscosity and be 'soft', and while it will be easier to change its shape during moulding, it may not retain its shape and is likely to flow during proof. When soft doughs are held in pans this may not be too much of disadvantage, but with freestanding, oven-bottom or hearth bread types, the subsequent flow may be to the detriment of final bread quality (see Fig. 2.4).

The optimum water level for a given dough varies according to the bread variety required, the breadmaking processes employed, and the methods by which it will be handled and processed, especially moulded. Reference has already been made to the undesirable flow that can occur with freestanding breads when the added water levels are too high, and it is common to use lower water levels with such breads than those used for pan breads. However, there are exceptions and optimum baguette qualities are obtained only with higher water levels than sometimes seen with pan breads (Collins, 1978a). For example, Collins (1978b) suggested that water levels for the production of baguette by the CBP could be up to 8% higher (based on flour weight) than those used for pan breads. Such soft doughs may be supported in cradles or shaped pans, at least during proof, if not throughout the whole of the baking process. In the case of baguette, the high water level and the soft dough consistency are an integral part of being able to form the required open cell structure and crisp crust in the baked product, but must be combined with a fully developed dough so that the gluten network can retain the expansion of the dough structure during proof and baking.

Fig. 2.4 Bread from a dough with more than the optimum water level.

During fermentation, bread doughs become softer as the gluten network relaxes under the influence of time and temperature, the effects of enzymic activity and the evolution of carbon dioxide gas by the yeast, which decreases dough density. The longer the fermentation time, the softer the dough becomes. The optimum dough water addition is dictated largely by the ability of bakers or their equipment to handle the dough, and it is therefore common practice to compensate for increased dough softening by reducing the level of water addition to the dough during mixing. In dough making processes that do not have a fermentation period after mixing and before dividing, the dough would have a much firmer consistency, and so it is common practice for levels of water addition with no-time doughs to be higher than that seen with bulk fermentation processes. This additional water in the dough is required to ensure that dough consistencies are the same for all breadmaking processes by the time of dividing.

The quantity of gas that is occluded in the dough during mixing affects its rheological properties; the more gas that is present in the dough (i.e. the lower its density) the softer it will be. This is one of the factors seen to affect the consistency of dough with increasing fermentation time. In the CBP, a partial vacuum may be applied to the dough during mixing to reduce the average size of the gas bubbles that are present (Cauvain, 1998a). This same action significantly reduces the overall quantity of gas present in the dough at the end of mixing, often by as much as 50% (Marsh, 1998), and gives a dough that is firmer to the touch. This change in dough rheology is usually offset by increasing the level of water added to the dough in order to produce a dough of suitable consistency for dividing and processing.

Typical levels of water addition to the same flour processed by different bread-making processes are given in Table 2.2.

In those breadmaking processes that require a significant input of energy to the dough during mixing, e.g. the CBP, optimisation of water levels plays a part in the energy transfer mechanism. In particular, the rate of energy transfer is affected by the consistency of the dough. Soft doughs offer less resistance to the action of the mixing tool, and energy transfer rates are therefore lower. However, within the range of dough consistencies that would give doughs suitable for handling and processing, the differences in energy transfer rate are small and therefore have only a small effect on mixing times. If doughs are mixed to a specified energy input, as in the CBP (Cauvain, 1998a), the impact of changes in dough consistency on dough development is minimal, but when doughs are mixed solely to time then the impact may be appreciable. In the latter case softer doughs may receive lower energy inputs, yielding doughs with less development and poorer gas retention and ultimately bread with less oven spring and smaller volume.

Table 2.2 Comparison of added water levels with different doughmaking processes (same flour).

Process	Water addition (% flour weight)
one-hour bulk	57
four-hour bulk	55
no-time, spiral mixer	58
CBP	60
CBP with partial vacuum	62

WHEAT FLOUR WATER ABSORPTION CAPACITY AND ITS DETERMINATION

In the manufacture of bread products, the production of doughs with unvarying consistencies (viscosities) is desirable so that process conditions and product quality can be optimised. Achieving an unvarying consistency depends to a large extent on being able to work with a known ratio of water to other recipe ingredients, mainly the flour, since that is the major component of all bread recipes. As discussed above, the ability of the flour to absorb water depends on its chemical and physical composition, which is influenced by wheat variety, environmental factors and agricultural conditions during growth, and the processing techniques used by the miller to convert wheat to flour.

It is inevitable that some (mainly small) variations occur in the water absorption capacity of flours, and it is these changes that millers and bakers seek to measure and predict. While the water absorption capacity of a flour may be the subject of a 'fixed' specification agreed between miller and baker, it is worth noting that the 'correct' water absorption is the one that provides the baker with a standard dough consistency that can be processed readily, and that the water absorption capacity of flour is therefore not an expression of a fundamental property of wheat flours. Also, because of the viscoelastic nature of gluten structures (see below), we cannot simply take a measure of dough viscosity as an indicator of dough consistency of performance in any given breadmaking process. These comments go some way to explain why different methods of determining the water absorption capacity of flours have been developed and continue to exist side by side.

For a given wheat, the flour water absorption capacity derived from it depends on the following properties:

- *Moisture content* – the drier the flour, the higher the water absorption capacity.
- *Protein content* – the higher the protein content, the higher the water absorption capacity.
- *Damaged starch* – the higher the damaged starch level, the higher the water absorption capacity.
- *Bran content* – the higher the bran content, the higher the water absorption capacity (compare white and wholemeal flours).
- *Pentosan level* – the higher the pentosan level, the higher the water absorption capacity.
- *Enzymic activity* – the greater the enzymic activity, the lower the water absorption capacity. This effect is seen most commonly in breadmaking processes with significant bulk fermentation (floortime) periods, and only when levels of enzymic activity are extremely high with no-time breadmaking processes.

Largely because of the empirical nature of the assessment of the water absorption capacity of a given flour, there have been attempts to develop mathematical models to predict water absorption from flour properties such as those described above. The most common models (Farrand, 1969; Dodds, 1971) have linked flour moisture, protein content and damaged starch. Cauvain *et al.* (1985) found similar correlation to those of earlier workers, and while they did not find that the best predictive equations included any measure of enzymic activity, they did find that their model over-predicted the water absorption for flours with low Falling Numbers (i.e. high cereal *alpha*-amylase levels). Given the very high water-absorbing capacity of flour pentosans, we could expect a term for this flour property to occur in correlations, but the relatively small variations in levels seen in pentosan quantity for different flours probably have too small an overall effect and are masked by the variability inherent in the measurement of flour water absorption. A similar reasoning applies to variations in bran content within a give type of flour (e.g. white) and the effects become evident only when there is a major change in flour type, e.g. from white to wholemeal, or when significant quantities of bran (more than 2%) are blended into a white flour base (Cauvain, 1987). Zhang and Moore (1997) also found that additions of bran increased dough water absorption but that the particle size of the bran had no effect.

Given the difficulties associated with predicting the water absorption capacity of a flour from its other chemical and physical properties, it has become common to make a direct measurement based on assessment of its performance in some form of dough mixing test. The basis of such tests is to mix a dough and measure aspects of its rheology, either during mixing or afterwards. The 'correct' water absorption is identified when the dough meets a predefined rheological condition (e.g. resistance to deformation or viscosity), which has been set by calibration with an expert assessor who has judged the 'correct' dough consistency based on a sensory evaluation and experience in dough processing.

The most common method for determining flour water absorption is based on the use of the Brabender Farinograph (e.g. CCFRA, 1991). With the Farinograph, the water absorption capacity is assessed by mixing a flour–water dough with known ratios of flour to water, and recording the resistance of the dough to the movement of the mixing blades. Initially there is little resistance from the mixture, but as the proteins hydrate and form gluten the resistance increases. The results are recorded graphically and the operator is required to add sufficient water to reach a predetermined height on the graph. It may take the operator two or three attempts with freshly mixed doughs each time to determine the necessary level of water addition to meet exactly the required height on the graph.

In the UK it has become the accepted practice to mix to a maximum viscosity on the 600 line of the Farinograph trace, but elsewhere the 500 line is still commonly used. Such differences arise from the use of different breadmaking processes and dough handling methods. If the same flour was used to make no-time and bulk fermented doughs, the optimum water level to achieve the same dough consistency at the divider would have to be reduced with bulk fermentation in order to compensate for the enzymic softening that would normally occur.

The value determined for the flour water absorption capacity should be taken only as a guide to the actual level of water to be added to the dough for mixing. Differences between the determined water absorption and the level of water used arise because it is common to determine water absorption based on a flour–water mix, while in baking other ingredients are present which will influence dough viscosity and its other rheological properties. The effects of some of these are discussed in subsequent sections.

WATER LEVELS IN RYE BREAD DOUGHS

The compositions of wheat and rye grains are similar, except that the latter have a much higher pentosan content (Prihoda *et al.*, 1993). The high levels of pentosans in rye flour largely inhibit their ability to form a continuous gluten network, but are important because they have a much higher water absorption capacity than wheat proteins. Despite the inability of rye flours to form gluten, added water levels in rye breads remains quite high and other water-binding substances may be added as improvers, e.g. up to 3% of pregelatinised potato, maize or rice starches, or a hydrocolloid or gum.

A sour dough process is commonly used in rye bread production to develop a specific flavour in the baked product (Cauvain, 1998b). The sour is commonly based on the production and fermentation of a soft rye flour dough. Dryness and crumbliness in rye bread can be avoided by presoaking or scalding part of the rye wholemeal flour before dough making. Typically between 10 and 20% of the wholemeal flour is scalded with an equal weight of water three hours or so before dough mixing and allowed to cool before use.

Triticale, a cross between wheat and rye, has similar water absorption properties to rye flour and the production of bread using triticale follows similar methods to that of rye (Achremowicz, 1993).

THE EFFECTS OF OTHER DOUGH INGREDIENTS ON WATER LEVELS IN BREAD DOUGHS

Dried gluten

The addition of dried gluten to flours to improve their quality for breadmaking purposes is relatively common (Cauvain, 1998c). Dried, vital gluten consists mainly of the water-soluble proteins extracted from flour derived from a shortened milling process. The addition of dried gluten to flours improves their gas retention properties, though the degree to which they are improved depends on the composition of the gluten (mainly its protein content) and the effects of processing (especially drying) on its functionality (vitality). The water absorption capacity of dried gluten is greater than that of wheat flour, weight for weight, and usually it is necessary to increase the addition of water in a dough to which dried gluten has been added by approximately one and a half times the weight of added dry gluten. Where the flour used in breadmaking already contains dried gluten before it arrives in the bakery, the water absorption capacity of the blend can be determined by any of the normal methods described above.

It is important that the dried gluten is rehydrated during dough mixing so that it can confer functionality to the dough. Rehydration is not usually a problem in mixing, even in the CBP, and it is not normally necessary to prehydrate the dried gluten before mixing, provided it is in the form of a fine powder. Rarely, unhydrated gluten particles may be seen as small white spots on product crusts.

Salt

Common salt or sodium chloride is added to most fermented products and strongly affects bread flavour (Cauvain 1998c). Sodium chloride is composed of sodium and chlorine ions ($NaCl \rightleftharpoons Na^+ + Cl^-$) and dissociates fully in water. The overall effect of increasing salt additions is to decrease the water absorption of the flour as measured with the Farinograph (Linko *et al.*, 1984).

Another effect of adding salt is to lower the water activity of the solution (*see* Chapter 6), which decreases the availability of water for other reactions. The strong affinity that salt has for water forms the basis of salting to preserve meats and protect them from microbial spoilage (Honikel, 1989). In breadmaking, the rate of yeast fermentation is related directly to the salt level in the dough (Williams & Pullen, 1998). This occurs because of the reduced water availability and because of the effect on the osmotic process of the yeast cells. Direct contact between yeast cells and salt should be avoided, otherwise the integrity of the cell wall can be compromised and yeast activity seriously impaired.

In addition to affecting the activity of microorganisms, the addition of salt makes water less available for the hydration and gluten development processes that take place in bread doughs. In general the overall effect is small compared with the development that comes from the energy transferred to the dough during mixing. With slower speed mixers, the overall transfer of energy to the dough is relatively small during mixing and so the effect of salt on dough development is greater and a 'delayed-salt' mixing process may be employed. This consists of delaying the addition of the salt until the dough has been formed and mostly developed. Because salt is readily soluble, there should be no specific problems with its dispersion and dissolution.

Sugars

Sucrose and other sugars are often added to bread doughs to produce a sweeter flavour, increase crust browning, and in some cases to support yeast fermentation. Sugar additions produce doughs that are softer, and therefore may require a reduction in the added water level in order to maintain dough consistency. Like salt, the addition of sugars lowers the water activity of the dough (Chapter 6); this has the effect of inhibiting gluten formation during mixing.

Enzymes

Enzymes need to have sufficient water available for them to be able to exert their various effects. In bread doughs, there is almost always sufficient water present to at least initiate the actions of enzymes during mixing, even if their effects on dough are not manifest until later in the process (e.g. the effects of *alpha*-amylase during baking, *see* Chapter 4). However, if sufficient enzymic action occurs during dough making, this usually leads to a softening of the dough which requires a compensatory reduction in added water levels in order to maintain optimum dough consistency. Not all enzyme additions result in dough softening; for example Gerrard *et al.* (1998) found that transglutaminase substantially improved dough water absorption, along with improved crumb strength and reduced work input.

Other ingredients

A number of ingredients become effective during dough mixing when they go into solution, including:

- *Ascorbic acid*, which acts as an oxidising agent and improves dough development (Williams and Pullen, 1998).
- *L-Cysteine hydrochloride*, which acts as a reducing agent and modifies dough rheology (Williams and Pullen, 1998). Usually there is a softening of the dough which may require a small reduction in the added water level.
- *Calcium phosphates*, which have been used in frozen dough production to increase dough firmness through gluten interaction and water binding effects (Anon., 1994/1995).

Some ingredients need to become hydrated in order to confer their special properties to bread products; they include *milk powders*, which affect product colour and flavour, although these have limited use in breads. The use of milk powders affects the water absorption capacity of the dough and added water levels should be increased by approximately the same weight of milk powders used.

Other ingredients may affect the level of water which is added to the dough to meet a specified consistency; they include:

- *Soya flour*, which is used to whiten bread colour and improve dough oxidation (Williams & Pullen, 1998). The addition of soya flour requires an increase in added water levels of about half the soya weight used.
- *Non-wheat fibres*, which covers a wide range of products used in specialised bread varieties. Added water levels are usually increased in proportion to the added fibre weight.
- *Gums and starches*, which may be used to make some specialised fermented products. Added water levels are usually increased in proportion to the added ingredient weight.
- *Other grains*, which are used in multigrain breads to add special textural characteristics, eating qualities and flavours (Cauvain, 1998b). They may be added in the whole, cracked or kibbled form, and will all affect the water absorption capacity in the dough to greater or lesser degrees. In some cases water will be absorbed slowly during post-mixing processes, and this makes it difficult to adjust water levels to provide an optimum dough consistency for moulding.

WATER IN BREWS AND SPONGES

Some breadmaking processes and fermented product types employ a pre-fermentation stage in which ingredients other than flour are mixed together and allowed to stand. These ingredients are water-based, and common ones include yeast and sugars; usually the mixture is known as a 'brew'. The aim of the pre-fermentation stage is to activate the yeast, and to encourage fermentation and the development of distinctive flavours, usually acidic in nature. The temperature, pH and total titratable acidity (TTA) of the brew are usually carefully controlled to ensure a consistent condition and flavour. Water brews are most likely to be encountered in the production of hamburger buns (Bent, 1998).

A number of breadmaking processes have evolved in which part of the flour and water used in doughmaking are mixed together as a preliminary fermentation stage. Such doughmaking processes are commonly referred to as 'sponge and dough', and comprise a two-stage process in which part of the recipe flour, water, yeast and some other ingredients are mixed as a first stage and fermented before blending with the remaining dough ingredients at a second mixing stage (Cauvain, 1998a). The initial consistency of the sponge may be made somewhat softer than a normal dough by adding water at levels above the determined flour water absorption level. The lower dough viscosity facilitates a more rapid expansion of the dough during fermentation and increases the water activity of the sponge. The greater yeast activity leads to rapid gassing in the sponge, which is usually controlled through the addition of salt or by lowering the temperature at which the sponge is held. In addition to yeast activity the production of a sponge encourages the action of (mainly) lactic acid bacteria, which leads to considerable flavour and pH changes in the sponge. The 'acid' flavour notes developed in the sponge will be carried through to the dough and confer an acidic bite to the final bread flavour.

In another form of prefermentation, a 'flour brew' may be produced. This contains some flour but less than is used normally to make a sponge. In the production of hamburger buns, flour brews have the advantage of being pumpable and are sometimes referred to as 'liquid sponges' (Bent, 1998). Flour brews were a traditional part of breadmaking for many years and were often called 'flying ferments'. They probably originated in the days before the introduction of standardised yeast, when it was common for bakers to use water ferments (barms) from the brewing industry and the addition of a small amount of flour was used to provide a substrate (food) for continued yeast activity before the main dough-making process was initiated.

Whichever form of prefermentation is used, it is important to control the system pH and TTA in order to ensure that the correct flavour is developed (Sutherland, 1989). This is because the optimum conditions for the activity of different micro-organisms vary, and if left uncontrolled will vary flavour development. In this context the effect of water hardness must be considered. As discussed in Chapter 1, the hardness of water varies according to geological and processing conditions, and the presence of calcium carbonate in water will act as a buffer and restrict the degree to which the pH of the brew or sponge will fall during storage. This buffering effect may be so marked that it becomes necessary to use softened water or add a suitable acid to lower the pH of the system. In the UK, the Bread and Flour Regulations (1995) require the addition of calcium carbonate to flour which creates a further problem for achieving a low pH in preferment systems.

OTHER FACTORS AFFECTING THE LEVEL OF WATER ADDED TO DOUGHS

In addition to the effects of flour properties, ingredients and formulation, other factors affect the level of water which is added to bread doughs. Some of these are process related, and others are related to the economics of the process.

The application of a partial vacuum towards the end of dough mixing when using the CBP has been shown to produce doughs that are firmer and drier to the touch (Cauvain, 1998a). This effect is usually compensated for in the bakery through the addition of extra water as noted above. The lower the pressure (i.e. the greater the vacuum) that can be achieved during mixing, the larger the quantity of extra water needed in order to adjust the dough consistency. However, as the mixing pressure falls so does the ability of the dough to form a normal bread structure. In most cases a practical limitation is about 0.3 bar of pressure.

Lowering the temperature of the dough at the end of mixing also produces a dough that is firmer to the touch. Once again the dough consistency may be adjusted through the addition of extra water, but lower dough temperatures do lead to less oxidation and development in the dough, as well as slower proof, unless extra yeast is added.

Bakers often judge the efficiency of their process based on the number of units that they obtain from a given combination of ingredients; this is their 'yield'. In those countries that have no minimum bread solids content, and where bread is sold by weight, there are advantages in being able to keep the level of added water to a maximum in order to maximise yield. As well as achieving a greater yield the resulting bread will also be softer and appear fresher to the consumer.

DOUGH AND WATER TEMPERATURES

The control of final dough temperature in the production of fermented baked products is the foundation of process and product quality control, and vitally important to consistent production and product quality. Because of these considerations it is common to control the final dough temperature at the end of mixing. However, there is no single 'correct' dough temperature and each baker must select the one that gives the appropriate dough and product quality consistency required.

The dough temperature at the end of mixing influences many aspects of dough and product quality, including:

- *Dough development* through chemical actions, e.g. ascorbic acid is temperature-sensitive, and there is less oxidation when dough temperatures are lowered.
- *Enzymic activity*, which proceeds more rapidly when the dough temperature is increased.
- *Yeast fermentation*, which proceeds more rapidly when the dough temperature is increased and therefore affects added yeast levels and process timings (*see below*).
- *Dough consistency and rheology*, which change with dough temperature, e.g. doughs become softer and less resistant as their temperature rises.
- *Dough tolerance* to processing delays, e.g. during dividing through the effect of temperature on dough rheology and yeast activity.
- *Proof time*, which will be increased with lower dough temperatures.

There is a close link between final dough temperature and the breadmaking process that may be used to manufacture the dough. In general, breadmaking processes that employ a period of bulk fermentation (floortime) require lower dough temperatures (23 to 26°C), depending on the length of bulk time. Shorter times require higher temperatures, while no-time dough making processes, e.g CBP, can employ higher temperatures (typically 28 to 31°C).

Environmental conditions vary around the world and with season so that ambient and ingredient temperatures vary within bakeries with time. Since control of final dough temperature is so important to final product quality, bakers have to modify ingredient temperatures to achieve a consistent dough temperature. In the manufacture of fermented products, only two ingredients are used in sufficient quantity to have a significant effect on final dough temperatures: flour and water. Flour is subject to environmental temperature changes and is a poor conductor of heat so that in practice bakers are left only with water as the ingredient with which to adjust dough temperatures.

Control of final dough temperatures is achieved by adjusting the dough water temperature mainly in response to variations in flour temperature, along with allowances for heat rise experienced during dough mixing. The latter varies according to the type of mixer being used. If bakers know the typical heat rise experienced by the dough ingredients for a given set of mixing conditions, they can quickly establish a protocol for adjusting final dough temperatures to meet specified limits.

The water temperature required for a given set of mixing conditions and flour temperature can be calculated using the following formula:

$$T_w = 2(T_d - T_r) - T_f$$

where T_w = temperature of the water required;
T_d = temperature of the dough required;
T_r = temperature rise during mixing;
T_f = temperature of the flour;
the constant 2 allows for flour having approximately half the thermal capacity of water.

For example:

Using a low-speed mixer and bulk fermentation time:

$T_d = 25°C$
$T_r = 0°C$
$T_f = 20°C$

then $T_w = 2(25 - 0) - 20 = 50 - 20 = 30°C.$

Using a high speed mixer:

$T_d = 30°C$
$T_r = 15°C$
$T_f = 15°C$

then $T_w = 2(30 - 15) - 15 = 30 - 15 = 15°C.$

The 'average' temperature rise for a given set of mixing conditions can be determined by making a series of doughs (probably eight to ten) and recording all ingredient and dough temperatures. By rearranging the equation above, the temperature rise for each mixed dough can be calculated and a mean value for T_r derived for general use.

For example, using a spiral mixer:

$T_d = 28°C$
$T_f = 18°C$
$T_w = 20°C$

then $T_r = (2T_d - T_f - T_w)/2$
$= (2 \times 28) - 18 - 20)/2$
$= (56 - 18 - 20)/2$
$= 18/2$
$= 9°C$

The precise temperature rise during mixing will be affected to a lesser degree by two other factors:

- *The ambient bakery temperature* – minor adjustments will be required for cold start-ups, or for low or high ambient temperatures. As a rough guide, the water temperature will need to be changed by 2° for every adjustment of 1°C needed to the dough temperature.
- *Heat of hydration from the flour*, which occurs with all flours but is normally only a problem with dry flours (less than 14% moisture). It can be calculated from the flour moisture content using a suitable equation (Wheelock & Lancaster, 1970). The effect of heat of hydration on temperature rise during mixing is small compared to that which comes from energy transfer, but it can make control of final dough temperature with high speed mixing more difficult.

The temperature rise experienced by the ingredients during dough mixing is related directly to the level of energy imparted to the dough (Cauvain, 1998b). In some breadmaking processes, such as the CBP, the energy levels are predetermined, while in others they are related to mixing speed and time. In general, the longer the mixing time the more energy is imparted to the dough.

Because of the relatively high energy level which may be imparted to the dough, considerable increases in temperature are encountered during mixing, so it will be necessary to reduce the temperature of the water by chilling it. The water temperatures required can be very low, especially with high speed or controlled-energy mixing, and often approach 0°C. In some cases crushed ice may be added to the mixer in order to try and achieve the necessary temperature control (Anon., 1997), but it should be noted that this will affect the hydration and dissolution processes that normally take place in the dough and may affect dough development. Indeed Campos *et al.* (1996) found that a uniform mixture of ice and flour that was warmed later gave a homogenous but undeveloped dough.

The application of cooling jackets to mixers provides another means of reducing or restricting the temperature rise during mixing (French & Fisher, 1981). The coolant may be chilled water or some other suitable refrigerant, such as glycol, circulating through the jacket. In general, the contact time between the dough and bowl surfaces during mixing is short and so the effect of the cooling jacket on temperature rise is limited. Very low refrigerant temperatures may lead to the formation of ice on the upper, inner surfaces of the mixing bowl, which may lead to problems of controlling ejection of the dough from the mixer. The higher energy levels needed for the development of doughs made with strong north American flours, up to 20 Wh/kg (Tweedy of Burnley, 1982), require the use of a suitable cooling jacket.

In its simplest form, control of the water temperature can be achieved by blending together quantities of hot and cold water until the required water temperature is achieved. Automatic metering of water levels at the appropriate temperatures can be achieved in virtually any bakery. The water meters concerned often contain a microprocessor capable of adjusting water temperatures to meet specified final dough temperatures, with the algorithms in the program taking into account mixing energy (or time), batch size, ingredient temperatures and even ambient bakery conditions.

In some cases, automatic systems are available which are capable of assessing the consistency of the dough part-way through the mixing process, usually via the stresses experienced by the mixer motor, with an allowance for the addition of extra water to optimise dough consistency if required. In such cases, the water level added intitially is slightly lower than the optimum to allow for the addition of extra water later during the mixing process. Should subsequent doughs become too soft then a reduction in initial added water has to be made. In high-speed mixing processes, e.g. the CBP, the mixing time is very short, so assessment of consistency must be made quickly and there may not be sufficient time to fully disperse any additional water uniformly throughout the dough. With spiral mixing, the slower mixing and longer timescale make the addition of extra water more practical (Ahlert & Gerbel, 1993; Gerbel & Ahlert, 1994).

WATER, DOUGH RHEOLOGY AND MOULDING

The ratio of water to flour used in breadmaking has effects of varying degrees on all of the rheological characteristics we encounter in the processing of doughs after mixing. Cauvain (1998b) considered that there were four dough physical properties of concern in bread doughs: resistance to deformation, elasticity, extensibility and stickiness. As discussed above, the consistency of the dough depends to a large extent on the level of added water: the higher the water level used, the softer the dough.

In practical terms, dough softness can be equated with resistance to deformation, since increasing water levels in bread doughs reduce their resistance. The effect of softer doughs on the rate at which energy is transferred to the dough during mixing has already been commented on above. The close link between dough water level, gluten formation and mixing makes the assessment of a suitable dough rheology for processing through a given set of equipment a complex issue, mostly outside the scope of this book. Numerous reviews of the subject are available, e.g. Rasper (1993). Dreese *et al.* (1988), when studying the fundamental rheological properties of doughs, related lower G' values (a measure of dough rheology) of doughs mixed past their optimum to a reduced water-binding capacity of the gluten network. Such observations are entirely consistent with the practical expedient of reducing added water levels in bread doughs whenever the dough becomes too soft.

In bread dough processing, the dividing and moulding operations subject the doughs to a variety of stresses and strains depending on the equipment used. The major stresses occur in the moulding stages, where the shape of individual dough pieces commonly undergoes considerable change; it is in these stages that the effects of differences in dough consistency are most often observed. Doughs that lack water and are 'tight' offer greater resistance to deformation and may lead to quality defects on the dough surface, e.g. tearing or rupturing of the dough surface.

In addition to the adverse changes that may occur on the surface, more serious defects may occur within the dough matrix itself. In particular, the internal structure of the dough may suffer 'damage' as the result of breakdown of the gluten strands within the dough matrix. This may lead to the formation of undesirable large holes or hard patches in the crumb. The basis of the adverse changes to bread quality which may occur with tight doughs is shown in Fig. 2.5. Within the dough matrix, individual gas bubbles of varying sizes are stabilised by the surrounding viscoelastic gluten network (Fig. 2.5a). If sufficient pressure is applied to the dough, the gluten network may be broken by the force and this may allow the coalescence of two or more adjacent bubbles (Fig. 2.5b), or gas bubbles may be eliminated from the dough matrix and amalgamation of gluten strands may occur (Fig. 2.5c). After the amalgamation of adjacent gas bubbles, the lower internal pressure of the new, larger bubbles allows them to grow at a faster rate than other smaller bubbles and they may become 'holes' in the crumb. When gas bubbles are eliminated from the dough matrix during moulding there are no opportunities for their re-introduction and the amalgamated gluten network cannot expand in the prover or the oven; hence the formation of hard, dense patches in the crumb. With sub-optimal dough consistency both effects may be observed to differing degrees in different places within the bread crumb.

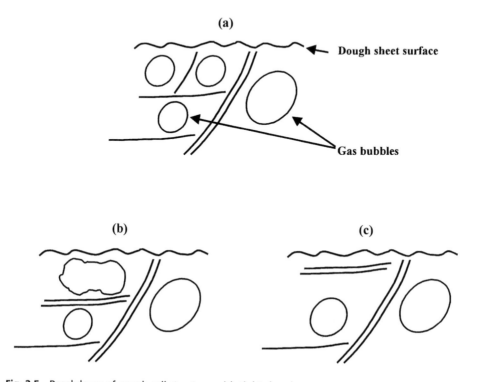

(a)

Dough sheet surface

Gas bubbles

(b)   **(c)**

Fig. 2.5 Breakdown of crumb cell structure with tight doughs.

   Doughs that lack water also exhibit greater elasticity and reduced extensibility, which increase the susceptibility of the dough to damage during dividing and shaping operations. There are limited opportunities to compensate for such deficiencies in dough rheology during post-mixing processing operations. Fermented doughs relax, i.e. become less resistant and less elastic, with increasing resting time, so it is possible to compensate for tight doughs to some extent by increasing any first (intermediate) proof time given to dough pieces. The potential for increasing first proof time is limited by other changes that will take place in the fermenting dough, namely the decrease in dough density which occurs with the evolution of carbon dioxide gas from yeast fermentation. The higher overall gas content after first proof increases the susceptibility of the dough to damage of the type described above.

   Water plays a significant role in relation to yeast fermentation in that the carbon dioxide gas which is evolved first goes into solution in the dough water. This process continues until the solution is saturated; thereafter the production of more carbon dioxide increases the pressure in the aqueous phase to such an extent that the gas comes out of solution to begin the inflation of the nitrogen gas bubbles present in the dough. Any oxygen that was present in the dough from air incorporation has been removed by the yeast (Cauvain, 1998a). If the density of dough is plotted against time after leaving the mixer, little change is observed in the first few minutes (*see* Fig. 2.6, which corresponds to the period during which carbon dioxide saturation of the dough water is being achieved).

   In practical doughmaking, the rheological terms softness (resistance to defor-

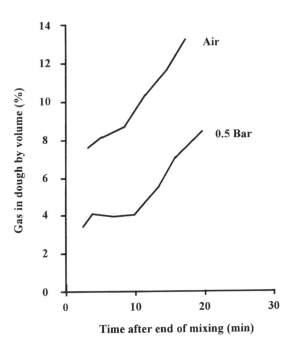

Fig. 2.6 Changes in dough density after mixing.

mation) and stickiness are often confused. It is possible to have doughs that are soft but not sticky and *vice versa*, or both soft and sticky. Stickiness is most often observed when doughs are subjected to the forces of shear rather than straight-forward compression. Many opportunities for the shearing of doughs occur in post-mixing processes, especially during dividing, rounding and moulding operations. Problems with doughs that exhibit stickiness during processing are often overcome by reducing the added water content and in some cases through the application of air-blasts to dry the surface of the dough during the first moulding stages (Marsh, 1998). The evaporation of a small amount of water from the dough surface helps to reduce dough stickiness while maintaining a high water level in the dough.

CONCLUSIONS

Water plays a critical role in the formation of fermented doughs, and it is important that the ratio of water to flour and other ingredients is optimised so that the dough has the 'correct' rheological characteristics for processing after mixing. The optimum water level in a fermented dough is affected by the properties of the flour used and some other ingredients that may be present in the formulation, so that determining the optimum level of water addition requires both measurement and expert opinion.

The role of water as a solvent and a means of achieving hydration of many of the recipe components is important, but often overlooked, in doughmaking. In some cases, e.g. in the use of brews and sponges, the preparation of solutions and soft doughs aids the mechanical operation of breadmaking plants.

As well as playing a key role in dough formation, water also plays a significant role in the control of dough temperatures and in turn in the activity of the yeast present in the formulation. Adjustment of dough temperature is best achieved by varying water temperature because other techniques for controlling dough temperatures (e.g. cooling jackets on mixers) have only limited potential.

REFERENCES

Achremowicz, B. (1993) Use of Triticale for bread production in Poland. *Chorleywood Digest*, **132**, Nov./ Dec., CCFRA, Chipping Campden, UK, pp. 115–20.

Ahlert, D. & Gerbel, D. (1993) Optimising of the mixing process. *Back Journal*, Sept., 75–7.

Anon. (1994/1995) Cafos Pyro, C14-01, in frozen dough processing. *Food Technology in Europe*, **1**, 202–203.

Anon. (1997) Supercool your dough by using ice's gentle touch. *British Baker*, **194**, 9 May, 14.

Bent, A.J. (1998) Speciality fermented goods, in *Technology of Breadmaking* (ed. S.P. Cauvain & L.S. Young), Blackie Academic & Professional, London, UK, pp. 214–39.

Bread and Flour Regulations (1995) *UK SI 3202*. HMSO, London, UK.

Bernardin, J.E. & Kasarda, D.D. (1973) Hydrated protein fibrils from wheat endosperm. *Cereal Chemistry*, **50**, 529–36.

Campos, D.T., Steffe, F.F. & Ng, P.K.W. (1996) Mixing flour and ice to form undeveloped dough. *Cereal Chemistry*, **73**, 105–107.

Catterall, P. (1998) Flour milling, in *Technology of Breadmaking* (ed. S.P. Cauvain & L.S. Young), Blackie Academic & Professional, London, UK, pp. 296–329.

Cauvain, S.P. (1987) Effects of bran, germ and low grade flour on CBP bread quality. *FMBRA Report No. 138*. CCFRA, Chipping Campden, UK.

Cauvain, S.P. (1998a) Breadmaking processes, in *Technology of Breadmaking* (ed. S.P. Cauvain & L.S. Young), Blackie Academic & Professional, London, UK, pp. 18–44.

Cauvain, S.P. (1998b) Other cereals in breadmaking, in *Technology of Breadmaking* (ed. S.P. Cauvain & L.S. Young), Blackie Academic & Professional, London, UK, pp. 330–46.

Cauvain, S.P. (1998c) Bread – the product, in *Technology of Breadmaking* (ed. S.P. Cauvain & L.S. Young), Blackie Academic & Professional, London, UK, pp. 1–17.

Cauvain, S.P., Davies, J.A. & Fearn, T. (1985) Flour characteristics and fungal *alpha*-amylase in the Chorleywood Bread Process. *FMBRA Report No. 121*, March. CCFRA, Chipping Campden, UK.

CCFRA (1991) Method No. 0004: Determination of water absorption and rheological properties of dough using a Brabender Farinograph. *CCFRA Flour Testing Panel Methods Handbook*. CCFRA, Chipping Campden, UK.

Collins, T.H. (1978a) The French baguette and pain Parisien. *FMBRA Bulletin*, June, CCFRA, Chipping Campden, UK, pp. 107–16.

Collins, T.H. (1978b) Making French bread by CBP. *FMBRA Bulletin*, Dec., CCFRA, Chipping Campden, UK, pp. 193–201.

Dodds, N.J.H. (1971) Damaged starch determination in wheat flours in relation to dough water absorption. *Starke*, **23**, 23–7.

Dreese, P.C., Faubion, J.M. & Hosney, R.C. (1988) Dynamic rheological properties of flour, gluten and gluten–starch doughs. II. Effects of various processing and ingredients changes. *Cereal Chemistry*, **65**, 354–9.

Farrand, E.A. (1969) Flour properties in relation to the modern bread processes in the United Kingdom, with special reference to *alpha*-amylase and starch damage. *Cereal Chemistry*, **41**, 98–111.

French, F.D. & Fisher, A.R. (1981) High speed mechanical dough development. *Bakers' Digest*, **55**, 80–82.

Gerbel, D. & Ahlert, D. (1994) Use of dough consistency to control the mixing process. *Getreide Mehl Brot*, **48**, 23–6.

Gerrard, J.A., Fayle, S.E., Wilson A.J., *et al.* (1998) Dough properties and crumb strength of white pan bread as affected by microbial transglutaminase. *Journal of Food Science*, **63**, 472–5.

Honikel, K.O. (1989) The meat aspects of water and food quality, in *Water and Food Quality*. (ed. T.H. Hardman), Elsevier Science Publishers Ltd., Barking, UK, pp. 277–304.

Hoseney, R.C. & Rogers, D.E. (1990) The formation and properties of wheat flour doughs. *CRC Critical Reviews in Food Science and Nutrition*, **29**(2), 73–93.

Hoseney, R.C., Zeleznak, K. & Lai, C.S. (1986) Wheat gluten: a glassy polymer. *Cereal Chem.*, **63**, 285–6.

Linko, Y.-Y., Harkonen, H. & Linko, P. (1984) Sodium chloride in bread making technology. *International Symposium on Advances in Baking Science and Technology*, 27–8 Sept., Kansas State University, USA.

Marsh, D. (1998) Mixing and dough processing, in *Technology of Breadmaking*, (ed. S.P. Cauvain & L.S. Young), Blackie Academic & Professional, London, UK, pp. 81–119.

Prihoda, J., Holas, J. & Kratachvil, J. (1993) Rye flour, wholemeal and rye breads, in *Advances in Baking Technology* (ed. B.S. Kamel & C.E. Stauffer), Blackie Academic & Professional, London, UK, pp. 20–37.

Rasper, V.F. (1993) Dough rheology and physical testing of dough, in *Advances in Baking Technology* (ed. B.S. Kamel & C.E. Stauffer), Blackie Academic & Professional, London, UK, pp. 107–133.

Stauffer, C.E. (1998) Principles of dough formation, in *Technology of Breadmaking* (ed. S.P. Cauvain & L.S. Young), Blackie Academic & Professional, London, UK, pp. 262–95.

Sutherland, W.R. (1989) Hydrogen ion concentration (pH) and total titratable acidity tests. *American Institute of Baking, Research Department Bulletin, No. XI*, May, p. 5.

Tweedy of Burnley Ltd. (1982) Dough mixing for farinaceous foodstuffs. *UK Patent GB 2,030,883B*, HMSO, London, UK.

Wheelock, T.D. and Lancaster, E.B. (1970) Thermal properties of wheat flour. *Starke*, **22**, 44–8.

Williams, A. and Pullen, G. (1998) Functional ingredients, in *Technology of Breadmaking* (ed. S.P. Cauvain & L.S. Young), Blackie Academic & Professional, London, UK, pp. 262–95.

Zhang, D. and Moore, W.R. (1997) Effect of bran particle size on dough rheological properties. *Journal of the Science of Food and Agriculture*, **74**, 490–6.

3 The role of water in the formation and processing of batters, biscuit and cookie doughs, and pastes

This chapter discusses the role of water in the formation of a wide range of bakery products, which are based primarily on a flour and water dough mix but which exhibit quite different characteristics to those observed with the bread and fermented doughs discussed in Chapter 2. The nature of the products covered in this chapter is diverse and there is no particularly unifying theme to their production, other than they are not usually classified as 'breads' and water is used in their preparation.

In the same way that the addition of water facilitates the formation of bread doughs, the addition of water to dry ingredients is a prerequisite for the formation of batters, biscuit doughs and pastes. There are, however, significant differences between bread doughs and the groups of products that are discussed in this chapter. Some of these differences are related to the ratio of water to solids in the recipes concerned, which has a major bearing on the formation, or not, of gluten. Other differences include the much wider range of ingredients that are used in the formulations, and which function to exploit and change particular flour properties during mixing and processing. Many of the ingredients that are used also confer particular flavours, textural and eating qualities to the final product.

The modification of flavour and eating qualities is probably the original reason for including many of the ingredients encountered in formulations for these product groups. For example, the use of sugars in the form of honey to make 'cakes' is known from ancient Greek literature, and the first mention of sugar cane is likely to be the 'sakcharon', or sweet reed, known to the natives of the Indian sub-continent at the time of Alexander the Great, around 300BC (Cauvain & Screen, 1990a). Once these 'additional' ingredients began to be added to the basic flour and water mix, water levels would need to be adjusted to take into account changes in dough rheological properties brought about by these additions. Gradually, probably through trial and error, a diverse range of products evolved based on the flour and water dough mix, each with their own special group of shape and texture characters and these have become the traditional cakes (sweet goods), biscuits, cookies and pastry products that are discussed in this chapter.

THE FORMATION OF CAKE BATTERS

In the formation of cake batters, we use the addition of water to achieve most of the same effects that were discussed above for the production of fermented doughs, namely to:

- Disperse uniformly the recipe ingredients;
- Encourage the dissolution and hydration of those ingredients;
- Incorporate air bubbles in the batter, which will act as nuclei for the carbon dioxide gas generated from the action of baking powder chemicals, where they are used;
- Provide a batter with suitable rheological properties for subsequent processing.

Missing from this list is the contribution of energy to the formation of a gluten network in the batter. There are several reasons for this omission:

- We do not wish to form a gluten network in these type of products because that would give a firmer, chewier eating quality than required from the products we commonly describe as cakes.
- The formation of a gluten network in the batter would impede its progress through normal cake batter processing equipment, e.g. depositors, and would necessitate a redesign of such equipment.
- The rheology of cake batters is such that their low viscosities do not provide sufficient resistance to the passage of the mixing tool in the bowl to permit the transfer of significant quantities of energy to the batter to facilitate gluten development.
- The ratio of water to flour solids in the formulation of cake batters is much higher than that used in the production of bread doughs.
- The water activities of typical cake batters are much lower than observed in fermented doughs because of the nature and concentration of ingredients used in the formulations, and because of this they both slow down and reduce the hydration of the flour proteins present.
- Cake batters typically contain much higher levels of oils or solid fats than fermented doughs, which slows down and reduces the hydration of flour proteins.

Cakes are produced by forming a complex emulsion and foam system – the batter – which is mainly processed by being heat set in an oven. In their simplest form, cake batters comprise wheat flour, sugar and whole egg, the latter traditionally contributing the necessary water in the recipe formulation (about 75% of whole egg is water). At the start of the traditional batter mixing process, the egg and the sugar are usually whisked together. The sugar goes into solution in the water present in the egg and large numbers of minute air bubbles are trapped in the batter by the surface active proteins in the egg. These proteins form a protective film around the air bubbles, preventing them from coalescing and escaping from the batter. As whisking continues, more air is incorporated until saturation is achieved and batter density reaches a minimum. When this point is reached the flour is added with a minimum of mixing to avoid destabilising the egg foam. The type of cake produced by this method is commonly referred to as a 'sponge' because of its open cellular structure, which gives it a similar appearance to natural and, more recently, synthetic sponges used in the bathroom.

Immediately after baking, the sponge cakes made using the traditional formula described above have a soft, tender eating quality, but this is soon lost during storage and the eating quality changes to one which is harsh and dry (*see* Chapter 5). Over the centuries bakers have discovered that the addition of oils and solid fats can improve both the initial eating quality of cakes and reduce the loss of desired qualities during storage. The addition of an oil or solid fat to a cake recipe changes the nature of the batter and it is now necessary to form an oil- (fat-) in-water emulsion where the aqueous, continuous phase contains the dissolved sugars, hydrated proteins and suspended flour, and other ingredient particles. Adding an oil or fat to the recipe considerably reduces the foam-stabilising properties of the egg, and the main aeration mechanism now involves the fat (Telloke, 1984) or the addition of some other suitable foam stabilising material, e.g. glycerol monostearate (Cauvain and Cyster, 1996).

DISSOLUTION AND HYDRATION OF INGREDIENTS IN CAKE BATTERS

The wider range of ingredients used to make cake batters means that there are many more materials to go into solution and become hydrated during the mixing process. Competition between ingredients for the available water is intense and there may be occasions when one or more of the ingredients used may not be fully dissolved or hydrated. There is no clear 'hierarchy' for the use of water by ingredients within cake batters since much depends on the proximity of water molecules to those other ingredient molecules with which they will interact. The speed of reaction with the water molecules will also depend on the nature of the molecular interactions, some taking place more rapidly than others. Since some water interactions are very rapid, the nature of the aqueous phase in cake batters changes quickly – even when water itself is added, and not as part of another ingredient (e.g. whole egg) – so that some of the later interactions during mixing will be between ingredient molecules and a 'solution' (usually sucrose) rather than pure water. A similar effect is observed with fermented doughs where, in the later stages of mixing, protein hydration takes place in a salt solution. Salt may also be present in cake batters, though the main solute to affect ingredient hydration will be sucrose or other sugars.

Some of the more important ingredients in cake formulations that need to go into solution or become hydrated include:

- *Salt* – used at similar levels to fermented doughs for its flavour and particularly for its effectiveness of lowering water activity and extending mould-free shelf-life (*see* Chapter 6).
- *Sucrose* – used to confer sweetness, but has a major effect on cake structure through its effect on starch gelatinisation (*see below* and Chapter 4), eating qualities (*see* Chapter 5) and product mould-free shelf-life (*see* Chapter 6). The rate of dissolution of sucrose depends on its form and crystal size; the granulated form dissolves less readily than the caster, pulverised and icing versions (*see below*).
- *Other crystalline sugars* – a wide range of sugars may be used for their effects on cake structure and shelf-life.
- *Baking powder components* – their rates of dissolution affect their rates of reaction and evolution of carbon dioxide gas in the batter (*see below*).

- *Flour* – hydration, swelling and gelatinisation of starch granules in batters are key elements in cake structure formation. Protein hydration does occur, although there is limited gluten development for the reasons discussed above.
- *Egg proteins* – need to be in the hydrated form in order to help with air bubble incorporation and bubble stability. They also contribute to cake texture and eating qualities.
- *Milk solids* – hydrated proteins make a limited contribution to cake structure formation. The lactose present dissolves and contributes to product flavour and colour.
- *Other cereal flours* – hydrated starches affect batter viscosity, cake structure and eating quality.

The mixing of ingredients to form cake batters is complex and, like breadmaking, a number of different mixing processes are in use to achieve the required batter (Street, 1991). In many cases the need for elaborate multistage mixing processes for cake batters is based on the use of ingredients in their 'traditional' form, e.g. milk, or to compensate for significant variations in ingredient character, e.g. butter composition. Today, provided that sufficient water is available to dissolve and hydrate the necessary ingredients, many cake batters can be based on a single-stage, all-in mixing method and little advantage will be gained from the more complex multistage methods (Telloke, 1984).

WATER LEVELS IN CAKE BATTERS

As discussed previously, water used in cakemaking formulations may be derived from a number of sources, although the major contributors in the more common cake types come from additions of whole egg (or egg albumen in the case of 'white' cakes), various forms of milk, and water. Because more than one water source may be used in cakemaking, it has become common for bakers to talk about 'liquid' additions, which can create some confusion. While it is acknowledged that different liquid additions may be made to cake formulations, for the discussion that follows references to water and its levels of addition should be taken to mean the *total quantity of water present in the batter, independent of its source*.

Factors to be considered when deciding upon the quantity of water to be used in cake recipe include:

- The necessity to achieve complete dissolution of soluble materials during mixing, or at least before the start of baking.
- The level of sucrose and other sugars in the formulation.
- The fluidity (viscosity) of the batter required for processing (*see below*).
- The capacity of the oven to remove moisture during baking (*see* Chapter 4).
- The moisture content required in the final cake because of its effect on product eating quality (*see* Chapter 5).
- The required cake water activity or equilibrium relative humidity (ERH), because of its relationship with product mould-free shelf-life (*see* Chapter 6).

The effects of changing water levels in sponge cake batters mixed with a continuous mixer–aerator were reported by Cauvain and Cyster (1996). They varied the level of added water but kept all of the other ingredients constant so that their water levels ranged from 28 to 34% of the batter weight. Batter viscosity fell as the water level increased, which affected the ability of the batter to pass through the mixer head and batter throughput rates for a constant pump speed. The more viscous batters experienced a greater heat rise during mixing. As the water content of the batter increased there was a linear increase in final cake moisture content (*see* Fig. 3.1) and a decrease in the sponge cake specific volume (*see* Fig. 3.2).

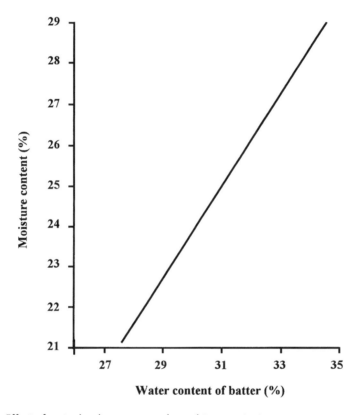

Fig. 3.1 Effect of water level on sponge cake moisture content.

Cauvain and Screen (1990b) studied the effect of changing ingredient levels with a high ratio unit cake formulation, and also found that cake specific volume decreased as the water level increased. Of the five ingredients they tested, the effect per unit of water on cake volume was much larger than the other four ingredients they tested (sugar, skimmed milk powder, fat and whole egg) (*see* Table 3.1). The appearance of a high ratio unit cake made with a high added-water level is illustrated in Fig. 3.3.

In cakemaking, a key issue is the ratio of water to soluble solids, particularly sucrose, in the formulation. This is because the gelatinisation temperature of wheat starch is affected by the presence of sucrose and other sugars. As the level of sucrose

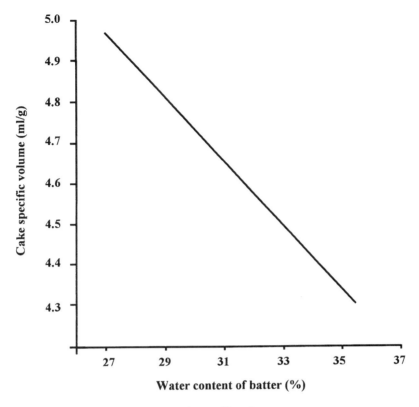

Fig. 3.2 Effect of water level on sponge cake specific volume.

Fig. 3.3 High ratio unit cake with high added-water level.

Table 3.1 Effect of ingredients on cake volume (Cauvain and Screen, 1990b).

Ingredient	Coefficient (ml)[a]
sugar	15.2[b]
skimmed milk powder	28.6[c]
fat	−14.4[b]
whole egg	−17.8[b]
water	−79.6[d]

[a] Values indicated are predicted increase (decrease if coefficient is negative) of the property value.
[b] Not statistically significant.
[c] Significant at the 1% probability level.
[d] Significant at the 0.1% probability level.

in the formulation increases, so does the gelatinisation temperature of the starch. The role of water and sucrose levels in controlling the expansion of batters and the formation of cake structures during baking is discussed in more detail in the next chapter.

The close relationship between water and sucrose in cake formulations has been recognised by practical bakers for many years and has become enshrined, along with other ingredient relationships, in a series of practical 'cake balance rules'. It is common in such recipe balance rules to try and achieve particular strengths of sucrose solution in the available water, the boundaries of which will always produce acceptable products. Examples of such rules, which link sucrose and water, can be found in Street (1991), in that for a given orthodox cake formulation "the sugar [level] should not exceed the liquids", and for high ratio cakes "Liquid should be about 1.4 times the flour [weight] when plastic shortening is used". Bent (1997) also offers examples of rules for the construction of cake recipes. More recently, computing technology has been used to develop rule-based programs that can perform many of the cake recipe balance functions required for product development (Young *et al.*, 1998).

FLOUR PROPERTIES AND WATER LEVELS IN CAKE BATTERS

In the production of many types of cakes, the 'standard' flour properties evaluated for bread have limited value in predicting cake baking performance. The two most important flour properties in cakemaking are the particle size distribution of the flour, and the application of some form of post-milling treatment, especially for the production of high ratio cakes.

Cauvain and Muir (1974) showed that the reduction of the maximum particle size of flour improved its cakemaking performance. This can be achieved by re-grinding flours or by using air-classification techniques. Essentially the process is one of detaching or separating the starch granules from the surrounding protein matrix, which allows more ready access of the sugar solution in the batter to the starch granule surface.

The two most common forms of post-milling treatment of flours for cakemaking are through exposure to chlorine gas (Telloke, 1986) or the application of heat treatment to the wheat, semolina (Cauvain *et al.*, 1976) or flour (Doe & Russo, 1968). The modification of cakeflour properties has been studied extensively, although the precise mechanism by which it works is still not fully understood. The application of heat to wheat and its products can result in flours with similar cakemaking properties to those of chlorination, but with one important difference in that the final flour will have a much lower final moisture content. This differ- ence has two important consequences: the level of added water (liquid) in batters must be raised in order to maintain a standard batter viscosity, and the hydration of the heat-treated flour during mixing leads to a marked increase in the tem- perature rise experienced during batter preparation (compared with effects in breadmaking, *see* Chapter 2). The latter effect needs to be regulated through the use of lower water (or liquid) temperatures, to ensure that baking powder reaction rates are not significantly increased with the premature release of carbon dioxide gas (*see below*).

GASES IN CAKE BATTERS

Some of the issues regarding the evolution of bubble structures in bread doughs discussed in Chapter 2 are relevant in the mixing of cake batters. The release of carbon dioxide gas first into solution and later to inflate the air bubbles that have been incorporated during mixing is an important part of the expansion mechanism in cakes. In this case, the carbon dioxide gas comes from the chemical reaction of baking powder components rather than yeast. The absence of yeast also means that the composition of the gas bubbles in the batter at the time of inflation will remain largely the same as observed in air (approximately 80% nitrogen and 20% oxygen), although this has little impact on the final product quality.

The rate at which carbon dioxide gas is generated from the baking powder components depends in part on the solubility of the ingredients in the aqueous phase in the batter. The more soluble the components, the faster they will act and the earlier the release of the carbon dioxide gas. Optimum cake volume depends in part on delaying the release of a portion of the carbon dioxide gas until the batter reaches the oven; regulating that release requires careful control of the acidic component of the baking powder. The rate of reaction comes in part from the particle size (the larger the particle size, the slower the rate of dissolution and reaction), and the choice of acid component.

Cauvain and Cyster (1996) showed that the evolution and loss of carbon dioxide gas could be relatively rapid in some circumstances – for example with extended mixing – even when one of the slower acting baking powder acids was used. Such observations partly explain the use of the traditional 'delayed soda' mixing proce- dure (Street, 1991), in which the sodium bicarbonate component of the baking powder is withheld from the mixing process until the very end. To facilitate its addition, the sodium bicarbonate is dissolved in a small portion of the recipe water. In some more traditional cakemaking procedures, hot water may be used to help dissolve the sodium bicarbonate before it is added to the other ingredients, though these days the fine grades of baking powder components available make such procedures largely unnecessary.

WAFER AND OTHER BATTERS

The manufacture of wafers encompasses a broad range of products based on the production of a low viscosity batter followed by depositing and, commonly, heating between two plates acting as two halves of a mould. Wafers are used for the production of ice-cream 'cones', chocolate-coated biscuits (*see* Fig. 3.4), caramel-filled sheets and 'bread' for use in holy communion. An example of a wafer sheet formulation is given in Table 3.2.

In wafer batter formulations, water is the major ingredient since it is necessary to produce a batter with a low viscosity which can be deposited on to the heated plates and which will spread quickly to the required size. The low viscosity of the batter

Fig. 3.4 Examples of chocolate-coated wafers.

Table 3.2 Example of wafer formulation.

Ingredient	Quantity (% flour weight)
wafer flour	100.0
water	147.0
powdered lecithin	1.0
oil	2.5
salt	0.25
sodium bicarbonate	0.30

also contributes to the absence of gluten formation during mixing in much the same way as discussed above for cake batters. Some biscuit wafer formulations may contain sugar, but at much lower levels than would be observed with cake batters, so the effects on water availability for gluten formation are somewhat less.

It is common in the large-scale production of wafers to recirculate the batter rather than leave it standing for any length of time before depositing; this can lead to gluten formation because of the extra 'work' done on the batter by the pumping systems and the shearing effects of the pipework. It is therefore very important that the solids content of the batter is strictly controlled; this is done largely by adjusting added water levels. Pritchard *et al.* (1975) showed that the main effects of increasing wafer batter solids content (i.e. reducing added water levels) were to increase wafer weight but not thickness, and increase wafer colour (i.e. make it darker). Low solids content wafer batters resulted in a low yield and low sheet moisture content (presumably because of excessive baking loss – *see* Chapter 4). The main contributor to the batter solids content was considered to be the damaged starch level in the flour.

In the last thirty years, there has been a steadily increasing demand for coated foods; this has led to a dramatic increase in the application of batters to meat and fish products. The batters used in the manufacture of such coated products cover a range of formulations and coating properties to deliver a wide range of textural and flavour sensations to the consumer. The formulations and technologies used are complex, but all rely on identifying and maintaining specific viscosity and batter rheological qualities. In these circumstances, the level of water used in the manufacture of the batters becomes very important, not just for dispersing and dissolving ingredients but also for ensuring hydration of many of the components that are responsible for the batter properties. These include the wheat flour components and additions of modified starches and gums.

CONTROL OF BATTER TEMPERATURES

Optimum batter performance and cake quality are achieved through control of batter temperatures at the time of depositing. This is especially true when the batter contains chemical aerating agents, such as baking powder, because the rates of chemical reaction are temperature-sensitive: the higher the temperature, the faster the reaction. In the case of cake batters, increased baking powder reactivity results in the premature release of carbon dioxide gas which will be seen as a lowering of the batter density (Robb, 1984) and ultimately a loss of baked product volume (Cauvain & Cyster, 1996).

Because of the low viscosity of batters, the transfer of energy during the mixing process is limited (Robb, 1968), although it does occur in some mixing situations and this may lead to an unacceptable temperature rise. As with bread dough mixing, the most common way to adjust batter temperatures is by adjusting the temperatures of any added liquids. This includes water additions, but in the case of batters may be extended to include liquid egg and liquid milk products. There is an additional advantage in using liquid egg products at lower than bakery ambient temperatures in that chill temperatures reduce the microbial risks associated with the storage of such products. Some cake mixers, e.g. continuous mixer–aerators, are fitted with a cooling jacket through which water or some other coolant may be circulated to assist in maintaining a constant batter temperature. Even though the batter residence times in the mixer head are low, e.g. less than 15 seconds, the high shear rates achieved between the mixer rotor and stator can lead to considerable temperature rises. The effects of using very dry or heat-treated cake flours on batter temperature rise have been commented on above.

BATTER VISCOSITY AND ITS MEASUREMENT

Fluids, such as water, have no particular shape of their own and flow under the influence of gravity to fill the space of a container. When held in a suitable container and stirred the fluid is pushed away by the front of the stirrer but flows to fill in the spaces behind as the stirrer moves on. In addition to noting the ability of the fluid to flow back into the shape of the container we would observe a resistance to the movement of the stirrer though the fluid. This frictional force which is encountered when moving through a liquid is described as its *viscosity*; the more viscous the fluid, the greater the frictional force observed. This type of viscosity is the one most commonly quoted in the technical and scientific literature and is known as *shear viscosity* (Menjivar, 1990).

Fluids have a measurable viscosity that varies with temperature; in general the higher the temperature, the less viscous the fluid. In batters, the presence of dissolved materials and suspended particulates, and even the numbers of air bubbles present, affect the viscosity of the system (Cauvain & Cyster, 1996). The shape, size, molecular weight distributions, inter-particle charges and concentrations all play their part in determining the batter viscosity. The key role played by water, either as added water or through its presence in other ingredients, has been discussed above. In most batter systems, the higher the water level, the less viscous the batter and the more readily it flows. The ability of batters to flow, particularly under the influence of heat, has a major impact on baked product quality as discussed in Chapter 4.

Batter viscosity may be measured either by assessing its ability to flow from a container under the influence of gravity or more commonly by using some form of recording mixing device, i.e. by measuring shear viscosity. When the viscosity of fluid is measured on its ability to flow under the influence of gravity, it is usual to measure differences based on the behaviour of the fluid with time, while shear viscosity is measured in terms of stress and strain rates (Menjivar, 1990).

Pritchard *et al.* (1975) used a standard Ford cup in their study of the influence of ingredients on the properties of wafer sheets. The technique they used was based on the time taken for a known volume of batter to drain from a cylindrical cup with a cone at the bottom and pierced by a hole (*see* Fig. 3.5). The time taken for the cup to drain is taken as an indication of the batter viscosity: the longer the time, the more viscous the batter. While related to fundamental properties that control batter viscosity, this techniques does not offer a fundamental measurement and so is not often seen quoted in the literature. However, the technique is particularly useful in a production environment because it is relatively simple to use, it is not sensitive to plant conditions, and it is inexpensive. In such cases, a trained operator can compare

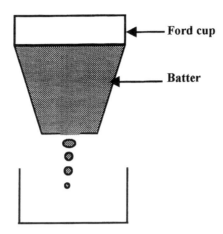

Fig. 3.5   Principle of assessing wafer batter viscosity with a Ford cup.

the flow-time for a given batter with that expected from the standard batter and adjust the viscosity of the batter accordingly to remain within specification, usually by adjusting water levels. The correlation between Ford cup flow times and some wafer properties can be very good.

A more popular way of assessing batter viscosity is by using a recording viscometer, such as the Brookfield viscometer. With this instrument, the stress placed on the batter during stirring with different strain rates may be recorded. The strain rates that are applied may be adjusted to more closely resemble those to which the batter will be subjected during processing. In the same way as would apply with the Ford cup technique, it is usual to establish a batter 'viscosity' profile from the Brookfield, which delivers a standard batter with appropriate processing qualities, and to assess test batters against that profile. Thus while more fundamental measurements of viscosity may be obtained with such viscometers, it will still be necessary to 'interpret' the data for a given process or product. This is particularly true of some of the other viscometers that may be encountered, e.g. Brabender Amylograph and Rapid Visco-Analyser, which have the additional facility of being able to apply heat to the batter according to a predetermined time–temperature profile. Such instruments have found particular use for the evaluation of the properties of flour–water slurries as a means of assessing and predicting flour performance during baking, but are not commonly used with full recipe batters (Faridi, 1990).

FORMATION AND PROCESSING OF BISCUIT AND COOKIE DOUGHS

The product groups covered in this section are those that may fit the general descriptors of hard-dough semi-sweet (e.g. Marie in the UK), rotary-moulded short-dough (e.g. Digestive in the UK) and wire-cut cookies. Crackers and other forms of laminated biscuits are discussed below. The individual groups may be distinguished from one another according to the degree to which gluten development occurs, or is desirable, as well as on the basis of the type of equipment used in their production. The key elements of the groups are summarised in Table 3.3.

Table 3.3 Key characteristics of biscuit and cookie doughs.

Type	Gluten development[a]	Equipment
crackers	modest	sheeter, laminator and cutter
hard-dough, semi-sweet	some to modest	sheeter and cutter
short-dough	limited	rotary moulder
cookies	limited	wire-cut

[a] By comparison with bread doughs.

The role of water in the production of biscuit and cookie doughs is very similar to that in fermented doughs and batters, with respect to the dispersion and hydration of ingredients. In biscuit- and cookie-making, high levels of added water at the doughmaking stage are avoided because most of it must be baked out in the oven in order to produce the crisp eating properties and long shelf-life that characterise biscuits. Typically, baked biscuit moisture contents fall well below 10% (*see* Chapter 4). This requirement limits the amount of water that is added to the other ingredients and the degree to which the softer dough types are mixed. In the case of short-dough and cookie dough, gluten development needs to be limited so that the forming processes for individual pieces can be easily accomplished, and so that changes in biscuit shape (e.g. shrinkage) after forming and during baking are minimised. This limited gluten development comes from water additions which are significantly lower than seen with fermented dough recipes (typically less than 15% flour weight), from the effects of sugars and other soluble materials on water activity, and through additions of fat.

In addition to the effects of recipe ingredients and their levels, the mixing method may be modified in an attempt to limit gluten formation. The most common variation is called 'creaming' because all the ingredients, except the flour and any nuts, fruits or chocolate pieces, are first mixed together. In this mixing stage, the sugars and other materials dissolve in the recipe water and the resulting solution becomes dispersed in the fat. The final mixture has a creamy-white colour and a soft consistency. The flour is blended through the cream mixture, giving a soft dough that lacks significant gluten formation because it is difficult for the flour proteins to become hydrated. However, protein hydration and gluten formation are possible, as shown by the fact that extended mixing when the flour has been added will lead to a much firmer, tougher mixture which is more difficult to process, and to loss of biscuit shape on baking.

Hard-dough, semi-sweet biscuits require a degree of gluten formation and so added water levels tend to be a little higher (typically 20 to 25% flour weight), and fat and sugar levels somewhat lower. An all-in mixing process tends to be used which also encourages gluten formation. Modification of the dough rheological character may also be undertaken through the addition of a reducing agent, commonly sodium metabisulphite, or a suitable proteolytic enzyme. If it is not possible to modify the dough rheological properties through the addition of a reducing agent, extra water may be used to give a softer, more machinable dough.

The important effects on biscuit processing which arise from varying added water levels have been studied by a number of workers. Gaines (1982) evaluated the consistency and stickiness of sugar-snap cookie doughs made with four different water levels. His data suggested a two-phase (initial and time-dependent) requirement for water by flour and sugar. In freshly mixed doughs, variations in water levels had approximately equal effects on dough consistency and stickiness, while in doughs that had been rested for 1 hour, changes in water level had twice the effect on dough consistency as on dough stickiness.

FORMATION AND PROCESSING OF SHORT PASTRY DOUGHS

Short-dough pastes are used in a variety of bakery applications and products. The main forms can be classified according to whether they are used for the production of sweet or savoury products, and are most commonly determined by whether sugar is present in the paste formulation. Examples of sweetened short-paste products include the various forms of filled fruit pies, while savoury pastries are most often associated with various meat and vegetable fillings. Savoury pastry forms are less common than the sweet type and derive mainly from British pie products. Once baked, the pie products made from savoury pastries may be eaten warm or cold.

Gluten formation in short-pastry doughs is not normally required, and if it occurs may lead to problems during processing and baking. The main problem will be related to shrinkage of the paste after forming (blocking) and during baking. Once again added water levels must be kept to a minimum because much of the water is baked out in the oven to give a crisp eating character to the pastry. Maintaining pastry crispness is a particular problem in this group of products because of moisture migration between the components (*see* Chapter 7).

Mixing methods for short-pastes may be all-in or multistage. As with short-dough biscuit pastes, the multistage methods aim to limit gluten formation. The three multistage methods in common use for short-pastry production are:

- *Rubbing-in*, in which the flour and the fat are first mixed together before the addition of the water and soluble materials.
- *Creaming*, in which only half the fat and the flour are mixed together, followed by the addition of the remaining fat, water and soluble materials (e.g. salt and sugars).
- *Boiling water*, in which the water (and sometimes the fat) is heated before being mixed with the other ingredients. This method is used only in the production of savoury pastes.

Taylor (1984) compared the all-in, rubbing-in and creaming mixing methods for short-pastry production and concluded that they had little effect on the handling properties of the paste or the final baked pastry. Such conclusions suggest that the concept of 'waterproofing' flour to prevent gluten formation has little credibility and it is more likely that the smearing of fat throughout the flour acts as points of discontinuity and weakness in the gluten network formed during mixing.

Cold water short-pastes are sensitive to the level of water used in the recipe. Hodge and James (1981) studied the effects on paste rheological properties of varying recipe water levels from 10 to 20% flour weight (the flour had 14% moisture) in 1% incremental steps. Using a form of penetrometer they showed that paste resistance to penetration gradually fell as the water level increased, reached a minimum at about 15% and then increased as recipe water levels continued to increase (*see* Fig. 3.6). It would appear from the data recorded in Fig. 3.6 that the development of a continuous gluten network did not occur until the added water level exceeded 15% of the flour weight.

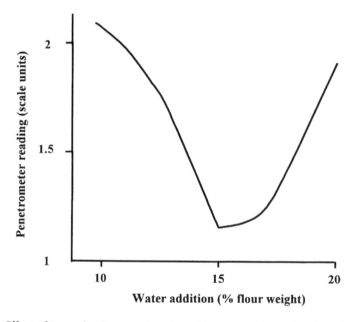

Fig. 3.6 Effect of water level on short-paste resistance to deformation (based on Hodge and James, 1981).

In the production of savoury short-pastes for pork pies, Mears and Wade (1969) concluded the properties of the paste did not appear to be particularly sensitive to variations in added water content, although the final paste temperature did vary with variations in added water temperatures, as would be expected. The same authors concluded that the temperature of the water at the time of addition to the other recipe ingredients during mixing also had little effect on paste properties.

FORMATION AND PROCESSING OF LAMINATED DOUGHS

One special group of bakery pastry products is characterised by the formation of alternating and largely discrete layers of doughs and fat (Cauvain, 1995). Because of the sheeting and folding processes used to achieve these structures the products are known collectively as 'laminated products' and they include both unyeasted and yeasted varieties. Unyeasted pastry forms are usually grouped under the heading of puff pastry (Thacker, 1997), while the yeasted forms are a more diverse group (most commonly recognised forms include croissant and Danish pastries (Bent, 1998)). The laminated structure, along with a low moisture content in some cases, gives the products a characteristic 'flaky' structure and eating quality.

The manufacture of all laminated products starts with the formation of a base dough. This is usually a relatively simple formulation of flour and water with some fat, salt, yeast (if required), and other functional ingredients. Some of the water used in the base dough formation in laminated products may come from additions of egg or milk products. The use of such ingredients is most common in the formulations for croissant and Danish pastries in order to confer particular flavours (Cauvain & Telloke, 1993). The levels of fat used in the manufacture of laminated products are much higher than those seen with bread, but most of the fat incorporation does not occur until after the dough has been formed. In these circumstances the fat plays little part in the formation of the base dough characteristics but does play a significant part during lamination (Telloke, 1991) and baking (*see* Chapter 4).

The formation of a gluten network in laminated products is important for the rheological properties of the base dough and their final structure formation. The energy imparted to the base dough for laminated products will be somewhat lower than that typically used for breadmaking because significant levels of work are imparted to the dough during the sheeting operations that characterise these products. The base dough rheology needs to be such that the dough has good extensibility, low elasticity and low resistance to deformation. Because of these requirements the level of water added in the formation of the base dough is particularly important.

Optimum water levels for laminated doughs vary with changes the flour characteristics in a similar manner to that seen with bread (*see* Chapter 2). However, the levels used in laminated product formulations are usually slightly lower (typically 3 to 7% lower, based on flour weight) than those used in breadmaking. These slightly lower water levels are required to compensate for the softening of the dough, which occurs because of the longer processing times that apply during the sheeting and laminating stages, in part because of the presence of the laminating fat. Telloke (1991) showed that, as expected, increasing the water level produced a softer dough with less resistance to deformation, but puff pastry lift was not affected by changes in added water from 52.5 to 62.5% of the flour weight. There was a slight decrease in pastry shrinkage over the same added water level changes.

These observations are interesting because the generation of steam from the dough water is an integral part of the mechanism by which puff pastry lifts during baking, but much of the steam generated does not take part in the aerating mechanism (*see* Chapter 4). Since only part of the added water provides steam for pastry lift, once a minimum level of addition is achieved the addition of further quantities becomes unnecessary, as shown by Telloke (1991). In puff pastry manufacture, it is far more critical to achieve a defined set of dough rheological properties for paste processing; it is these requirements that decide the level of water to be added to the base dough.

Optimising dough rheology, and therefore dough water levels, is also important in the production of croissant and Danish pastry. Cauvain and Telloke (1993) considered that maintaining the correct dough consistency was more important for croissant and Danish pastry than for puff pastry, partly because firmer doughs were more difficult to process and this resulted in less regular separation of the dough and fat layers. Firmer croissant and Danish pastry doughs expand less readily during proof so that by the end of a given proof time the dough pieces will be lower in proof height, which in turn will be reflected as a lower product volume. An increase in proof time can compensate for the loss of proof height, but this may lead to other quality losses, e.g. increased oiling of the laminating fat which would reduce product lift.

Control of base dough temperature in the production of puff pastry is less critical than control of the laminating fat temperature and the paste processing temperatures. Knight *et al.* (1967) found no significant effects resulting from a 5°C increase in base dough temperature, and Telloke (1991) studied the effects of changing added water temperature to give base doughs with temperatures spanning a 10°C range without finding any significant effects. In the case of croissant and Danish pastry, variations in water temperature led to variations in base dough temperature – which had a more profound influence on final quality because of the effect on yeast activity, as well as dough rheology. Higher dough temperatures lead to softer doughs and increased yeast activity which leads to faster proof and potential losses of final product quality (Cauvain & Telloke, 1993).

Another type of yeasted laminated product is the biscuit cracker. In this case, the layering technique is normally based on forming a dough sheet on to which is added a 'cracker' dust comprising a mixture of fat and flour, with some minor ingredients. This technique gives a product that has some limited flakiness after baking, but which is able to withstand a considerable degree of mechanical handling, including the application of butter by the consumer before consumption. The formation of the base dough depends on the development of a gluten network with the correct rheological characters so that optimising added water levels is as critical with crackers as with any other laminated product. The precise level of added water will be influenced by the method used to make the dough, although with all methods the added water levels are lower than would typically be seen with the same flour in a bread dough.

There are three main groups of dough mixing methods for crackers: straight dough with no fermentation (floor) time; straight dough with fermentation time; and sponge and dough. Each dough mixing method requires its own combination of ingredient formulation and plant, and each produces a slightly different final product. Dough water levels will vary between the methods because of changes in dough rheology, which typically occur after mixing and during dough processing. The changes in dough properties are greatest when they are given some fermentation after mixing and before processing, or when a sponge and dough process is used. With both of these methods, enzymic (or chemical) softening means that a lower water level can be used in the initial doughmaking stage.

BISCUIT DOUGH AND PASTE RHEOLOGICAL PROPERTIES

It is clear that the rheological properties of biscuit doughs and pastes are very important to both processing of the intermediate and to final product quality. In this context, the level of water and the formation (or not) of gluten play major roles in determining the required rheological character. There are a number of rheological testing methods available that can be used to assess the biscuit dough and paste properties. A selection of these, and some brief comments on the effect of water on the readings obtained with each method, are given below.

Compression–extrusion tests

In this type of test, the dough or paste is held within a container with specified geometry and a force applied. The general principles are illustrated in Fig. 3.7a for a closed container and one that has an orifice through which the dough or paste may pass after compression. With the closed container, it is usual to measure the force required to achieve a given penetration depth in the sample; softer doughs or pastes, such as those obtained with higher water levels, require less force to achieve a given penetration. Compression devices are known as *penetrometers* or *compressimeters*. Compression measurements commonly relate to the sensory properties (touch or feel) so often used by craft bakers. For example, Miller (1985) found that the subjective assessment of short biscuit doughs on a seven-point scale from very soft to very tough correlated reasonably well with compressive force measurements.

Compression–extrusion tests may be used to measure the force required to extrude the sample through the orifice, but it is more common to measure the time taken for a given quantity of material to pass through the orifice (*see* Fig. 3.7b). The higher the water content, the softer the dough and the faster the extrusion time. The forces experienced by the dough or paste during extrusion may be equated roughly to those that might occur when a biscuit passes through a rotary moulder, or when a paste is formed in a die (blocked) or sheeted between pairs of rolls. Hodge and James (1981) used an extrusion test to assess the properties of savoury pie pastry, and Shekara *et al.* (1986) used a 'Research' water absorption meter to evaluate changes in short biscuit dough consistency.

Recording dough mixers

Included in this category are mixers such as the Farinograph and Mixograph, which measure the torque that results from mixing a dough at constant speed. Such instruments are most commonly used in the assessment of flour properties (Catterall, 1998), but may also be used with full recipe doughs to make assessments of biscuit dough and paste properties. Changes in dough or paste resistance to mixing are usually recorded on a chart. Initially there is little resistance to mixing, but the resistance soon increases and this is recorded as a steep rise on the graph; continued mixing results in a rapid fall (the fall is less gradual when assessing flour–water doughs). Hodge and James (1981) used the Farinograph with full recipe savoury pastes and found that paste consistency as measured with this technique was sensitive to added water levels, with higher water levels giving softer doughs with

(a)

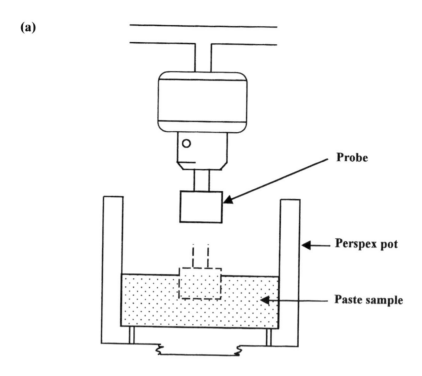

Probe

Perspex pot

Paste sample

(b)

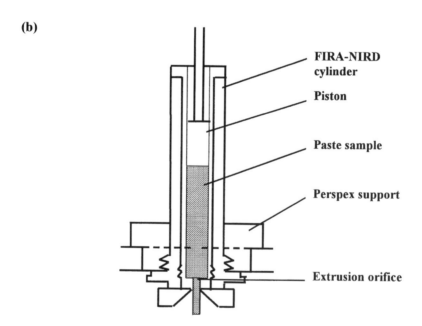

FIRA-NIRD
cylinder

Piston

Paste sample

Perspex support

Extrusion orifice

Fig. 3.7 General principles of compression extrusion tests for biscuit dough and pastes. (a) Detail of assembly fitted to Instron Universal Tester for measuring penetration of paste. (b) Detail of FIRA-NIRD extruder assembly fitted to Instron Universal Tester for measuring extrusion of paste.

lower Farinograph heights. More fully developed doughs, e.g. puff pastry and crackers, will show Farinograph curves closer in form to the standard flour–water tests in common use.

Load–extension tests

In this case, a prepared dough is subjected to some form of stretching stress. Instruments used with flour–water doughs include the Extensograph, the Alveograph, the Consistograph and the Dough Bubble Inflation device (Dobraszczyk, 1997). Their use with many biscuit doughs and pastes is limited because such products do not have a highly developed gluten structure with reasonable extensional properties.

Load extension tests have been devised by some workers to evaluate full recipe pastes. For example, Hodge and James (1981) devised a tensile strength test and applied it to savoury pastes. They used a 'bone'-shaped portion of a sheeted paste held in suitable clamps and stretched the sample at a predetermined rate. As would be expected, they found that the extensibilities of the pastes were low because of limited gluten formation, and the test offered limited information of likely paste behaviour during processing.

Telloke (1991) developed load–extension tests for measuring the properties of base doughs and laminated pastes used in the production of puff pastry, croissant and Danish pastry. Measurements were made of the resistance of a suspended sheet of dough or paste to deformation forces, and were shown to be highly correlated with dough behaviour during processing and final product quality. Increasing the level of added water in puff pastry doughs decreased the resistance of the dough to deformation but appeared not to significantly affect its elastic recovery. Telloke concluded that changes in dough water level affected only the viscous component of the dough. Morgenstern *et al.* (1996) used a similar method to produce stress–elongation curves for pastry sheets and showed that the 'pseudoplastic behaviour' of the dough became less pronounced at higher levels of water addition.

Fundamental tests

Small-scale deformation tests have been developed which apply shear deformation to a sample held between two parallel plates (Menjivar, 1990). Such tests are more readily related to fundamental measurements of rheology and are used when the deformation history of the sample is well defined. A potential drawback of such testing methods is that the size of the stresses and strains applied to the sample are lower than might be experienced during normal processing of doughs and pastes in the bakery. Nevertheless, appropriate instruments have been used in the study of biscuit doughs. For example, Oliver *et al.* (1995) used a Bohlin VOR-controlled strain rheometer to study the changes in semi-sweet biscuit dough rheology associated with additions of sodium metabisulphite (SMS) and increases in added water level. In their study they showed for a range of wheat varieties that increased levels of water addition could be used to produce biscuit dough rheologies similar to those obtained with lower water levels and added SMS. This similarity was achieved even though water and SMS changed biscuit dough rheology by different mechanisms.

CHOUX PASTRIES

The production of eclairs and other forms of choux pastries depends on specialised mixing methods to develop a viscous fluid with an egg protein matrix capable of expanding to a high specific volume, which dries during baking to give a crisp eating shell. The baked shell will later be filled with a high moisture content filling (e.g. dairy cream). In the initial stages of mixing, a mixture of water and fat (usually margarine) is heated until the water boils. Flour is then stirred in to make a smooth paste. During this part of the mixing stage, the hot water begins to gelatinise the starch and the mixture forms a thick paste (a roux). Whole egg is then added gradually to the roux and beaten after successive additions until a smooth depositable paste is achieved. The viscosity of the final mixture is usually controlled with the addition of the egg rather than through adjustment of the added water content.

In some modern processing methods, pregelatinised flour and starch mixtures are used to eliminate the need for boiling the water. In such cases a mixture of water and egg may be used to achieve the required paste viscosity. The water and the egg are not interchangeable because the proteins present in the egg are needed to help form the final product structure and to give strength and crispness to the baked case.

BAKERY PRODUCTS NOT BASED ON FLOUR

There are a number of products manufactured in bakeries that are not based on wheat flour but in which the addition of water plays a significant role. They include some items that will go on to be baked, but a much larger number of items that remain unbaked. The latter group comprises the various creams, fillings and toppings that fill or decorate the base products. The range of products embraced under this heading is too large to be considered in detail and the following comments are intended only as a brief introduction to the various classes of such items.

Baked products

Amongst the most common non-flour baked products are those based on egg white – meringues. They have a crisp, brittle texture and are very sweet because of their high sugar content. The egg whites are used for the incorporation of air to create a foam structure and, along with added water, to dissolve the large quantities of sugar that are used in the recipe. The mixture may be acidified to improve the stability of the albumen proteins in the egg white.

Macaroon products are based on ground almond nuts; here water is required to wet the mixture rather than truly hydrate it and to dissolve the added sugar. As with meringue products, the level of sugar is very high and the resulting strength of the sucrose solution may lead to recrystallisation in the baked product. Some recrystallisation may be desirable because this confers a 'crunchy' texture to the final product (*see* Chapter 5).

Fillings

A wide range of fillings may be used with bakery products. In all cases water plays a significant role in dissolving materials and contributes to a generally soft eating texture. Water may come directly from added recipe water or through the addition of other water-containing ingredients, such as dairy cream or fruits. In all cases a most important issue is the retention of water within the filling and prevention of its loss or migration to some other component in the composite product. Water retention in the filling is controlled by adjusting its water activity and through the use of stabilisers. Control of water activity in fillings and moisture migration in composite products are discussed in more detail in Chapter 7.

Toppings and icings

All of the common toppings that are used with bakery products contain high levels of added sugars. The main role of the water in the formulation is to dissolve the sugars and to disperse and suspend some of the other ingredients. The strength of the sugar solution in the topping has a major impact on its sensory qualities and its behaviour during storage. In many cases the topping has undissolved sucrose present and is therefore hygroscopic, which leads to particular problems with moisture migration (*see* Chapter 7).

A common form of icing for use as a bakery topping is called 'fondant' in the baking industry. Essentially, fondant is a suspension of sugar crystals in a sugar syrup. It is made by heating a water–sucrose mixture (1:3 parts by weight) until it boils, and then beating the solution as it cools. Other sugars may be present, e.g. glucose. The resulting product requires re-heating before it can be used; after being applied to the finished product is has a soft, plastic texture with a slight crust, and is very sweet. Other forms of icing may be based on unheated mixtures of sugar and sugar syrups (water icing), or with the addition of egg whites (royal icing).

Marshmallow

These products are similar to meringues in that they are often based on egg white and sugar with the addition of a suitable gelling agent, e.g. gelatin or modified starch. Unlike meringue, however, marshmallow products are usually soft-eating. Both the sugar and the gelling agent act to hold the water within the matrix of the marshmallow.

Jams and jellies

The various forms of jams and jellies used in the bakery are based on mixtures of fruit and sugars, with some form of stabilising agent, commonly pectin. The water needed to dissolve the sugars that are present may come from the fruit alone or through the addition of extra water in the formulation. As with marshmallow, the combination of sugars and stabiliser acts to keep the water held within the product matrix.

CONCLUSIONS

Even when gluten formation is not desirable in bakery products, water plays a major role in the formation of their structures. In products that contain relatively high levels of sugar, the formation of a sugar solution in the aqueous phase is important so that the right conditions for the necessary starch gelatinisation processes are set up or initiated. Higher levels of fat also characterise many types of cakes, biscuits, cookies and pastries, with the fat contributing to the inhibition of gluten formation and also conferring soft and tender eating qualities.

REFERENCES

Bent, A.J. (1997) Cakemaking processes, in *The Technology of Cakemaking,* 6th edn (ed. A.J. Bent), Blackie Academic & Professional, London, UK, pp. 251–74.

Bent, A.J. (1998) Speciality fermented goods, in *Technology of Breadmaking* (ed. S.P. Cauvain & L.S. Young), Blackie Academic & Professional, London, UK, pp. 214–38.

Catterall, P. (1998) Flour milling, in *Technology of Breadmaking* (ed. S.P. Cauvain & L.S. Young), Blackie Academic & Professional, London, UK, pp. 296–329.

Cauvain, S.P. (1995) Putting pastry under the microscope. *Baking Industry Europe,* 68–9.

Cauvain, S.P. & Cyster, J.A. (1996) Sponge Cake Technology. *CCFRA Review No. 2.* CCFRA, Chipping Campden, UK.

Cauvain, S.P., Hodge, D.G., Muir, D.D. & Dodds, N.J. (1976) Improvements in and relating to treatment of grain. *British Patent No. 1 444 173.* HMSO, London, UK.

Cauvain, S.P. & Muir, D.D. (1974) High-ratio yellow cakes: the effect of flour particle size. *FMBRA Report No. 61.* CCFRA, Chipping Campden, UK.

Cauvain, S.P. & Screen, A.E. (1990a) Sugars, sweeteners and low-sweetness bulking agents. *FMBRA Bulletin No. 2,* April, CCFRA, Chipping Campden, UK, pp. 62–9.

Cauvain, S.P. & Screen, A.E. (1990b) Effects of some ingredients on cake texture. *FMBRA Report No. 142.* CCFRA, Chipping Campden, UK.

Cauvain, S.P. & Telloke, G.W. (1993) Danish pastries and croissants. *FMBRA Report No. 153.* CCFRA, Chipping Campden, UK.

Dobraszczyk, B.J. (1997) Development of a new dough inflation system to evaluate doughs. *Cereal Foods World,* **42,** 516–19.

Doe, C.A.F. & Russo, J.V.B. (1968) Flour treatment process. *British Patent No. 1 110 711.* HMSO, London, UK.

Faridi, H. (1990) Application of rheology in cookie and cracker industry, in *Dough Rheology and Baked Product Texture* (eds H. Faridi & J.M. Faubion), Van Nostrand Reinhold, New York, USA, pp. 363–84.

Gaines, C.S. (1982) Influence of dough absorption level and time on stickiness and consistency in sugar-snap cookie doughs. *Cereal Chemistry,* **59,** 404–7.

Hodge, D.G. & James, C.D. (1981) Pastry technology: factors affecting the consistency of short paste. *FMBRA Report No. 96.* CCFRA, Chipping Campden, UK.

Knight, R.A., Mears, K. & Robb, J. (1967) Puff pastry: a test bakery investigation of a shortened process of manufacture using the 'English' method. *FMBRA Report No. 2.* CCFRA, Chipping Campden, UK.

Mears, K. & Wade, P. (1969) The manufacture of meat pies: some factors affecting the properties of boiling water paste. *FMBRA Report No. 26.* CCFRA, Chipping Campden, UK.

Menjivar, J.A. (1990) Fundamental aspects of dough rheology, in *Dough Rheology and Baked Product Texture* (eds H. Faridi & J.M. Faubion), Van Nostrand Reinhold, New York, USA, pp. 1–28.

Miller, A.R. (1985) The use of a penetrometer to measure consistency of short doughs, in *Fundamentals of Dough Rheology* (ed. H. Faridi), American Association of Cereal Chemists, St. Paul, USA, pp. 117–32.

Morgenstern, M.P., Newberry, M.P. & Holst, S.E. (1996) Extensional properties of dough sheets. *Cereal Chemistry,* **73,** 478–82.

Oliver, G., Thacker, D. & Wheeler, R.J. (1995) Semi-sweet biscuits: 1. The influence of sodium meta-bisulphite on dough rheology and baking performance. *Journal of the Science of Food and Agriculture*, **69**, 141–50.

Pritchard, P.E., Emery, A.H. & Stevens, D.J. (1975) The influence of ingredients on the properties of wafer sheets. *FMBRA Report No. 66*. CCFRA, Chipping Campden, UK.

Robb, J. (1968) Effect of work input in different mixers on Madeira cake. *FMBRA Bulletin No. 5*, October, CCFRA, Chipping Campden, UK, pp. 340–5.

Robb, J. (1984) The practical implication of baking powder reaction rates. *FMBRA Bulletin No. 6*, December, CCFRA, Chipping Campden, UK, pp. 215–24.

Shekara, S.C., Haridas Roa P. & Shurpalekar, S.R. (1986) Studies on the consistency of biscuit doughs using a 'Research' water absorption meter. *Journal of Food Science & Technology*, **23**, 208–12.

Street, C.A. (1991) *Flour Confectionery Manufacture*. Blackie Academic & Professional, London, UK.

Taylor, S.L. (1984) The mixing of short paste. *FMBRA Bulletin No. 5*, October, CCFRA, Chipping Campden, UK, pp. 200–9.

Telloke, G.W. (1984) The mixing of cake batters. *FMBRA Report No. 114*. CCFRA, Chipping Campden, UK.

Telloke, G.W. (1986) Chlorination of cake flour. *FMBRA Report No. 131*. CCFRA, Chipping Campden, UK.

Telloke, G.W. (1991) Puff pastry I: Process and dough ingredient variables. *FMBRA Report No. 144*. CCFRA, Chipping Campden, UK.

Telloke, G.W. (1991) Puff pastry II: Fats, margarines and emulsifiers. *FMBRA Report No. 146*. CCFRA, Chipping Campden, UK.

Thacker, D. (1997) Pastries, in *The Technology of Cakemaking* (ed. A.J. Bent), Blackie Academic & Professional, London, UK, pp. 239–50.

Young, L.S., Davies, P.R & Cauvain, S.P. (1998) Cakes – getting the balance right. *Proceedings of ES98, the Eighteenth Annual International Conference of the British Computer Society Specialist Group on Expert Systems* (eds R. Milne, A. Macintosh, & M. Bramer), Springer, London, UK, pp. 42–55.

4 The contribution of water during processing, baking, cooling and freezing

After mixing and forming (depositing), doughs, pastes and batters need to undergo heat setting before they can truly be called baked products. In some cases (i.e. fermented doughs), another processing stage that must occur before baking is proof – the expansion of the structure to a suitable size before the dough goes into the oven. After baking, the product must be cooled and in some cases this may be to temperatures low enough to freeze it for long-term storage. In the thermal processing stage, water continues to play a key role as the relatively fluid dough, paste or batter structures become immobile through baking. That is not to say that water itself has become immobile, because in many cases it remains sufficiently 'free' to take part in a range of different reactions during storage, many of which are discussed in the subsequent chapters.

Many of the transitions from relatively fluid to rigid structures during baking require the overall loss of water from the product and its redistribution, both on the macroscopic and microscopic scales, within the product structure. It is because of the loss of water from the product during heating that some of the key transitions occur during baking as, in many cases, the matrix moves from a glassy to a rubbery state. Water plays a major role as a plasticiser in this context because of its low molecular weight, and the transitions invite parallels with changes in synthetic polymers where low molecular weight plasticisers also affect glass transitions. The special properties of wheat flour, namely the formation of gluten and the gelatinisation of the starch, also become critical to the formation of baked product structures.

WATER IN RETARDED AND FROZEN FERMENTED, UNBAKED DOUGHS

The process of retarding refers to the specialised refrigerated storage of unproved, yeasted dough pieces for many hours, commonly 16 to 72 hours, to allow bakers to 'time-shift' their production (Cauvain, 1992). During the retarding period, the activity of the yeast in the dough slows down to a considerable extent, and if the storage temperature falls low enough the dough may be held in what approximates to a state of suspended activity (Cauvain, 1998a). However, there are some important changes which take place in retarded doughs during storage, and water plays a significant role in most of these.

The relative humidity of fermented dough pieces is around 90 to 95% and much higher than the relative humidity of the air in a retarder (commonly around 60% at loading). Soon after entering the retarder the dough pieces begin to lose moisture and will continue to do so throughout the storage period. The longer the storage period, the greater the moisture loss. An example of moisture losses from dough pieces during retarded storage is given in Fig. 4.1 for four typical dough storage temperatures. Unlike the situation in dough provers (*see below*), it is not practical to introduce water vapour into a retarder to limit relative humidity differentials and therefore moisture losses between dough and atmosphere by raising the relative humidity of the latter. There are two main reasons for this restriction: the water vapour will be at a higher temperature than the air within the cabinet and will thus be trying to raise the cabinet temperature; and moisture in the atmosphere will condense as ice on the cold surfaces, especially the evaporator (cooling) coils, within the cabinet.

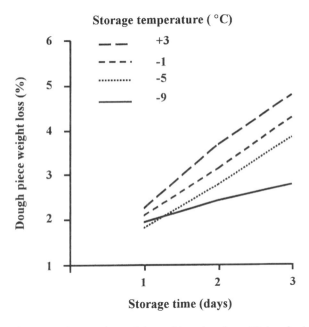

Fig. 4.1   Effect of storage time on the weight moisture loss from 60 dough pieces.

The basic design of the cooling coils in retarders and retarder–provers with their larger surface area limits the potential for condensation of moisture on the surfaces of the cooling coils (Cauvain, 1998a), but inevitably some condensation and ice formation does occur. Provided the efficiency of the evaporator coils is not too badly affected, the formation of ice is of no great consequence. Indeed, in some retarder–provers the melting of the ice when the cabinet begins to warm provides some of the water vapour required for the proving conditions.

The data illustrated in Fig. 4.1 show that moisture losses decrease as the storage temperature falls. This is because the saturated vapour pressure of air is lower at lower temperatures (*see* Chapter 1) and thus less water needs to be lost from the dough pieces in order for them to achieve equilibrium with the cabinet atmosphere.

At any given storage temperature, the velocity of the air across the surface of the dough pieces will affect the rate at which they lose water: the higher the air velocity, the greater the rate of moisture loss. For this reason, air velocities in retarders and retarder–provers are usually kept to a minimum, just enough to ensure uniform air circulation and temperature distribution. Many retarders and retarder–provers are designed with some form of baffle to assist air distribution (Cauvain, 1998a), but in some cases this may result in an unduly high air velocity in places within the unit and may cause skinning and misshapen products. The dough pieces illustrated in Fig. 4.2 show a characteristic 'leaning' shape towards a perforated baffle fitted to one side of a retarder–prover to aid air distribution. The shape comes from the skinning of the surface nearest to the air inlet, which restricts its expansion, while the trailing surfaces have a higher moisture content and allow the dough to continue to expand during storage.

Fig. 4.2   Dough piecies 'leaning' towards the air inlet during retarded storage because of surface water evaporation.

The greater the surface area of the dough piece during storage in the retarder or retarder–prover, the greater the potential for weight loss through increased evaporation. This means that dough pieces with large surface areas will lose water faster than smaller ones. The surface area is related roughly to the weight of the dough piece and its shape. Thus a 450 g dough piece in a pan has a much smaller exposed surface area than the same weight of dough formed into a baguette shape. Expansion of dough pieces during retarded storage is not uncommon. It occurs through yeast fermentation, which may continue at relatively low temperatures, even at around –5°C. With this increase in dough piece volume comes an increase in surface area, and with this, increased evaporation which may lead to greater skinning.

THE INFLUENCE OF MOISTURE ON WHITE SPOT FORMATION DURING THE RETARDING OF FERMENTED DOUGHS

One of the most common quality losses associated with retarded and frozen fermented doughs is the formation of small, translucent blisters or 'white spots' on the crust of the baked product. They may occur for a number of reasons, but are associated mainly with lack of gas retention in the dough or excessive gas production before or in the early stages of retarded storage (Cauvain, 1992). In the case of retarded pan breads, these white spots may merge to form patches with a 'waxy' appearance (Cauvain, 1996) and are sometimes referred to as 'condensation spotting' (Sluimer, 1978). This latter reference suggests that water plays a role in the manifestation of the spotting phenomenon, and this is indeed the case.

The key role of water in the formation of white spots is confirmed by the observation that dough pieces which lose water from their surfaces during retarded storage typically skin and do not show white spot formation. Where dough piece surfaces are protected and water cannot evaporate, skinning cannot occur and there is thus the potential for white spot formation. In free-standing breads this will apply to the base resting on a tray, and in pan breads to the base and sides where the dough touches the pan. If storage or subsequent warming conditions cause excess moisture to condense on dough piece surfaces this may well increase the risk of spot formation, but only if the other qualities of the dough referred to above are present. A slight loss of water from the surface of retarded doughs during storage would appear to be desirable and such circumstances also apply to the proving of fermented dough pieces, as discussed below.

The white spots seen on retarded products are visible to the naked eye only when the dough pieces have been proved and placed in the oven to bake. As the crust colour begins to form, the white spots become visible. When viewed under a microscope, there is some evidence for water droplets suspended within voids under the dough surface, which probably become white spots (Cauvain, 1998a), and this water may well be reducing the local concentration of the sugars that take part in the normal Maillard browning reactions. With less or no Maillard browning (*see below*), the spots become visible in an otherwise brown area of crust.

THE IMPORTANCE OF RELATIVE HUMIDITY DURING PROOF OF FERMENTED DOUGHS

The gradual release of carbon dioxide gas from yeast fermentation inflates the air bubbles trapped in bread doughs during mixing and causes the dough to expand. It has become traditional for bread to be fermented (expanded) before it enters the oven to develop an aerated (foam) structure, which leads to a more palatable product after baking. Over the centuries, fermentation of the individual dough pieces has become an essential part of the breadmaking process and it has become commonly known as 'proof'. It has become common practice in most industrial environments to raise the temperature of the dough to around 40°C to encourage maximum gas production by the yeast present in the dough and to keep production times as short as conveniently possible. (But note that some production processes may benefit from cooler proving temperatures, e.g. during retarding (Cauvain, 1998a) and the production of baguette (Collins, 1978).)

As discussed above, when a dough piece stands for any length of time it is likely to lose water from the exposed surface and dry out over a range of temperatures. If the moisture loss is excessive, this may lead to the phenomenon that bakers refer to as 'skinning', restricting expansion of the dough piece (even though the yeast is still active) and leading to an unacceptable crust character and lack of baked product volume. In addition to the effects of the relative humidity of the atmosphere surrounding the dough piece, the velocity of the air over the dough piece and the surface area of the dough piece, the water activity of the dough piece also influences skinning.

Most bread doughs have a 'lean' formulation, that is they contain few ingredients other than flour, water, salt and yeast. The proportion of water in the dough is such that the relative humidity of the solution within the dough is high, typically above 95%. The relative humidity within a bread dough will fall as the proportion of soluble materials in the formulation (usually sugars) increases, but seldom falls much below 90% for fermented products. The dough relative humidity is therefore almost invariably higher than that of the air in the bakery and so moisture is inclined to move from the surface of the dough piece to the surrounding atmosphere. By placing the dough in an enclosed space for proof – the prover or proof box – it is possible to control not only the temperature of the air in the cabinet but also its relative humidity and, in turn, the potential for skinning of the dough.

Successful proving demands that the relative humidity of the air in the cabinet should be close to, but slightly lower than, that of the dough. In practice this means around 80 to 85% relative humidity at about 40°C. Lower relative humidities can be used at lower proving temperatures or when doughs have been retarded or frozen (Cauvain, 1998a). A small difference between the relative humidity of the dough and the air in the cabinet promotes a slight moisture loss from the dough surface so that it is slightly dry to the touch. This delicate skin is useful in helping the dough piece to retain its desired shape during proof. Raising the air relative humidity up to and above that of the dough results in a moist, permeable surface through which some of the carbon dioxide gas generated by yeast fermentation may be lost. With free-standing, oven bottom and hearth breads, air relative humidities above that of the dough lead to flowing (spreading) of the dough piece in the prover, and ultimately loss of product volume and shape (*see* Fig. 4.3). For these reasons prover relative humidities tend to be lower for such products, typically around 65 to 70%. Low prover humidities may also be used with baguette (Collins, 1978). Condensation of water of the surface of dough pieces arising from excessive relative humidity in the prover may also lead to unsightly surface streaks on the baked product.

The humidity in provers is raised by the introduction of water into the cabinet or chamber atmosphere, usually in the vapour state (steam). This means that the temperature of the water vapour is higher than that of the dough pieces when they enter the cabinet or chamber, and as the vapour condenses on the dough and pan surfaces, if used, it gives up its latent heat. The temperature gradient that is established by the condensing water vapour provides a driving force for heat transfer by conduction to the centre of the dough and helps increase yeast activity. Later in the proof cycle when the dough temperature has stabilised to that of the cabinet heat, transfer to the dough causes evaporation of moisture from its surface. At the start of proving, dough pieces gain weight; later they lose it. Wiggins (1998) reported that there was a nett weight loss from dough during proof, which was typically about 3 g from an 880g dough piece.

The potential loss of water from the dough piece during proof will also be affected

Fig. 4.3   UK 'bloomer'-style breads, proved at (top) 95% and (bottom) 80% relative humidity.

by the air movement across its surface. The circulation of air throughout the cabinet or chamber is required to ensure uniformity of heating and distribution of water vapour. High air velocities may lead to excessive moisture loss from the dough with subsequent skinning and loss of product quality. Condensation on the internal surfaces of the prover may lead to hygiene problems and corrosion of the materials used in the cabinet structure.

THE CONTRIBUTION OF WATER (STEAM) TO EXPANSION AND PRODUCT STRUCTURE DURING BAKING

The reactions that take place in the conversion of dough or batter to bread or cake are many and diverse, and water is involved in almost all of them. The key reaction is usually the loss of water from the unbaked matrix, although this simple statement hides a multitude of complex reactions dictated in part by product formulation, and in part by the mechanisms and rates of heat transfer during the baking process itself. Underpinning the heat setting process called baking are the key transformations associated with products made from wheat flour – the gelatinisation of the starch and the coagulation of the gluten – both of which are concerned with the movement of water from and within the product matrix.

Along with the physicochemical changes occurring within the dough or batter, it is necessary to consider the expansion forces created by the gases present in the dough or batter. These forces are derived from three sources:

- *Thermal gas expansion.* As the temperature in the dough or batter increases, trapped gas bubbles expand according to the gas laws defined by Charles and

Gay-Lussac, which means that for no change in pressure, gas volumes increase by approximately $\frac{1}{273}$ for each kelvin (1 kelvin = 1 degree Celsius) rise in temperature.

- *Release of carbon dioxide.* This may be provided by yeast (in bread) or through the action of an acid and sodium bicarbonate (leavening agents commonly combined as baking powder in cakes, biscuits and cookies). Release of carbon dioxide occurs at relatively low temperatures during baking (e.g. yeast starts to be inactivated at about 45°C (113°F)) but can continue to make an increasing contribution through thermal gas expansion. The contribution of carbon dioxide to product expansion depends on the quantity of aerating material present in the dough or batter. The greater the initial quantity, the greater will be the potential expansion, provided that the dough or batter is capable of retaining quantities of the gas produced.

- *Water vapour.* As the temperature in the dough or batter increases, some of the water is turned to vapour and adds to the gas expansion of the matrix. Water can only turn to steam and contribute to product expansion when the temperature in the dough or batter exceeds 100°C. Thus steam expansion contrasts with thermal gas expansion and evolution of carbon dioxide, which occur at much lower temperatures and therefore earlier in the baking process. The contribution of the steam to expansion depends in part on the level of water present in the dough or batter, where and how it is held in the matrix, and the rate at which heat is provided. Bloksma (1990) calculated values for the theoretical expansion of bread during baking and considered that 60% of the volume increase in the oven, i.e. the difference between proof volume and baked volume (oven spring), came from the steam generated.

If product expansion involves all three sources of gas expansion; the order of magnitude for individual contributions is usually least from thermal gas expansion, and approximately equal for that from the release of carbon dioxide and steam generation (but varying with product type and formulation, i.e. level of carbon dioxide generating agent). When only two gas expansion mechanisms are present in baking, it is usually only thermal gas expansion and steam generation, with the latter making the major contribution. Because baked product formulations and processes vary widely it is useful to consider the role of water and steam during baking under several different product group headings.

Baking is a process of heat gain and moisture loss. In general, the faster the heat input, the more rapid the moisture loss. However, other aspects of product character are related to heat input rate and these do not always benefit from faster heat input. Conventional oven baking is based on conduction of heat from the surface to the centre of the dough or batter matrix so that a temperature gradient exists throughout a given product cross-section in an oven. This means that the transformation from unbaked matrix to baked structure takes place at different moments within a given product cross-section with the areas at and close to the surface baking far earlier than the centre during the oven residence time for a given product. Baking conditions are commonly set according to the time–temperature combination required to achieve a given set of quality criteria and vary widely, not just for different product groups but also for individual products within particular groups. In the discussion of the role of water in baking that follows, it is as well to remember that baking is not a single, instantaneous event, and that this has its impact on many aspects of product quality (including those to be discussed in Chapter 5).

Bread and fermented products

When dough pieces first enter the oven, the water present is largely uniformly distributed throughout the matrix. As discussed in Chapter 2, the main water-absorbing components are the water-soluble proteins (pentosans), bran, gluten-forming proteins and starch. The latter two components form the bulk of the water-absorbing materials and so most of the changes in dough during baking are related to them. As the temperature of the matrix begins to rise, the starch granules begin to swell (from about 45°C (113°F)) and gelatinise (from about 60°C (140°F)). When the dough enters the oven and its temperature begins to rise, the polymers in the starch granules vibrate. This breaks the intermolecular bonds and allows hydrogen bonding sites in the granules to engage more water. With more heat input there is a complete loss of crystallinity. Gelatinisation therefore involves a change from an ordered, crystalline state to a disordered, amorphous state. To achieve this transition, the starch granules need more water than is usually held in their mass and there is a loss of water from the gluten network to the gelatinising starch. At this time the gelatinised starch takes over the structure supporting role from the gluten network in the dough.

As discussed previously (*see* Chapter 2), damaged starch has a much higher water-absorbing capacity than the undamaged form. As the temperature rises in the product matrix during baking, enzymic activity increases and the amylase enzymes present begin to attack the starch granules, and in doing so increase their ability to absorb water. The action of amylase in bread doughs is complex however, as continued action by the enzymes will break down the starch granules and ultimately release water within the dough matrix. The effect of the amylase action on final bread quality depends on the type of amylase present or added to the dough; for example, higher levels of cereal *alpha*-amylase (either natural or added via malt products) can lead to bread collapse and slicing problems (Chamberlain *et al.*, 1977), while additions of fungal *alpha*-amylase lower dough viscosity, improve bread volume and avoid collapse (Cauvain *et al.*, 1985; Cauvain & Chamberlain, 1988). The different effects are related to the temperature at which the particular form of *alpha*-amylase is inactivated during baking; the fungal form is inactivated at a lower temperature than the cereal form (Williams & Pullen, 1998), thus giving more potential benefit and fewer problems.

During baking the rheological character of bread doughs undergoes profound changes that appear to become irreversible between 55 and 75°C (131 and 167°F) (Dresse *et al.*, 1988). This temperature range encompasses the two major events in structural formation in bread: starch gelatinisation (discussed above) at the lower end and protein coagulation at the upper end. The viscosity of the dough at this stage increases by many orders of magnitude; however, the product is not 'baked' at this point since if it is removed from the oven it cannot support itself and will collapse under the influence of gravity. Practical observations have shown that it is necessary to continue heating many types of bread products to achieve a core temperature of between 92 and 96°C (198 and 205°F) before a sufficiently rigid 'loaf' structure is formed. Heating dough pieces beyond the gelatinisation/coagulation temperatures undoubtedly involves continued loss of water from the matrix, but other changes are taking place, which need to be considered.

In its unbaked form, bread dough (and cake batters) may be considered as a complex *foam* in which the gas bubbles (cells) are intact and discrete from one another. It is because they are intact that they are able to receive carbon dioxide gas from yeast fermentation and enable the dough to expand (Cauvain, 1998b). The 'surface' of the gas bubbles is stabilised by a combination of gluten and other ingredients in the dough, for example fat and emulsifiers (Williams & Pullen, 1998). During baking, the bubble-stabilising components in dough gradually lose control. Fat and emulsifiers will have melted by 65°C (149°F) and the internal bubble pressure becomes so great that the bubbles begin to become buoyant and try to escape, but they are still restrained by the gluten network. As discussed above, the gluten network is losing water to the gelatinising starch and in consequence is losing much of its extensibility. Once the gluten protein structure sets there is no bubble-stabilising mechanism left and the gases are free to escape from the baking dough. At this point the foam becomes a *sponge* (in the generic rather than the specific cakemaking sense), i.e. all of the cells are interconnected and vapours and liquids may move freely through the matrix. The properties of sponges can be fully appreciated with a few simple experiments in the bathroom.

This transition from foam to sponge in bread baking is very important because it makes the matrix permeable to vapours and liquids. Because of the temperature gradient set up during bread baking, the surface of the dough piece reaches the sponge stage long before the centre and quickly becomes permeable. This permeable surface is known as the crust and it is through this porous crust that the water vapour generated during baking can escape; as discussed previously moisture loss during baking is essential to the formation of a bread structure. Wiggins (1998) described the heat transfer mechanism of baking dough in terms of evaporation front and heat pipe effects. Evaporation of moisture can occur only once the liquid boiling point has been reached. The low concentration of soluble materials in bread doughs means that the boiling point is not much higher than 100°C.

Crust formation is not merely the loss of water from the dough, although the very low moisture content does contribute significantly to the crisp eating character of the crust (*see* Chapter 5). The crust of most baked products is characterised by the formation of a darker, commonly brown, layer which penetrates for a few millimetres into the crumb. The colour comes from the complex Maillard reactions that occur at temperatures approaching 150°C (302°F). The application of steam in the early stages of baking to affect crust formation is discussed below.

Cakes

The heating of a batter to form a baked cake also depends on the transformation from foam to sponge (again in the generic sense). The fact that cake batters are foams is perhaps more readily appreciated than with bread doughs because of the manner in which cake batters are prepared; that is the ingredients are commonly beaten or whisked during which the volume of batter considerably increases as air is incorporated during the mixing process. The formation of a stable cake batter is complex and several ingredients play significant roles in achieving batter stability, most notably fats (Telloke, 1984) and emulsifiers such as glycerol monostearate (Cauvain & Cyster, 1996). In the formation of stable cake batters, proteins play a less significant role, with the exception of egg proteins in some types of cakes (Street, 1991). The gluten-forming proteins of wheat play an insignificant role in the baking of cakes (although coagulation does occur) and the major role in structure formation is taken over by the starch in the flour.

Far higher levels of soluble ingredients are present in cake batters than in bread doughs, and this affects the manner in which water is held in the unbaked matrix. Both the gelatinisation characteristics of the starch and the boiling point of the aqueous phase are affected. The most commonly used group of soluble materials in cake batters is the sugars, in particular sucrose. When sucrose is used in a cake formulation, it dissolves readily in the aqueous phase that forms in the batter, and helps to stabilise the foam by controlling the viscosity of the continuous phase by interacting with the starch chains to stabilise the amorphous regions within them. The addition of sucrose increases the temperature at which egg proteins coagulate and, most importantly, increases the gelatinisation temperature of the starch in the flour (Spies & Hoseney, 1982).

The increase in starch gelatinisation temperature in cake batters is related directly to the sucrose concentration in the formulation and therefore the water activity of the batter. The higher the sucrose concentration, the higher the gelatinisation temperature and the longer the batter will stay fluid during baking, thereby allowing the cake to achieve larger volume (Cauvain & Screen, 1994). Street (1991) suggested that a 50% sucrose solution would increase the gelatinisation temperature of wheat starch by 23°C (41°F) so that for a sponge cake batter the gelatinisation temperature would be in the order of 80°C (176°F). With an optimised sucrose solution, the disruption of the starch granules at gelatinisation also allows the release of the expanding gases in the batter matrix and the structure will set firm on cooling. If the sucrose solution is too concentrated, the starch gel may not form a stable structure and the cakes will collapse on cooling (*see* Fig. 4.4). Thus, in cake making a critical 'rule' relates the level of water to the level of added sugar in the formulation (e.g. Street, 1991).

Similar effects are seen with concentrations of sugars other than sucrose, or for combinations of other sugars with sucrose. However, not all of the effects on cake quality of sugars other than sucrose are desirable, and generally their levels of addition are limited by comparison with sucrose. For example, Cauvain and Screen (1994) observed that when high levels of glucose replaced sucrose in a standard high-ratio cake, the crust of the cakes set earlier and permitted the early release of carbon dioxide and steam thereby limiting cake volume.

Laminated products

The generation of steam from within the dough layers makes a major contribution to the mechanism by which laminated products rise in the oven. Telloke (1991) studied the aeration of puff pastry under the microscope and showed that the thickness of the individual dough layers hardly increased during baking. These

Fig. 4.4 Effect of sucrose level on cake structure, left 57.5%, centre 115%, right 172.5%, flour weight basis.

observations confirmed the view that most of the lift in puff pastry comes from diffusion of steam into the fat layers (Tscheuschner & Luddecke, 1972) where its diffusion to the atmosphere is impeded by the melted fat and the increase in vapour pressure forces the dough layers apart. This process is shown in Fig. 4.5. In this mechanism the solid fat index and the melting point of the laminating fat used play a significant role in controlling the degree of lift that can be achieved. In general, the higher the fat melting point, the greater the pastry lift. Telloke (1991) provides a comprehensive review of the role of laminating fats in the production of puff pastry.

The stability of the laminated product structures after the steam has finally escaped from the matrix comes in part from the formation of bridges between the dough layers. The individual dough layers are never completely discrete from one another. Even in the most uniform of laminated pastes, some bridging occurs

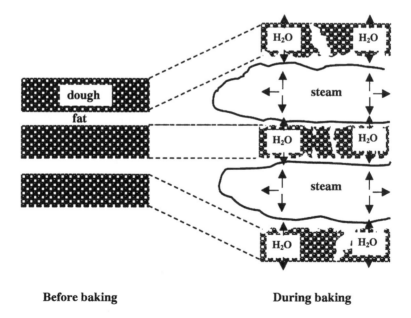

Fig. 4.5 Representation of mechanism of lift in puff pastry.

between dough layers; this becomes particularly true as the number of laminations increases in the paste. Further structural rigidity comes from the loss of water from the gluten structure formed in the base dough both during and after mixing, the latter coming from the energy transferred to the dough during the sheeting action in the lamination process.

The relationship between the loss of water during the baking of puff pastry and product lift is illustrated in Fig. 4.6. As the time the product spends in the oven increases, the moisture content continues to fall. Pastry lift on the other hand increases quickly in the first half of the baking period, but thereafter there is no change because any steam generated escapes readily from the product matrix through the liquid fat. While the products may have achieved maximum lift after half the baking cycle, the products are not stable and collapse readily when taken from the oven. As commented above, the continued loss of moisture is required to achieve structural rigidity, as well as a crisp eating character (*see* Chapter 5). Telloke (1991) calculated the volume of steam lost by the time the product reached maximum lift, compared that with a typical increase in product volume, and showed that the generated steam volume was more than one hundred times greater than the product volume increase.

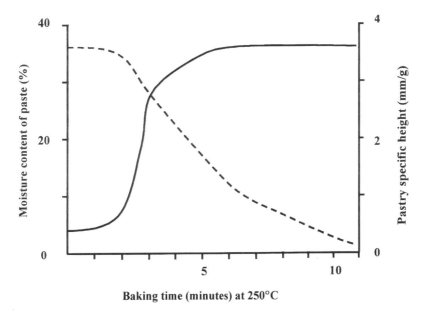

Fig. 4.6 Effect of baking time on puff pastry lift (———) and moisture content (– – –).

A similar aeration mechanism to that described above applies to fermented, laminated products, although the presence of yeast interferes with the integrity of the dough layers and provides carbon dioxide for volume expansion (Cauvain & Telloke, 1993). The production of crackers also relies to a significant extent on lift generated from steam trapped in the dough layers of the laminated structure.

Biscuits and pastries

The formation of a gluten structure in most biscuits, cookies and short pastries is limited. Also the levels of water that are commonly used are too low to permit full gelatinisation of the starch present (Abboud & Hoseney, 1984). All of these factors limit the expansion seen in such products, and minimise the contribution of steam to product volume. Because of the limited addition of water but high levels of sugars in biscuits and cookies, the glass transition temperature of the matrix is commonly above room temperature. When the doughs reach the oven, the sugars (and fat) melt and allow the flour to form the continuous phase. Continued heating drives off water and allows the gluten in the flour to move from the glassy to the rubbery state, and the matrix stops spreading and sets. Thus the level of sugar in the formulation plays a significant role in structure formation, especially spread. In practice this can be seen with high-sugar products, such as gingernuts in the UK, and sweet wafers that can be folded or shaped at the end of the baking cycle because they are still relatively plastic and flexible.

Audidier and Battail (1968) showed that the initial temperature rise of biscuit doughs was faster in an oven with a moist rather than a dry atmosphere. In the early stages of baking, a high humidity increased the rate of temperature rise either by reducing the moisture evaporation from the dough piece or by causing some condensation on the piece surface. Wade (1995) reported that the humidity in the first zone of biscuit ovens affected both the appearance and dimensions of products. The stack heights of semi-sweet biscuit and crackers fell as the oven humidity increased because the products were thinner, but the thickness of short dough biscuits was not affected (Lawson *et al.*, 1979).

Choux pastry

The development of a partially gelatinised, (egg) protein-enriched and high moisture content matrix for the preparation of choux pastries was described in Chapter 3. In the oven, the generation of steam within the choux case is an important part of its expansion mechanism. Unlike bread and cakes, the desirable internal structure for choux products comprises large cavities with limited membrane formation. To achieve this requires the generation of large quantities of steam or other gases while the paste matrix is still capable of expanding. The steam is derived from the high moisture content of the unbaked roux encouraged by the partial gelatinisation of the starch and subjected to rapid heat transfer using high oven temperatures. Other gases may be contributed through the use of baking powder, or sodium bicarbonate or ammonium bicarbonate (Vol).

Once the crust of choux products forms, it becomes permeable to water vapour and expansion ceases (as with all other baked products). Traditionally, large-volumed choux products were achieved by covering the products as they entered the oven with a large, loose fitting lid (commonly known as a 'coffin' in the UK). While this lid slows down the heat transfer rate to the product it does encourage the development of a localised area of high humidity, which delays the onset of the product crust and reduces water vapour loss from within the baking product. The extra vapour pressure generated by this action helps increase product volume.

Eventually steam does begin to escape from under the loose fitting lid and continued heating permits crust formation. In some cases the rate of moisture loss may be encouraged by the removal of the lid before the end of baking.

Doughnuts

Doughnuts may be yeast- or powder-raised, but in both cases the heat setting of the product matrix is achieved by totally or partially immersing the dough in hot oil – frying. Heat is transferred through the product by conduction and a temperature gradient is established through the dough piece cross-section in a similar manner to baked products. As the temperature of the piece increases, the water vapour pressure inside the piece increases and gas bubbles expand in a similar manner to that seen in other baked products. Because of the relatively high levels of sugar in doughnut formulations, setting of the product structure again follows the lines seen with cakes, i.e. setting is delayed to temperatures approaching 80°C (176°F).

The transition from foam to sponge makes the structure porous and in this case provides the points of entry for the hot oil. The absorption of oil into the product matrix gives doughnuts a characteristic bite, eating quality and flavour. However, excessive absorbtion of oil leads to unacceptable 'greasy' eating qualities. As long as the pressure within the dough matrix is greater than that of the atmosphere surrounding it, and the foam is intact, oil cannot be absorbed. In this respect increasing the added water level in the dough offers some advantage in reducing fat absorbtion through increased vapour pressure.

Wafers

Traditional forms of wafers are baked by depositing batter on to one of a pair of plates, with the top plate closing on the lower to seal the batter between the two (Wade, 1995). The plates are heated rapidly, usually by direct-fired gas burners, and the rapid heat transfer quickly turns the water in the batter to steam. Considerable steam pressures are generated (up to 2.1 kgf cm^{-2} has been reported by Pritchard and Stevens (1973)), and vents in the edges of the plates permit escape of the steam (and a very small quantity of batter). The number and dimensions of the steam vents both affect wafer sheet thickness (Pritchard and Stevens, 1973). Wafer sheets are commonly baked in 1.5 to 3 minutes to a moisture content of less than 3%.

APPLICATIONS OF STEAM DURING BAKING

Water in the form of steam may be introduced deliberately into the oven chamber to raise the humidity and influence the final product character. The steam may introduced into the oven chamber in a number of ways:

- As vapour generated from a source separate and external to the oven (e.g. a boiler).

- Through the introduction of water to a heating mechanism outside of the chamber but part of the oven construction (e.g. water running over heated surfaces).
- As an atomised spray (mist) introduced directly into the oven chamber.

Bread

In the manufacture of many bread and fermented products, the use of steam will add to the appearance through the formation of a *gloss* on the surface and influence the texture and eating qualities of the crust. In general, with bread and fermented products the aim of using steam is to increase the 'crustiness' of the products, although it may also be used to achieve a more uniform expansion of the product in the early stages of baking.

The formation of a gloss on the surface of bread products derives directly from the introduction of steam and control of the quantity that is made available for a given mass of dough in a given baking chamber. When dough pieces are first placed in the oven, their surface temperature is low – typically below 45°C (113°F) – and the introduction of steam at 100°C (212°F) results in some condensation on the surface of the dough piece. This excess of water combines with the starch and with the action of the enzymes present and encourages the formation of dextrins and sugars (mainly maltose) on the dough piece surface. As the temperature begins to rise the surface begins to dry and the enzymic activity ceases but the dextrins and sugars remain and will colour as baking proceeds. The dextrins are the components that are mainly responsible for the formation of the surface gloss. The whole process is very short because the crust temperature climbs rapidly above the boiling point of water. The length of time over which steam will be introduced into the oven temperature is short, commonly less than 90 seconds and typically less than 60. Wiggins (1998) discussed the importance of having an excess of water vapour introduced into the oven. He considered that an excess is needed to encourage paste-type gelation, which leads to gloss formation, whereas insufficient steaming leads to crumb-type gelation and lack of crust gloss.

In addition to changing the appearance of the product, steaming will affect product crustiness: the thicker the gelatinised starch layer that is formed, the greater will be the cracking of the crust on the baked product. This cracking occurs when the product leaves the oven and begins to cool. The crumb of the product has a higher moisture content and is more flexible than the lower moisture content crust and so readily contracts as the temperature of the air within the cells falls. Being less flexible, the crust is not able to contract as fast or to the same degree as the crumb, and the strains placed on the crust by attached portions of crumb become such that splits begin to occur in the surface. A similar effect occurs when baked products are frozen, as discussed below.

Part-baked breads

Part-baking is a process in which proved doughs are baked just sufficiently to inactivate the yeast and enzymes, and set the structure with a minimum of crust colouration and moisture loss. A second baking stage is used to refreshen the crumb properties and develop a normal crust colour. Steam may be applied during one or both of the baking stages. In the first baking stage, baking temperatures are lower and times longer than used in scratch production, and steam may be used to help control the oven spring, or break. Collins and Ford (1985) studied the application of steam in the production of part-baked soft rolls and French bread, and found that limited steaming improved product quality. In the preparation of part-baked rolls in a rack oven, only a 'few seconds' was required and longer steaming led to severe wrinkling of the product. Steaming times of 18 seconds were recommended for part-baked French breads, and extending the steaming period led to product collapse and severe wrinkling. Collins and Ford (1985) also studied the application of steam at bake-off and found that it improved final product appearance.

Cakes

It is not common to introduce steam into ovens for cake baking, since the formation of a hard, glossy crust is not normally required. There is evidence, however, that the humidity level in the oven during cake baking can affect aspects of product quality. To a large extent differences in humidity levels during cake baking come from the use of different types of oven with their different heating methods. The effect of extraction systems in most ovens is to lower chamber humidity, which leads to drier baking conditions.

Robb (1987) experimented with the introduction of humidity using water injected into a tunnel oven and examined the effect on the quality of sponge cakes. The introduction of steam had no direct effect, but did change the effects of baking times and temperatures. Steam injection with combinations of lower temperatures and longer baking times reduced sponge cake volume. The introduction of steam appeared to have no effect on cake weight losses during baking.

Choux pastry

The benefits of raising atmospheric humidity during the baking of choux pastry have been discussed above. In cases where the use of lids or coffins would be difficult, e.g. in a tunnel oven, similar improvements to product quality have been obtained through the introduction of steam into the oven soon after the point at which the product enters the chamber.

Rye breads

Gluten formation in rye bread doughs is restricted by the lack of any significant quantities of gluten forming proteins, and starch gelatinisaton plays a much greater role in structure formation than in wheat breads. Bread baked from 100% rye flour is much denser compared with wheat flour bread, and it is common for rye and wheat flours to be mixed to improve bread volume and palatability. Baking times for rye and mixed rye–wheat breads are much longer than 100% wheat (typically 45 to 55 minutes compared with 25 to 30 minutes for the latter). The length of time over which steam is applied is also greater, possibly as much as 20 minutes. This extended steaming period helps to improve bread volume and softness by allowing greater expansion of the dough before gelatinisation of the starch occurs.

Pumpernickel and wholemeal rye breads may be produced by the specialised Horlbeck steam-baking process, which utilises a steam baking chamber which might best be described as a steam pressure vessel. The dough pieces are packed tightly into closed pans and steam baked for many hours. Baking conditions may vary from 16 to 24 hours at 100°C (212°F), to 5 to 8 hours at 200°C (392°F). The product crumb darkens considerably during the baking process but moisture retention is higher in the product due to increased solubilisation of the carbohydrates which are present.

Chinese steamed breads

Chinese steam bread, or 'man-t'ou', has a long history in China, probably stretching back for more than 3000 years. It is the staple food of the wheat-growing areas of northern China. The key features of Chinese steam bread are their semi-circular shape, white crust colour, smooth surface and shiny skin. The latter characteristic derives from the heat setting process carried out by baking the proved dough pieces in an atmosphere of steam until the structure has become set. The high level of water that condenses on the surface of the heated dough pieces enourages starch gelatinisation but discourages the usual Maillard browning reactions.

SURFACE TREATMENTS WITH WATER AND WATER-BASED SOLUTIONS

The use of steam during baking is not the only way in which water may be used to modify baked products. Water or water-based solutions and suspensions may be applied directly to the surface of unbaked and baked products to enhance the product surface appearance, colour, eating qualities and flavour. In a simple form of treatment, water may be sprayed on to the surface of products in advance of baking to help with the coating or adherence of particulate materials. For example, hamburger bun doughs commonly pass through a water mist before the application of sesame seeds (Bent, 1998).

A common form of water-based treatment is the application of various solutions or suspensions before baking to modify baked product colour and appearance. Whole egg and milk are probably the most common materials used on unbaked dough and pastry products. Sugar solutions may be used, although it is more common for these to be applied after baking to sweetened doughs, for example hot cross buns and fruited buns.

Starch pastes are sometimes applied to the surface of bread doughs to create a special surface finish. Since the heat from the oven will quickly gelatinise the starch paste, the surface finish becomes dry and hard and cracks to give a distinctive surface appearance. One such example, tiger- or leopard-skin bread, is illustrated in Fig. 4.7. Collins and Ford (1985) applied a water-based starch paste on to the surface of cooled, part-baked bread and rolls before freezing and found that it improved product appearance after bake-off but not when steam was also used at bake-off.

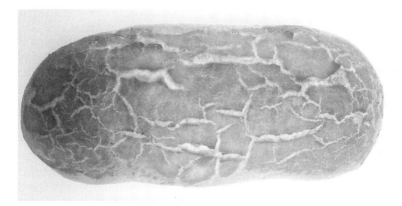

Fig. 4.7 Tiger- or leopard-skin bread.

The use of boiling water is the essential processing feature that distinguishes bagels from other roll-type products. After being formed into a ring shape and proved for a short time (typically 15 to 20 minutes), bagel dough pieces are immersed in boiling water or a boiling water–sugar solution for about 10 to 15 seconds. After this treatment, the dough pieces are removed for baking. The boiling water treatment encourages the formation of a surface gloss, which is considered an important characteristic of the finished product.

Water may also be used for cutting or marking the surface of bread doughs before they enter the oven so that expansion of the pieces may be controlled. The 'water splitter' consists of a jet of high pressure water with which the depth of the cut can be adjusted by adjusting the jet pressure. Water splitters are also used to give a clean cut through delicate baked products such as cake.

WATER AND MICROWAVE BAKING

As discussed in Chapter 1, water molecules are dipoles, that is each molecule has an asymmetric charge centre. Microwave radiation is based on the exposure of materials to an electric field in which the polarity is changing many millions of times per second. As the field strength builds in a material, dipoles (like water) are momentarily aligned with the field direction, and as it decays they return to their random orientation. This rapid building and decay of the field causes frictional heating in the water molecules which is converted first to potential energy in the water and then to thermal energy. With continued exposure to microwaves water becomes heated, and if present in bakery food will transfer that energy to surrounding materials.

In most bakery products, the water present will contain dissolved substances, many of which are ionic in character. These ions also react to the introduction of microwaves into the product matrix. They will be moved in the opposite direction to their polarity so that the change in field direction causes them to move one way and then quickly in the reverse. As they move backwards and forwards in the matrix they may collide with water molecules and become part of the energy transfer mechanism by which products are heated.

In the application of microwave heating to bakery foods, water plays a major role in facilitating the transfer of energy within the product matrix. In general, the higher the moisture content of a given product matrix, the faster it will heat. This relationship goes some way to explaining why many microwavable cake mixes have much lower viscosity than would be seen with batters to be baked by conventional means. Schiffman (1993) provided a comprehensive review of the application of microwave technology to baking and its use with part-baked (brown and serve) products, doughnut processing, and bread and cake baking.

One of the limiting factors in the application of microwaves to baking is the microwave absorption potential of the water, and this is affected by the degree to which it is bound within the product matrix. Bound water is not rotationally free and therefore has poor microwave absorption properties. The microwave absorption properties of ice are much poorer than those of water because the ice acts like a large polymer and vibrates slowly. When a few ice crystals have melted during exposure to microwaves, those water molecules begin to absorb the energy and are heated quickly. The water molecules continue to absorb energy and become hot even though ice crystals may remain elsewhere in the product matrix. This 'localised' heating makes the defrosting of frozen products with microwaves difficult.

LOSSES OF WATER DURING BAKING AND COOLING

The processes of baking and, to a lesser extent, cooling involve the loss of water from the product matrix. The role that the loss of water plays in helping to expand and set the structure of products has been discussed above. In some cases, e.g. bread and cakes, bakers seek to limit moisture losses during baking and cooling because of the organoleptic benefits of water in the final product (*see* Chapter 5). The magnitude of the losses that occur during baking are related directly to the quantity of energy input: the greater the energy input, the greater the moisture loss.

Robb (1987) showed that weight losses for sponge cakes deposits of 200 g (7 oz) varied between 16 and 22 g ($\frac{1}{2}$ to $\frac{3}{4}$ oz), depending on baking times and temperatures. Cauvain and Screen (1988) also studied the effects of heat input during sponge cake baking. They measured heat flux (J cm^{-2}) and integrated it with time, and found a correlation with weight loss that was curved, although it could be approximated with a straight line. There was no significant correlation when the same baking losses were plotted against an integral of time and temperature. In their study, Cauvain and Screen (1988) recorded weight losses that varied from 12 to 20 g from a 200-g deposit of sponge batter. They also showed that changing evaporation rates by changing air velocities in a tunnel oven, by opening and closing dampers, independently of oven temperature, had a profound affect on weight losses. Wiggins (1998) gave weight loss figures for UK plant bread (800 g at point of sale) of between 50 and 55 g (1.8 oz). Losses will be much higher for crusty, free-standing and hearth breads.

During cooling there will be further losses from baked products as moisture evaporates from the product surface because of the temperature differential between the still warm product and the colder air to which it has been exposed. Variations in air flow rates and temperatures across the product affect the rate at which it cools and loses moisture. As might be expected, moisture losses are higher for higher air flow rates. Wiggins (1998) suggested a 20 to 25 g (1 oz) weight loss for typical UK plant bread during cooling. The humidity of the air used in the cooler may be increased in an attempt to reduce moisture losses from the product. In some cases (Allied Bakeries, 1986), water may even be sprayed on to the surface of the product to aid cooling. Vacuum cooling may also be used with bakery products, although moisture losses are not improved (i.e. lessened) with this method of cooling.

WATER IN FROZEN BAKERY PRODUCTS

Freezing is applied to many bakery products, both unbaked and baked, in order to retain their organoleptic properties for extended periods of time (*see* Chapter 5). As the temperature in the product matrix falls below 0°C (32°F), the water present begins to freeze and ice crystals form. Bakery products are complex systems in which polymers (e.g. starches and proteins) and low molecular weight solutes (e.g. sodium chloride) are dispersed or dissolved in the aqueous phase. The freezing of such matrices takes place under non-equilibrium conditions so that the normal phase change from liquid to solid is not observed in the product. Thus, the behaviour of the aqueous phase during freezing and thawing is affected significantly by the product formulation and the degree to which the water is 'bound' within the product matrix.

The term 'bound water' has been used to refer to water in a product that does not freeze when the matrix temperature falls below 0°C (32°F). Referring to water as bound does not imply that it is energetically bound in the matrix and therefore that the input of measurable quantities of energy are required to free it, but that the water is loosely held and may diffuse out of the matrix, usually over relatively long periods of time, because this '*non-freezable*' water remains relatively mobile compared with the mobility of water within ice. A simple analogy may be water held in a bath sponge: if pressed (i.e. energy applied) the sponge releases water readily, while if left to stand it will gradually dry out as the water evaporates from within the sponge structure. Inevitably the behaviour of non-freezable water in a frozen matrix is more complicated than this simple analogy, although evaporation of non-freezable water can be seen as the formation of frost or snow when products are stored for long periods of time in deep freeze in moisture impermeable bags. This loss of water from products usually has a detrimental effect on product quality, some aspects of which are discussed in Chapter 5.

The presence of solutes in a product formulation lowers the freezing point of water. The greater the concentration of the solute, the lower the freezing point. The everyday proof of these comments is seen in those climates where ambient temperatures can fall to below 0°C, so that salting becomes necessary to avoid ice formation on the roads. Baked product formulations contain many soluble ingredients, the most common of which are salt and sugar, and thus the freezing point of the water in such matrices is considerably lower than 0°C. For example, unbaked bread dough formulations in the UK typically freeze around –6°C (21°F) (Cauvain, 1996) and unbaked cake batters between –12 and –20°C (10 and –4°F) (Screen, 1988). After baking, the loss of moisture increases the solute concentration and the freezing points become lower still, which can affect final product quality (*see* Chapter 5). As the temperature during freezing falls, some of the water in doughs, batters and baked products turns to ice and is effectively 'removed' from the aqueous phase. The concentration of the solutes in the aqueous phase is therefore increased, so the freezing point of the remaining water becomes even lower. Eventually solutes will reach their limits for solubility and freeze concentration can no longer occur. At this point, the freezing point of the solution may be so low that it does not freeze under normal conditions, e.g. –20°C (–4°F).

When water turns to ice there is an increase in volume of about 10% and this change can have a significant effect on the physical nature of the product matrix. In the case of frozen unbaked bakery products, e.g. doughs and pastes, the growth of ice crystals within the matrix can lead to the formation of stress cracks on the product surface. These cracks may carry through to the thawed and baked product and lead to quality losses. Robb (1985) studied the formation of cracks on the pastry lids of meat pies because such cracks allowed the loss of gravy from within the pie during subsequent baking. He found that very small cracks, sometimes too small to be seen with the naked eye, formed when the unbaked product was frozen and the crack later increased in size when baked. Cracking was worst when recipe water levels were lowest, probably because gluten formation was restricted at low water levels and the paste lacked the necessary elasticity to withstand the mechanical stresses introduced during freezing and thawing. Cauvain (1996) noted a similar problem of surface crack formation when unproved fermented doughs were frozen. In addition to stress induced by ice crystal formation, other stresses were introduced from continued gas production for some time after entering the freezer by the yeast in the centre of the dough piece.

CONCLUSIONS

The transition from a mixed batter, dough or paste to a baked product is complex and varied. In all cases water plays a significant role in these transitions even though it is most often being lost from the product matrix. Indeed, the loss of water from the matrix during baking is essential to the formation of the many different baked product structures, because of the contribution of steam both to expansion and ultimately to the formation of a rigid matrix in the baked product.

Controlling the timing and rate at which moisture is lost from the matrix also makes a positive contribution to product quality. In some cases, for example during the proof of fermented doughs, it is necessary to delay the loss of water until the dough has been sufficiently expanded, while in others control of humidity or the use of steam during baking makes a positive contribution to final product quality.

REFERENCES

Abboud, A.M. & Hoseney, R.C. (1982) Differential scanning calorimetry of sugar cookies and cookie doughs. *Cereal Chemistry*, **61**, 34–7.

Allied Bakeries Ltd (1986) Method for cooling of baked goods. *GB Patent 2 134 636B*, 20 August, HMSO, London, UK.

Audidier, Y. & Battail, J. (1968) Changes occurring during the baking process. *Brot und Geback*, **22**, 41–6.

Bent, A.J. (1998) Speciality fermented goods, in *Technology of Breadmaking* (eds S.P. Cauvain & L.S. Young), Blackie Academic & Professional, London, UK, pp. 214–39.

Bloksma, A.H. (1990) Rheology of the breadmaking process. *Cereal Foods World*, **35**, 228–36.

Cauvain, S.P. (1992) Retarding. *Bakers' Review*, March, 22–3.

Cauvain, S.P. (1996) The freezing and retarding of fermented doughs. *CCFRA Review No. 3*. CCFRA, Chipping Campden, UK.

Cauvain, S.P. (1998a) Dough retarding and freezing, in *Technology of Breadmaking* (eds S.P. Cauvain & L.S. Young), Blackie Academic & Professional, London, UK, pp. 149–79.

Cauvain, S.P. (1998b) Breadmaking processes, in *Technology of Breadmaking* (eds S.P. Cauvain & L.S. Young), Blackie Academic & Professional, London, UK, pp. 18–44.

Cauvain, S.P. & Chamberlain, N. (1988) The bread improving effect of fungal *alpha*-amylase. *Journal of Cereal Science*, **8**, 239–48.

Cauvain, S.P. & Cyster, J.A. (1996) Sponge cake technology. *CCFRA Review No. 2*. CCFRA, Chipping Campden, UK.

Cauvain, S.P. & Screen, A.E. (1988) Heat-flux measurement and sponge cake baking. *FMBRA Bulletin No. 4*, CCFRA, Chipping Campden, UK, pp. 156–62.

Cauvain, S.P. & Screen, A.E. (1994) The role of sugars in cakes. *FMBRA Report No. 155*. CCFRA, Chipping Campden, UK.

Cauvain, S.P. & Telloke, G.W. (1993) Danish pastries and croissant. *FMBRA Report No. 153*. CCFRA, Chipping Campden, UK.

Cauvain, S.P., Davies, J.A.D. & Fearn, T. (1985) Flour characteristics and fungal *alpha*-amylase in the Chorleywood Bread Process. *FMBRA Report No. 121*. CCFRA, Chipping Campden, UK.

Chamberlain, N., Collins, T.H. & McDermott, F.F. (1977) The Chorleywood Bread Process: the effects of *alpha*-amylase on commercial bread. *FMBRA Report No. 73*. CCFRA, Chipping Campden, UK.

Collins, T.H. (1978) The French baguette and Pain Parisien. *FMBRA Bulletin No. 3*, June, CCFRA, Chipping Campden, UK, pp. 107–16.

Collins, T.H. & Ford, W. (1985) Part-baked soft rolls and French bread. *FMBRA Bulletin No. 3*, June, CCFRA, Chipping Campden, UK, pp. 128–34.

Dreese, P.C., Faubion, J.M. & Hosney, R.C. (1988) Dynamic rheological properties of flour, gluten and gluten–starch doughs. *Cereal Chemistry*, **65**, 348–53.

Lawson, R., Miller, A.R., Steele, I.W. & Thacker, D. (1979) Rotary-moulded short dough biscuits. Part I: The effects of oven conditions on the properties of Lincoln biscuits. *FMBRA Research Report No. 87*. CCFRA, Chipping Campden, UK.

Pritchard, P.E. & Stevens, D.J. (1973) The influence of processing variables on the properties of wafer sheets. *Food Trade Review*, **44**, 12–18.

Robb, J. (1985) Pastry technology: cracking of frozen meat pie pastry. *FMBRA Report No. 126*. CCFRA, Chipping Campden, UK.

Robb, J. (1987) Cake baking conditions. *FMBRA Bulletin No. 4*, CCFRA, Chipping Campden, UK, pp. 151–8.

Schiffman, R.F. (1993) Microwave technology in baking, in *Advances in Baking Technology* (eds B.S. Kamel & C.E. Stauffer), Blackie Academic & Professional, London, UK, pp. 292–315.

Screen, A.E. (1988) Producing frozen cake batters. *FMBRA Bulletin No. 3*, CCFRA, Chipping Campden, UK, pp. 126–32.

Sluimer, P. (1978) An explanation of some typical phenomena occurring during retarding. *Bakkerswereld*, **19**, 14–16.

Spies, R.D. & Hoseney, R.C. (1982) Effects of sugars on starch gelatinization. *Cereal Chemistry*, **59**, 128–31.

Street, C.A. (1991) *Flour confectionery manufacture*. Blackie Academic & Professional, London, UK.

Telloke, G.W. (1984) The mixing of cake batters. *FMBRA Report No. 114*. CCFRA, Chipping Campden, UK.

Telloke, G.W. (1991) Puff pastry II: Fats, margarines and emulsifiers. *FMBRA Report No. 146.* CCFRA, Chipping Campden.

Tscheuschner, H.-D. & Luddecke, J. (1972) Steam leavening in the production of baked goods. *Backer. u. Konditor,* **20,** 325–6.

Wade, P. (1995) *Biscuits, Cookies and Crackers. Vol. 1: The Principles of the Craft* (2nd edn). Blackie Academic & Professional, London, UK.

Wiggins, C. (1998) Proving, baking and cooling, in *Technology of Breadmaking* (eds S.P. Cauvain & L.S. Young), Blackie Academic & Professional, London, UK, pp. 120–48.

Williams, A. & Pullen, G. (1998) Functional ingredients, in *Technology of Breadmaking* (eds S.P. Cauvain & L.S. Young), Blackie Academic & Professional, London, UK, pp. 45–80.

5 Effects of water on product textural properties and their changes during storage

After baking and cooling, baked products will commonly undergo a period of storage before consumption. This storage period may be as short as a few hours or as long as a year, depending on the type of product and the storage environment. During this period, a number of significant changes take place which affect, individually and collectively, the organoleptic properties of bakery foods and sometimes their physical appearance. These changes are most often linked with the movement of water both within and out of the product matrix. Some occur because of the inherent properties that have been built into the product during the baking process itself, while others are a consequence of the storage environment. The organoleptic changes are most commonly referred to as *staling*, although loss of (perceived) freshness may be a better descriptor of the process of change in product character during storage since quite diverse changes may occur, yet still be referred to as staleness.

THE CONTRIBUTION OF PRODUCT MOISTURE CONTENT TO BAKED PRODUCT CHARACTER

Before considering the changes in product character that occur during storage, and how the presence of water influences those changes, it will be helpful to examine the contribution that water makes to the underlying characters of bakery foods. Water in baked products plays a major 'lubricating' role when the product is eaten, and because of this the product moisture content has a profound effect on the perception of quality, whether the product has been freshly made or stored. As discussed previously, the level of moisture in a particular baked product is an essential part of the properties that characterise that product. Thus bread has a much higher moisture content than biscuits and as such is not expected to have the crisp and hard eating character of the latter. On the other hand, the crust of baguette has a lower moisture content than the baked crumb and is therefore expected to have a hard, crisp eating character compared with the softer, chewier character of the crumb.

Bread and fermented goods

Bread and other fermented goods fall into the intermediate moisture range of foods and have the highest water levels of virtually all baked products. They are characterised by a relatively high moisture content in the baked crumb of the product and a lower moisture content in the crust. This moisture differential is essential in those fermented products that are expected to have a hard or crisp eating crust which contrasts with the softer, chewier crumb, such as baguette. The moisture content of fermented products varies according to the required crust character for the product and is mainly a consequence of the heat input during baking. The longer the baking time, the thicker the crust region will be for bread (Wiggins, 1998) and therefore the perception of crustiness.

The data for the average moisture content of UK breads given in Table 5.1 are taken from Chamberlain and Knight (1987) who derived their figures from a nationwide survey of the nutritional composition of bread undertaken by the UK Ministry of Agriculture, Fisheries and Food (Wenlock *et al.*, 1983). The data show that 'crusty' bread products have a lower average moisture content, and also show the effect of wrapping in retaining moisture in the product during storage. The data given in Table 5.1 are averaged for the combination of crust and crumb so that breads with a higher ratio of crust to crumb, e.g. French bread, will have a lower average moisture content but possibly the same crumb moisture content, as breads with thinner crusts, e.g. sandwich-tin breads.

Table 5.1 Average moisture contents for UK breads (based on Chamberlain & Knight, 1987).

Bread type	Moisture content (%)
800 g, tin, white, wrapped	40.4
800 g, tin, white, unwrapped	37.6
800 g, free-standing (crusty), unwrapped	35.6
800 g, tin, wholemeal, unwrapped	38.6
400 g, tin, white, wrapped	37.3
400 g, tin, white, unwrapped	35.4
400 g, tin, wholemeal, unwrapped	36.8
400 g, French bread (baguette)	29.2
60 g, crusty roll	26.4

It is well known that the moisture content of bread crumb is a major contributor to the perception of product freshness and that, within limits, the higher the moisture content, the fresher the bread will be perceived by the consumer. Some of the influence of a higher crumb moisture content is seen when bread crumb is compressed with the fingers: the higher the moisture content, the easier it will be to deform the crumb and the softer (fresher) it feels. Too much water and the crumb may be easily deformed but it may not recover to the shape that it was before compression. This combination of easy compression with good recovery is commonly assessed by the 'squeeze test' carried out by consumers at the point of purchase, especially when the bread is cold on the store shelf and the direct link between product warmth and freshness has been lost. Increasing the thickness of the crust on such products will often result in a loaf that is firm or hard to the touch and may be rejected as stale by the consumer.

Cakes

The baked moisture content of cakes is somewhat lower than that of breads, but cake products still fall within the intermediate moisture range of foods. The crust formed on cakes during baking is usually considerably thinner than that of breads; the formation of a hard crust on cakes is not usually seen as desirable by the consumer. Nevertheless, the moisture content of cake crumb has a major impact on the perception of freshness in cake products. Guy *et al.* (1983) used a sensory panel to relate cake moisture content and freshness ratings. They showed that as the moisture content of the cake increased so a sensory panel perceived that the cake was fresher (*see* Fig. 5.1). Raising the moisture content of the crumb may have other less desirable effects on cake quality, such as increasing the product ERH and decreasing its mould-free shelf-life (*see* Chapter 6).

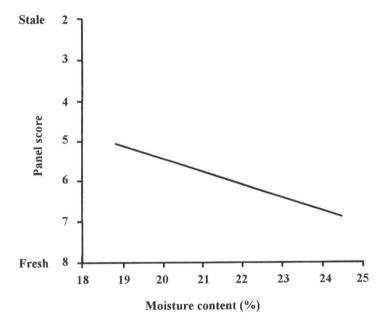

Fig. 5.1 Relationship between panel score and moisture content of cake crumb (based on Guy *et al.*, 1983).

Cauvain and Screen (1990) examined the effects of some ingredients on the properties of cake crumb and found that the level of water used to make up the batter and the baked crumb moisture content had a significant effect on the textural properties of cakes, as assessed with textural profile analysis. In part, the effects were the result of changing water levels on cake crumb density; however, when the data were corrected for variations in crumb density, increasing the cake moisture content still affected the cake texture profile making the crumb more cohesive, chewy and gummy.

Pastries and laminated products

The moisture content of pastries and laminated products is usually much lower than that of cakes, ranging from around 5% for puff pastry up to around 17% for short and Danish pastries. This means that the eating qualities of such products are characterised largely by their dryness or crispness. If the pastries have higher moisture contents, e.g. as a result of moisture migration from creams or fillings (*see* Chapter 7), such products are generally considered to be unacceptable in terms of eating quality and may be classified as stale. There are no precise limits to the level of moisture acceptable in pastry products because they vary according to product type and consumer preference.

Butcher and Hodge (1984), in a study of the causes of softening of pork pie pastry during storage, used a five-point panel rating for pastry crispness, where 0 rated soft, and 4 rated crisp, with a '*neutral crispness point*' (i.e. neither soft nor crisp) at 2. They correlated their neutral crispness value with pastry hardness measured using a puncture test with an Instron and established a force value that corresponded with their neutral crispness point (*see* Fig. 5.2). In the same study, they correlated crispness values with pastry moisture contents; by extrapolating their data, the neutral crispness value for side-wall pastry corresponds with a moisture content of around 11%. This would mean that moisture contents above 11% in side-wall pie pastry were likely to be considered unacceptable to their panel. Robb (1991) studied moisture migration in apple pies and found that his panel rating of neutral crispness for the sweetened pastry corresponded to a moisture content of about 17%. The difference between the two neutral crispness moisture contents may arise from the use of two different panels, but is more likely

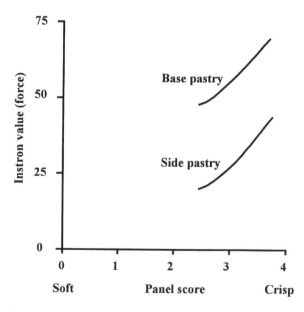

Fig. 5.2 Relationship between sensory rating and pastry crispness (based on Butcher & Hodge, 1984).

to be associated with the level of moisture content considered to be acceptable for the two different product groups.

Biscuits and cookies

The moisture contents of freshly baked biscuits and cookies are usually below 5%, with a water activity of around 0.2. Prolonged exposure of the product to many ambient storage conditions can lead to the absorption of water from the atmosphere into the biscuit matrix, making the biscuit soft. It is therefore common to seal biscuits in a moisture impermeable film to prevent this moisture uptake. As biscuits absorb moisture from the atmosphere they lose their crispness, and become soggy (Manley, 1983) and less acceptable to most consumers. Even biscuits that may eventually be 'dunked' (deliberately immersed in a suitable hot liquid such as tea) benefit from having a low initial moisture content; otherwise they are prone to falling to pieces in the liquid during dunking.

The absorption of moisture by dry products such as biscuits and cookies can lead to a change in product dimensions, even though the structure has been set during baking. The usual form of change is an increase in size, commonly diameter or length, although an increase in thickness is possible. Such dimensional changes can lead to quality problems where the biscuits have been coated, for example with chocolate. Barron (1977) studied the effect of moisture absorption by wafers on the cracking that occurred in the chocolate coating. He observed a gain in length of between 0.33 and 0.42% of the original dimension for each 1% increase in wafer sheet moisture content (storage relative humidities ranged from 11.7 to 75.5%). The time taken for cracks to occur in the coating depended on the initial moisture content of the wafer sheet and the relative humidity of the atmosphere, as well as the thickness and completeness of the chocolate coating.

LOSS OF PRODUCT FRESHNESS (STALING)

Changes in bread character during storage

Some of the most important changes that take place in bakery products post-baking are listed in Table 5.2. The relative importance of each of these changes in baked product character will depend on the type of product being made. For example, loss of crust crispness will be less important in pan breads than in hearth breads or baguette. The changes listed in Table 5.2 are all affected to some extent by water, whether it is because of its loss (e.g. crumb firming) or its gain (e.g. loss of crispness). The changes that occur during storage are called staling, although loss of perceived freshness may be a more appropriate term, because for cereal scientists staling has become associated with the changes that occur in the crystallinity of the wheat starch in baked products during storage. Such changes are discussed in more detail below.

When baking is finished, the crusts of all bread types will have a lower moisture content than those of their respective crumbs. This lower moisture content is an intrinsic part of the product and makes a very significant contribution to the crisp

Table 5.2 Product characters that change during storage.

crust or product crispness
crumb and crust moisture
crumb firmness
crumbliness
taste
aroma

eating character of the crust. Gradually, depending on the storage conditions, the moisture held within the crumb migrates to the areas of lower moisture content closer to and at the crust surface, causing the crust to lose its crisp eating character and become soft. This phenomenon is most readily observed in oven-bottom or hearth breads, baguette and crusty rolls, where the softening of the crust detracts from the product character and leads to loss of consumer appeal as the formerly crisp eating crust assumes a 'chewy' character. Pan breads, on the other hand, actually benefit from this moisture migration phenomenon during storage since a crisp crust is largely undesirable with such products when they are sliced or eaten.

The migration of water from the bread crumb to its crust causes a lowering of the crumb moisture content so that it acquires a firmer texture and a drier, harder eating character. The rate at which this change in crumb character occurs depends on the storage conditions, the thickness of the crust and the ratio of crust to crumb in the product. The role of the latter two effects in loss of bread freshness is not always fully appreciated. The degree to which a bread crust softens and the crumb firms depends in part on the relative masses of the dry (crust) and moist (crumb). This can be appreciated by the following example for a rectangular loaf:

Example A

800 g rectangular loaf measuring 12.5 cm × 23.5 cm × 10.5 cm
Therefore loaf volume = 3084 cm^3
Crust thickness = 1 mm; moisture content = 15%
Crumb moisture content = 44%
Assume average loaf density is 0.26 g/cm^3 (usually the crust is more dense than the crumb)

Volume of crumb without crust = 2952 cm^3 (12.3 × 23.3 × 10.3)
Mass = 765 g (density × volume)
Therefore mass of available water = 336 g

Volume occupied by crust = 132 cm^3 (total loaf volume − crumb volume)
Mass = 34 g

At equilibrium crumb moisture will be 42.3%, representing a loss of about 1.7%.

Example B

800 g rectangular loaf with volume 3084 cm³
Crust thickness 2 mm; moisture content = 15%
Crumb moisture content = 44%
Assume average density = 0.26 g/cm³

Volume of crumb without crust = 2823 cm³ (12.1 × 23.1 × 10.1)
Mass = 731 g (density × volume)
Therefore mass of available water = 322 g

Volume occupied by crust = 261 cm³ (total loaf volume – crumb volume)
Mass = 68 g

At equilibrium crumb moisture will be 41.1%, representing a loss of about 2.9%.

From these examples, we can see that doubling the crust thickness on bread increases considerably the loss of crumb moisture at equilibrium. Such considerations go some way to explaining why the crumb of crusty bread loses its apparent freshness more rapidly than that in pan breads. In crusty breads, the more open cell structure increases the rate of moisture diffusion though the crumb, which also encourages crumb drying and crust softening.

The loss of crust crispness is an important and beneficial change in sandwich bread types, since it adds to the perception of freshness by the consumer. This is because the consumer confronted with a cold loaf in the store has no means of assessing freshness other than by carrying out a 'squeeze test': consumers know that fresh bread has little resistance to squeezing but it quickly springs back to its original shape. Softness or resistance to deformation and recovery from deformation are important crumb characteristics and are affected directly by the level of moisture remaining in the product, coupled with a fully developed and resilient crumb structure.

The type of the packaging used for bread products also influences the rate of moisture movement both within and from the product, and therefore influences product freshness. With a moisture-impermeable film, the product reaches equilibrium fairly quickly, with the crust softening but with little loss of moisture from the product overall. This situation is suited to pan bread character but not to crusty breads. In crusty breads, some extension of freshness, i.e. retention of crust crispness, can be achieved by allowing some moisture to escape from the product to the surrounding atmosphere so that there is always a moisture gradient throughout the product. The negative side to this approach is that the crumb moisture content falls rapidly to a level that is organoleptically unacceptable. A perforated film is most commonly used to slow down moisture loss from crusty products while trying to retain crust crispness.

Changes in the character of cakes, biscuits and pastries

Loss of freshness in cake products follows much the same lines as those for bread. Changes in cake texture and eating quality are a result of loss of moisture from the crumb and the intrinsic firming of the structure associated with staling (*see below*).

When stored, cakes become firmer and drier to eat, although the timescale over which these changes happen is often much longer than that for bread. The lower rate of firming arises because of differences in formulation between bread and cakes. Generally it is the presence of higher levels of sugar in cakes that lowers the product water activity and therefore moisture evaporation rates, which accounts for the difference in product behaviour during storage.

Cakes are not usually expected to have a crisp eating crust, and so changes in crust character are not a critical issue with such products. In general, cakes are wrapped in moisture-impermeable film to retain the moisture necessary for their soft and tender eating character, but this does mean that they are particularly susceptible to spoilage during storage unless steps are taken to control mould growth (*see* Chapter 9).

In products like biscuits and pastries, the water activities and moisture contents are so low that moisture may migrate from the atmosphere into the product, rather than from product to atmosphere as with bread and cakes. This is the mechanism by which cookies and pastries go soft or stale. Such products are wrapped in a moisture-impermeable film to prevent moisture uptake, but this does not encourage any significant mould growth because the product moisture contents and water activities are so low (unless the basic product has been combined with a higher water activity filling; *see* Chapter 7). A major driving force for the softening of biscuits and pastries is the lack of equilibrium between product and atmospheric relative humidities, accelerated in many cases by the presence of undissolved or recrystallised ingredients, especially sugars, which confer so-called 'humectant' properties to the product. In such cases the driving force is for water to be absorbed by the product in order to achieve equilibrium. Many toppings and fillings used in the manufacture of composite bakery products show humectant properties and will absorb water from either the surroundings or other parts of the composite products. Moisture migration between components in composite bakery products is discussed in detail in Chapter 7.

Checking in biscuits and crackers

Checking is the formation of cracks and splits in biscuits and crackers without the products being subjected to external forces strong enough to fracture the product. It is the result of moisture migrating within the product after baking (Dunn and Bailey, 1928). When many biscuit and cracker products leave the oven and begin to cool, the moisture content at the edges of the biscuits is lower than that at the centre. Gradually as the biscuit cools and after wrapping, moisture moves from the moist centre to the drier parts of the product and stresses are developed within the product, causing the product to break. The cracks often develop along lines of inherent weakness within the product, both macroscopic and microscopic. The cracks are often radial in round products, although apparently more randomly distributed cracks may occur in products like crackers (*see* Fig. 5.3).

In products like biscuits and crackers, which have a large surface area relative to their thickness, it is inevitable that a moisture gradient will be present in the product as it leaves the oven. To avoid checking, this moisture gradient should be as small as possible, which requires that the baking conditions are adjusted. This may require

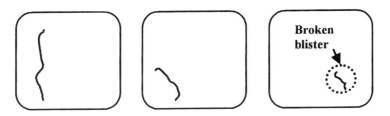

Fig. 5.3 Checking patterns in cream crackers.

the lowering of baking temperatures with a corresponding increase in baking time. If changes to the baking conditions are not acceptable, radio frequency or microwave heating can be used to reduce the moisture gradient in the product. There is no evidence to suggest that the ingredients or dough preparation play a role in biscuit checking (Fearn *et al.*, 1982).

Water and staling in bread

The water level in bakery foods is also related to physicochemical changes in product character that occur during storage and to which we refer collectively as staling. During baking, the starch present in bread doughs and cake batters undergoes the transformation known as *gelatinisation*. This is a complex process but essentially involves a transition of the starch from an ordered (crystalline) to a disordered state. In the unbaked starch, it is the amylopectin fraction which contains ordered regions and is embedded in the non-crystalline matrix of the amylose, the other main constituent of the lenticular wheat starch granules (Schoch, 1945).

The starch granules present in wheat flour are largely insoluble in cold water, but when heated in an aqueous medium they begin to absorb water and swell. Penetration of the warm water into the granule contributes to a loss of crystallinity in the granule structure, and as the temperature begins to rise, the intermolecular bonds of the starch polymers begin to break. This increases the number of hydrogen bonds available for the water present, and the viscosity of the starch–water mixture begins to increase. Further heating of the mixture results in a change from a viscous liquid to a solid, and this point is regraded as the gelatinisation temperature of the starch. In bread, gelatinisation occurs in the region of 60 to 65°C (140 to 149°F) while in cakes where large quantities of sugar in the batter are present, the gelatinisation temperature may rise to 90°C (194°F).

On cooling, the polymers begin to lose their mobility and the disordered starch state created during baking gradually begins to re-order, or '*retrograde*'. This retrogradation continues during storage and contributes to the firming that typically occurs with bread and cake crumb. Retrogradation of starch in bread crumb is both time- and temperature-dependent, with the maximum staling rate for bread occurring around 4°C (39°F) (*see* Fig. 5.4). These time- and temperature-related phenomena have been noted by a number of workers, including Cornford *et al.* (1964) who studied the relationship between bread crumb elastic modulus and firming rate using Avrami-type equations.

The availability of sufficient water is a key requirement for starch retrogradation

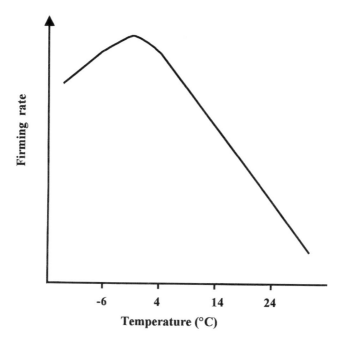

Fig. 5.4   Effect of temperature on firming rate of bread.

to occur in bread crumb. It is generally considered that the water level in the baked product needs to be greater than 20 to 30% for retrogradation to occur and, as shown in Table 5.1, the moisture content of bread products readily exceeds such levels. In the baked loaf, water acts as a plasticiser, which aids the mobility of the long polymer chain segments of the amylopectin component of wheat starch. This allows gelatinised starch granules to re-associate to form the double helix crystalline structures that increase crumb firmness.

During storage, water is redistributed throughout the loaf structure. On the macroscopic scale this involves the movement of moisture from crumb to crust as discussed above. The movement of water between crumb components at the 'microscopic' level is likely to occur, although there is no common agreement on the nature of that movement. The two main components that have been cited for the microscopic movement of moisture are the starch and the gluten structures in the baked loaf. Wilhoft (1973) favoured a loss of moisture from the gluten to the starch during storage, while Cluskey *et al.* (1959) and D'Appolonia and Morad (1981) favoured a mechanism for moisture movement in the reverse direction.

This lack of clarity on the direction of moisture movement between bread crumb components arises partly from the overlap in the glass transition ranges for the two main polymers (starch and gluten) at a given moisture content, and partly from the close physical relationship of the polymers in the crumb. In bread crumb, the starch granules are attached to the continuous gluten network that has been formed in the dough, expanded during proof and set during the baking process (Rao *et al.*, 1992). This close physical association provides a ready opportunity for moisture migration between the two components by diffusion, and water is clearly present within both in the bread crumb. In a recently reported study, Chinachoti (1998) used nuclear magnetic resonance (NMR) to study bread staling, and suggested that the water in bread crumb was in close proximity to the protein surfaces and plasticised the gluten more than in the starch. Variations in the crumb moisture content, the ratio of water to starch and the ratio of water to gluten in bread will clearly have an effect on the staling rate. Since there is a moisture gradient in the crumb, it is important to recognise that the rates of firming during storage will vary throughout the product during its storage life.

Whatever the precise mechanism by which bread stales, if we store a product in a moisture-impermeable film it goes firm and becomes less palatable. However, if we take old bread and reheat it, the softness of the crumb (and to a lesser extent the crispness of the crust) is restored. In this second heating process, there will be some further loss of water from the product, especially in the crust region, and a moisture gradient will be re-established in the baked and cooled product. Overall, re-heating results in a lower product moisture content, which ultimately affects adversely the perception of product freshness (although short-term, the renewed softness is the more important effect for product quality). The crumb-softening occurs because the heat-reversible aggregation of the amylopectin fraction in the starch is mainly responsible for bread staling (Schoch and French, 1947). After being refreshed, the subsequent rate of staling in the crumb increases by comparison with that which previously prevailed. This particular phenomenon explains practical observations that part-baked products stale at a faster rate than freshly baked ones, and repudiates the unsubstantiated claims made by Kear (1995) for products made by the Milton Keynes Process.

Cakes

Cake crumb also loses its freshness and becomes firmer during storage. As with bread this may arise even when the conditions are such as to prevent moisture loss. Guy *et al.* (1983) considered that two sub-processes contributed to the staling of cake crumb: the loss of moisture from the crumb by diffusion to the crust, and an intrinsic firming of the cell wall material. The two sub-processes had different temperature relationships, the first having a positive and the second a negative temperature coefficient. Both crumb-firming effects are similar to those observed with bread, but with cake the maximum firming (staling) peak occurs at a higher temperature, typically between 15 and 20°C (59 and 68°F). This change in peak staling rate comes from the differences in formulation between bread doughs and cake batters, and is accounted for mainly by the high levels of sugar and water in the cake batter, which raise the gelatinisation temperature of the starch and the glass transition temperature of the baked product.

The relationship between consumer perception of freshness and the moisture content of cakes was examined by Guy *et al.* (1983), who showed that increasing the water content of the cake crumb gave products that were perceived as being fresher by a taste panel. This example illustrates the important role played by moisture content in the perception of quality. But, as will be noted in Chapter 6, there is a direct link between product moisture content and a product's water activity and shelf-life: the higher the product moisture content, the higher the water activity and the shorter the product's shelf-life.

EFFECTS OF FREEZING AND THAWING ON PRODUCT TEXTURE AND EATING QUALITY

The transition of water to ice was discussed in Chapter 1. When bakery products are cooled to a low enough temperature the water present within the structure freezes (forms ice crystals). However, the transition is not a simple one. The aqueous phase in bakery products contains the dissolved ingredients from the product formulation and their presence prevents the liquid water phase making the transition to the solid ice form. In fact the freezing point (the temperature at which the whole of the product matrix becomes solid) can be very much lower than the freezing point of pure water, as noted in Chapter 4.

Initially during the freezing of bakery products, heat is removed quite quickly and the product cools. As the freezing point is approached, cooling slows down and considerable quantities of heat must be removed to overcome the effects of latent heat. Once ice crystals have formed, the rate of cooling increases again. The process by which ice crystals form is referred to as '*nucleation*', which may occur in homogeneous or heterogeneous forms. Homogeneous nucleation occurs at a temperature sufficiently low to induce spontaneous formation of ice crystals and may be as low as –40°C (–40°F) according to some studies (e.g. Bigg, 1963). Heterogeneous nucleation is more likely to occur in the aqueous phase of food systems where the various particulates provide the sites for ice crystal formation. Such processes occur at temperatures much higher than –40°C. More detailed considerations of the processes of nucleation are given by Reid (1998) and Kennedy (1998), who also discuss the potential control of ice crystal formation by physical stimuli.

The rate at which ice crystals grow and their relative sizes depend to a large extent on the rate of heat removal from the product. Rapid cooling favours the formation of small ice crystals, while lower freezing rates favour the formation of larger crystals. As will be discussed below, the formation of smaller ice crystals generally has a less damaging effect on bakery food quality. Because of their complex formulations and relatively small surface areas compared with their cross-sections, bakery products are not good conductors of heat, so the freezing point is reached in different parts of the product at different times during the freezing operation. This has significant implications for the quality of many bakery products. During the defrosting of frozen bakery products, similar considerations apply as the product begins to receive heat and once again has to pass through the latent heat barrier before the ice turns to water. The rate at which the transition from solid to liquid occurs also affects product quality.

Unbaked bread doughs

Freezing has been applied to many unbaked products as a means of preserving them for later use. Frozen fermented doughs that can be defrosted, proved and baked after a period of frozen storage have been particularly popular in the in-store bakeries of north America (Best, 1995) and parts of Europe (Brummer, 1995). Bread doughs may be produced and frozen centrally, and then distributed to satellite in-store bakeries (Cauvain and Collins, 1978), removing the need for a 'scratch' bakery operation. However, careful control of storage, defrosting and baking of the dough is still required if baked product quality is to be optimised.

The successful production of frozen doughs can be achieved only by balancing a number of conflicting requirements. They include:

- Restriction of the yeast activity in the dough, both before freezing and during the cooling process.
- Preservation of the viability of the yeast cells so that they remain capable of producing carbon dioxide gas after defrosting.
- Minimisation of dough dehydration during the freezing process.
- The encouragement of the formation of small ice crystals.

Yeast fermentation in the dough before freezing can have an adverse effect on final product quality and on the survival of individual yeast cells (Cauvain, 1998a). Loss of yeast cell viability is shown mainly as a loss of gassing power in the dough when it is defrosted, and a weakening of the dough structure resulting from the impact of the contents of dead yeast cell on the dough gluten structure. The poor conductivity of dough means that the dough piece surface may become frozen some time before its centre. This means that in larger diameter dough pieces gassing at the centre may continue for some time after the surface has become frozen; in such cases the force arising from the fermentation may be sufficient to split the frozen surface (Cauvain, 1996). The reader is referred elsewhere for more detailed considerations of the technology of frozen doughs; comprehensive reviews are given by Brummer (1995), Lorenz and Kulp (1995) and Cauvain (1998a).

During the freezing process some dehydration of the dough surface occurs as water is removed by the air passing over the dough piece. This loss of surface water contributes to the inelastic nature of the dough surface and plays a part in the formation of the problem of surface cracks noted above. The higher the air velocity across the dough surface, the greater the dehydration of the dough, but in general the faster it will freeze. As noted above, the freezing rate affects the size of the ice crystals that form in frozen bakery products; fast freezing favours the formation of small ice crystals.

In the freezing of bread doughs, the size of the ice crystals that form may have effects on both the dough structure and the viability of the yeast cells. The formation of ice crystals leads to a reduction of the mass of the aqueous phase, which may be considered as a dehydration process. The loss of water from the gluten in bread doughs leads to a loss of elasticity and hardening of the structure (e.g. skinning in retarding or proof). Provided that the water which forms as ice in the dough can return to the gluten structure on defrosting, no permanent damage to the structure appears to occur. However, if moisture is lost during storage, a permanent loss of structural quality can occur.

Not all of the water present in frozen fermented doughs (and baked bread and cakes; *see below*) exists as ice. As freezing proceeds and ice crystals form, the concentration of solutes and the viscosity of the aqueous phase both increase. At a certain temperature, known as the *glass transition temperature* (T_g), the mobility of the aqueous phase becomes so restricted that the rates of chemical and physical reactions reach a minimum. If held above its T_g, the aqueous phase in the product is still unstable enough to take part in reactions or for moisture to evaporate. The T_g for bread doughs can be relatively low – certainly below –10°C (14°F) – and frozen storage temperatures should be well below such values.

Unbaked cake batters

The concentration of solutes in powder-raised bakery products (e.g. cakes and cookies) is much greater than that typically seen in fermented doughs so that freezing points and T_gs are much lower. Screen (1988) gave freezing points for high ratio cake batters between –12 and –20°C (10 and –4°F). The higher temperature was obtained for a point close to the surface of the batter and the lower one for the centre of the same unit. These differences in temperature may well relate to the different freeze-concentration effects in the aqueous phase and different rates of ice crystal formation at different points in the batter unit. Screen's freezing curves (*see* Fig. 5.5) show some similarity with those of Hsu *et al.* (1979), who showed how the freezing point in bread doughs varied with the temperature in the freezer, i.e. with variations in freezing rate.

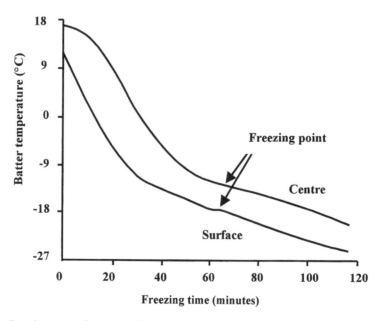

Fig. 5.5 Freezing curves for cake batters.

Unbaked pastries

Large numbers of pastry products may be frozen in the unbaked form. In the UK, these commonly include products based on savoury and sweetened short pastries. In the freezing process, the water present in the pastry and the filling expands while the fat present contracts. These changes place the pastry under some stress and may precipitate the formation of cracks in the pastry surface. Often these cracks form along lines of microscopic imperfections, which remain after the sheeting and blocking processes. After defrosting and during subsequent baking these cracks may further increase in size and allow the boil-out of the filling to leave unsightly surface blemishes. Once formed, there is no remedial action that can be taken, so their avoidance is based on adjusting the rheological properties of the paste by changing ingredient qualities or pastry formulation. Low water or high fat levels in the formulation exacerbate the problem, while reduced mixing, reduced inclusion of trimmings and improvements to the freezing process are all of potential benefit in overcoming the problem (Robb, 1985).

Bread

It has been known for some time that the staling rate of bread increases with the temperature at which it is stored, and that it reaches a maximum at around 4°C (40°F) (Russell, 1985). Two physicochemical changes affect the process of recrystallisation of gelatinised starch in bread products: crystal nucleation and growth (Morris, 1990). The optimum rates for nucleation and growth are different and in opposite directions, i.e. nucleation increases as the temperature falls, while crystal growth decreases. For bread, the overall starch recrystallisation reaches a maximum around 4°C, and so this is the temperature at which its maximum staling rate occurs (Pateras, 1998).

Once frozen and stored below its T_g, bread does not stale and can be kept for considerable periods of time provided there are no significant moisture losses during storage. If any moisture is lost from the frozen product, there will be a lower moisture content in the final product which may well lead to the product being interpreted as 'staler' by consumers. Even if no moisture is lost from the frozen product the defrosted bread crumb will be firmer due to staling. This occurs because the process of freezing and defrosting bread is the equivalent of 24-hour storage at ambient temperature (20°C, 70°F) (Pence & Standridge, 1955) with the bread having to pass through the point of maximum staling (4°C) twice, once while cooling and once while defrosting.

When the temperature of frozen bread (or any other product) is allowed to rise above its T_g some of the moisture present can evaporate into the surrounding atmosphere. This leads to a lowering of the moisture content of the product so that the concentration of the solutes increases and its T_g changes (usually decreases). Should the defrosting and moisture loss process be repeated, the product T_g will fall again. In many practical situations, it is unusual for the whole of the product to become defrosted during frozen storage; the more likely occurrence is for only the outer layers of the product to become defrosted and refrozen. This cycle of defrosting followed by moisture loss and then refreezing often leads to the phenomenon known as 'freezer burn' in bakery products. An example of the problem is illustrated in Fig. 5.6, where changes introduced by the freeze–thaw cycle show as a white ring running around the roll cross-section a few millimetres under the crust. The eating qualities of this portion of the crumb are much harsher and drier than the rest of the product, and the physical changes to the crumb structure cannot be reversed.

Fig. 5.6 Freezer burn.

Shelling with frozen crusty breads and part-baked products

The essential features of a crusty bread have been discussed above. They arise largely from a lower moisture content in the crust than the bread crumb. This being the case, the concentration of solutes is different in the two bread components so that they will each have a different T_g and will freeze and thaw at different rates. This places a considerable strain on the crumb linkages with the crust and may lead to a rupturing of those linkages. The net result may be that the crust and crumb become separated from one another, either in the freezer or when defrosted. This phenomenon is commonly referred to as 'shelling' and may be seen with other bread products, for example part-baked rolls and breads (Cauvain, 1998b).

Cakes

As discussed above, cakes contain large quantities of sugars and these depress product freezing point to a much lower temperature than seen with bread. As a result the staling of cakes continues until the storage temperature is at least less than –15°C (5°F). The range of actual freezing points for cakes is considerable, and some high-sugar and fruited cake formulations are not frozen at typical domestic freezer store temperatures, e.g. –20°C (–4°F). This leads to a lack of storage stability in the product and limits its shelf-life. On the other hand, the high concentration of soluble materials gives the products much lower water activities, and so reduces the potential for moisture evaporation during frozen storage.

To keep cakes for very long periods of time, it is necessary to store them below their T_g. In some cases, these are so low that they fall below typical frozen storage temperatures. If lower storage temperatures are not available, the alternative is to reformulate to raise the T_g above that of the frozen store. Cakes offer greater, but not limitless, opportunities for reformulation by comparison with bread. Cauvain (1998b) gave data for a cooling profile of a cake made with sucrose and compared the results when sucrose was substituted with Lactitol or sorbitol. Lactitol raised, and sorbitol lowered, the freezing point compared with the sucrose cake.

Two cake crumb texture properties that show significant changes during frozen storage are crumb hardness and cohesiveness. Cauvain and Pateras (unpublished observations) studied changes in cake crumb during frozen storage and found that the moisture content had no effect on changes in crumb firmness with time. There was, however, a clear moisture-related effect on cohesiveness (*see* Fig. 5.7), with the higher moisture content cake being more cohesive after freezing and having a slightly slower rate of change during the first four weeks of storage. The cakes with the higher moisture content also had a less sticky crumb. The underlying reasons for the difference in crumb cohesiveness between the two types of cakes were not entirely clear since both formulations were balanced to have different moisture contents but the same water activities. Differences in the ratio of water to flour components (principally the starch) and potential differences in crumb cohesiveness in the nature of the ice crystal formation may be involved. The data given by

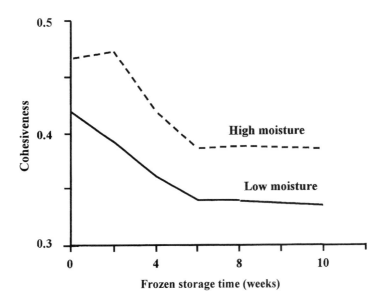

Fig. 5.7   Effect of cake moisture content on crumb cohesion after freezing and thawing.

Cauvain and Pateras for changes in crumb cohesiveness appear to confirm the commercially held view that some cakes become softer eating after a period of frozen storage.

Composite products

Many bakery products are composed of two or more components, e.g. a sponge cake filled with jam and cream. This increases the complexity of the considerations of storage life because each component will have its unique water activity, freezing profile and T_g. Because of these differences, there is always the potential for moisture migration between components; such issues are discussed in Chapter 8. The freezing and frozen storage conditions for the individual components will have different optima, which means that any set of conditions chosen for a composite product will compromise the quality of one or more of the components.

The formation of ice crystals in many bakery creams may disrupt the interfacial films that are essential to their stability. When the ice crystals melt, the effect of gravity on the water molecules causes their migration down through cream foams (drainage) and their absorbtion at the interface with other cake or pastry components, assuming that they do not escape completely from the product. The structural integrity of bakery creams for freezing is commonly achieved through the addition of a suitable stabilizer. Ito and Hodge (1985) studied a number of possible stabilisers for frozen dairy creams and found that guar and xanthan gums were particularly effective in improving cream stability.

In some frozen cake products, moisture migration appears to have some positive benefits in delaying staling. Cauvain (1998b) reported that this could be the case for composite cakes when the water activity was higher than that of the filling. This difference in the water activity between components contrasts with the situation with the same product stored at ambient temperatures when the formulation strategy is usually to balance component water activities, as much as is possible, in order to limit moisture migration, especially from cake or pastry component to filling, or *vice versa* (*see* Chapter 8).

CONCLUSIONS

The textural properties of bakery products are complex, although many can be defined for the various groups of products. Water plays a major role in both the formation of the initial product textural properties and the manner in which they change during storage. Many of the changes in product texture are influenced strongly by the absolute level and the movement of moisture. Even when preservation techniques such as freezing are used, water continues to influence product texture as it first turns to ice and then back to water during defrosting. The management of water within baked products is critical to achieving, influencing and maintaining product textural properties as well as those aspects of product spoilage associated with microbial activity (discussed in the next chapter).

REFERENCES

Barron, L.F. (1977) The expansion of wafer and its relation to the cracking of chocolate and "bakers' chocolate" coatings. *Journal of Food Technology*, **12**, 73–84.

Best, D. (1995) Economic potential of frozen and refrigerated doughs and batters, in *Frozen and Refrigerated Dough and Batters* (eds K. Kulp, K. Lorenz & J. Brummer), American Association of Cereal Chemists Inc., St. Paul, Minnesota, USA, pp. 1–18.

Bigg, E.K. (1963) The supercooling of water. *Proceedings of the Physical Society, London, section B*66, 688–694.

Brummer, J-M. (1995) Bread and rolls from frozen dough in Europe, in *Frozen and Refrigerated Dough and Batters* (Eds K. Kulp, K. Lorenz & J. Brummer), American Association of Cereal Chemists Inc., St. Paul, Minnesota, USA, pp. 155–66.

Butcher, G.J. & Hodge, D.G. (1984) Pastry technology: the softening of pork pie pastry during storage. *FMBRA Report No. 116.* CCFRA, Chipping Campden, UK.

Cauvain, S.P. (1996) The freezing and retarding of fermented doughs. *CCFRA Review No. 3.* CCFRA, Chipping Campden, UK.

Cauvain, S.P. (1998a) Dough retarding and freezing, in *Technology of Breadmaking* (eds S.P. Cauvain & L.S. Young), Blackie Academic & Professional, London, UK, pp. 149–79.

Cauvain, S.P. (1998b) Improving the control of the staling in frozen bakery products. *Trends in Food Science and Technology*, **9**, 56–61.

Cauvain, S.P. & Collins, T.H. (1978) Centralised production of fermented goods for satellite in-store-bakeries and hot-bread shops. *FMBRA Bulletin No. 2*, CCFRA, Chipping Campden, UK, pp. 64–9.

Cauvain, S.P. & Screen, A.E. (1990) Effects of some ingredients on cake texture. *FMBRA Report No. 142.* CCFRA, Chipping Campden, UK.

Chamberlain, N. & Knight, R.A. (1987) The water content of bread – background notes. *FMBRA Bulletin No. 5*, CCFRA, Chipping Campden, UK, pp. 179–81.

Chinachoti, P. (1998) NMR dynamics properties of water in relation to thermal characteristics in bread, in *The Properties of Water in Foods, ISOPOW 6* (ed. D.S. Reid), Blackie Academic & Professional, London, UK, pp. 139–159.

Cluskey, J.E., Taylor, N.W. & Senti, F.R. (1959) Relation of the rigidity of flour, starch and gluten gels to bread staling. *Cereal Chemistry*, **36**, 236–46.

Cornford, S.J., Axford, D.W.E. & Elton, G.A.H. (1964) The elastic modulus of bread crumb in linear compression in relation to staling. *Cereal Chemistry*, **41**, 216–29.

D'Appolonia, B.L. & Morad, M.M. (1981) Bread staling. *Cereal Chemistry*, **58**, 186–90.

Dunn, J.A. & Bailey, C.H. (1928) Factors affecting checking in biscuits. *Cereal Chemistry*, **5**, 395–430.

Fearn, T., Miller, A.R. & Thacker,D. (1982) Checking in cream crackers. *FMBRA Report No. 98.* CCFRA, Chipping Campden, UK.

Guy, R.C.E., Hodge, D.G. & Robb, J. (1983) An examination of the phenomena associated with cake staling. *FMBRA Report No. 107.* CCFRA, Chipping Campden, UK.

Hsu, K.H., Hoseney, R.C. & Seib, P.A. (1979) Frozen dough II: Effects of freezing and storage conditions on the stability of yeasted doughs. *Cereal Chemistry*, **56**, 424–6.

Ito, S. & Hodge, D.G. (1985) Some proposed new cream stabilizers. *FMBRA Bulletin No. 5*, CCFRA, Chipping Campden, UK, pp. 204–9.

Kear, H. (1995) The Milton Keynes Process. *Proceedings of the 79th Conference of the British Society of Baking*, November, 1995.

Kennedy, C.J. (1998) Formation of ice in frozen foods and its control by physical stimuli, in *The Properties of Water in Foods, ISOPOW 6* (ed. D.S. Reid), Blackie Academic & Professional, London, UK, pp. 329–64.

Lorenz, K. & Kulp, K. (1995) Freezing doughs for the production of bread and rolls in the United States, in *Frozen and Refrigerated Dough and Batters* (eds K. Kulp, K. Lorenz & J. Brummer), American Association of Cereal Chemists Inc., St. Paul, Minnesota, USA, pp. 135–54.

Manley, D.J.R. (1983) *Technology of Biscuits, Crackers and Cookies.* Ellis Horwood Ltd., Chichester, UK.

Morris, V.J. (1990) Starch gelation and retrogradation. *Trends in Food Science and Technology*, **1**, 2–6.

Pateras, I. (1998) Bread spoilage and staling, in *Technology of Breadmaking* (eds S.P. Cauvain & L.S. Young), Blackie Academic & Professional, London, UK, pp. 240–61.

Pence, J.W. & Standridge, N.N. (1955) Effect of storage temperature and freezing on the firming of a commercial bread. *Cereal Chemistry*, **32**, 519–26.

Rao, P., Nussinovitch, A. & Chinachoti, P. (1992) Effects of surfactants and amylopectin recrystallization and recoverability of bread crumb during storage. *Cereal Chemistry*, **69**, 613–18.

Reid, D.S. (1998) Freezing – nucleation in foods and antifreeze actions, in *The Properties of Water in Foods, ISOPOW 6* (ed. D.S. Reid), Blackie Academic & Professional, London, UK, pp. 273–84

Robb, J. (1985) Pastry Technology: cracking of frozen meat pie pastry. *FMBRA Report No. 126*. CCFRA, Chipping Campden, UK.

Robb, J. (1991) Moisture migration in apple pies. *FMBRA Report No. 145*. CCFRA, Chipping Campden, UK.

Russell, P. (1985) Shelf-life and staling, in *The Master Baker's Book of Breadmaking* (2nd edn) (ed. J. Brown), Turret Wheatland, Rickmansworth, UK, pp. 431–40.

Schoch, T.J. (1945) The fractionation of starch, *Advances in Carbohydrate Chemistry*, **1**, 247–8.

Schoch, T.J. and French, D. (1947) Studies on bread staling. 1. Role of starch. *Cereal Chemistry*, **24**, 231–49.

Screen, A.E. (1988) Producing frozen cake batters. *FMBRA Bulletin No. 3*, CCFRA, Chipping Campden, UK, pp. 126–32.

Wenlock, R.W., Sivell, L.M., King, R.T. *et al.* (1983) The nutritional composition of British bread – a nationwide study. *Journal of Science, Food and Agriculture*, **34**, 1302–18.

Wiggins, C. (1998) Proving, baking and cooling, in *Technology of Breadmaking* (eds S.P. Cauvain & L.S. Young), Blackie Academic & Professional, London, UK, pp. 120–48.

Wilhoft, E.M.A. (1973) Recent developments on the bread staling problem. *Bakers' Digest*, **47**, 14–21.

6 Water activity

In the finished baked product there are two important aspects related to the presence of water: the moisture content in the final baked product, and its water activity (Young, 1997). The ingredients that comprise the product, including the liquids, dictate the final product characteristics and to a large extent include the product structure, texture and the eating characteristics as discussed in the previous chapters.

In this chapter we shall consider the differences and the links between moisture content and water activity in baked products. The concepts of water activity and equilibrium relative humidity will be explained, and their relationships with respect to microbial shelf-life and other forms of spoilage will be explored in some detail. Glass transition temperatures and their relationship with water activity will also be considered. The potential effects that individual ingredients and changes in product formulation have on water activity will be explored, and the ways in which moisture and water activity can be used to manipulate specific product characteristics and keeping qualities will be introduced.

SOURCES OF MOISTURE IN BAKERY PRODUCTS

The moisture remaining in products after baking comes mainly from the ingredients used in the recipe since the vast majority of baking operations are associated with a loss of water. The exceptions to this rule are usually products that have been steamed, examples of which include Christmas and similar types of puddings in the UK, but not the Chinese steamed bread discussed in Chapter 4. The most obvious contributor of moisture to baked products from the ingredients list is added water, but other less obvious sources include ingredients such as flour, eggs, fruit, and many others that have significant amounts of water held within their structures, e.g. carrots or apples. The moisture contents of some commonly used bakery ingredients are given in Table 6.1. Some groups of ingredients, like glucose syrups, may have varying moisture contents (*see* Table 6.2). The moisture content variation for these ingredients may need to be taken into account when changing one material for another in product formulations where the intention is to adjust a particular product characteristic other than moisture content, e.g. sweetness, otherwise unwanted changes in moisture content and product shelf-life may occur.

Each of the individual ingredient moisture contents contributes to the total moisture content of doughs, batters, pastes and final products. During the processing, baking, cooling and storage stages, the moisture that was originally present in a particular ingredient will move within the product matrix. The moisture content of

Table 6.1 Moisture content of typical bakery ingredients.

Ingredient	Approximate percentage
flour	14
fat	0
whole egg	75
yeast	70
sucrose	0
sultanas	18

an individual ingredient may change several times, and may no longer be held within the original contributing components, many of which will have undergone considerable change themselves. For example, whole egg contributes about 75% of its mass as water, which is held loosely within a protein structure, mainly the albumins. During heat setting (baking), the proteins undergo coagulation, which affects their ability to bind water and this change, along with the stronger affinities for water associated with other ingredients, e.g. sucrose, will mean that the quantity of water associated with the original egg proteins is considerably less than was originally the case. Many such changes in ingredient moisture contents take place and it would be very difficult to quantify the changes that have occurred, but they do play a significant part in determining product characters as discussed in earlier chapters.

As described previously, moisture in different ingredients is held in different ways with different strengths of attraction between the water and the other molecules comprising the ingredient. By contrast to the example for whole egg described above, moisture in dried fruit is more strongly held within the ingredient matrix. This is because the sugars within the fruit attract and hold on to the water, and because the wall of the fruit itself acts as a physical barrier preventing the use of that moisture in hydrating and dispersing other ingredients. Ingredients like apple or carrot, with moisture contents of around 90%, yield their water particularly easily during the baking process but are often forgotten in the wider picture of moisture content when used as ingredients in recipes, especially their impact on batter viscosity in the oven and the product shelf-life after baking.

In yeast, the water is held within the cells by the cell wall membrane and is not bound in any way. Compressed yeast comprises approximately 70% water (Williams & Pullen, 1998). The osmotic properties of the cell allow moisture and nutrients to pass through the cell walls in both directions in fermented doughs so

Table 6.2 Water content of sugar syrups.

Ingredient	Approximate percentage
high fructose 42%	29.0
high fructose 90%	20.0
glucose 42 DE	18.0
glucose 63 DE	18.0
invert sugar	20.0

that fermentation and the production of carbon dioxide (essential for the production of bread and other fermented products) can occur. In the baked product, the yeast cells are no longer viable and the cell walls no longer intact, so the water is released to be redistributed throughout the product matrix. In some bakery fats, e.g. butters and margarines, water is suspended as a water-in-oil emulsion. In such cases the water is given up easily, especially when the fats are heated and the solid material turns to liquid, and water vapour can escape readily from the product structure to take part in other physical and chemical reactions, as occurs in the expansion of puff pastry (Cauvain, 1995). In order to keep the water stable in margarines for long periods of time and over a range of temperatures, it is common to use an emulsifying agent (Podmore, 1997).

PRODUCT MOISTURE CONTENT

The moisture content, expressed as a percentage of the total product mass, is often used as an indication of the 'moist eating' characteristic, much sought after in bread and cakes but shunned in biscuits, hard cookies and pastry products. As discussed in Chapter 5, bread products have moisture contents of around 40%, while that in cakes and sponges is between 15 and 25%. Biscuits and cookies are usually much lower in moisture, with levels below 10%, except for some soft eating cookies which are closer in eating character to cakes and may have moisture contents of around 15%. Some typical moisture contents for bakery products are shown in Table 6.3.

Table 6.3 Moisture levels in typical bakery products.

Product	Approximate percentage
breads	38–44
cakes	15–25
biscuits and cookies	5–10
pastries	up to 15

The moisture content of an unbaked product can be expressed as the sum of the proportions of water in each of the ingredients, for example 100 g of flour with 14% moisture content would contribute 14 g of water to the total moisture and about 86 g solids in a recipe. Moisture content can also be measured directly using the methods described in Chapter 8. In the case of calculated moisture contents, once all the individual moisture contributions have been summed for each ingredient in a recipe, the moisture content can then be expressed as a percentage of the total recipe weight. An example of a recipe moisture content calculation is given in Chapter 8.

THE IMPORTANCE OF WATER ACTIVITY

Water activity, a_w, is a term used frequently in the description of bakery products as a means of explaining the potential for how water may behave within products or between components in a composite product. Simply, it is a measure of how mobile water is within a product and how it may therefore take part in a whole range of physical and chemical processes. As a measure of how well moisture is 'locked up' by ingredients or within a given product matrix, it is particularly useful as an indicator of the availability of water for microbial growth that may lead to food spoilage.

The growth of microorganisms is generally considered to be inhibited if the osmotic pressure of the medium on or in which the organism is located is sufficiently high (i.e. lower water activity). In many of the spoilage mechanisms that concern bakery foods, individual cells must feed before they can begin the process of multiplication that eventually leads to food spoilage. High osmotic pressures within the potential growth medium (the food) inhibit the movement of nutrients through microbial cell membranes and likewise inhibit the activity of enzymes released through the cell membrane to break down the available nutrients into forms suitable for use by individual microorganisms.

Franks (1991) considered that the cellular response of a microorganism to lower water activity was not clearly understood but was known to be energy-consuming, which led to a reduction in growth rate. If the water activity is sufficiently low, growth rates can be extremely slow and in practice are considered to have been stopped. While Franks expressed concern over the lack of fundamental understanding, he considered that water activity was still an adequate way in which to assess the potential for microbial growth.

Water activity may also give significant information on potential changes in food properties that are not related to microbial spoilage. Many of these changes relate to the loss of freshness in the food, loss of intrinsic characteristics or to other adverse changes in the quality. The importance of water activity in predicting these changes is discussed in more detail below.

THE LINK BETWEEN MOISTURE CONTENT AND WATER ACTIVITY

For each bakery product, there is a unique relationship between its moisture content and water activity; this can be expressed as a simple curve, which takes the general form shown in Fig. 6.1. The precise relationship depends on whether the material being assessed is undergoing dehydration (e.g. drying or baking) or hydration (e.g. wheat flour proteins forming gluten, or the absorption of water by starch). The two different processes are usually described as *desorption* and *adsorption* respectively, and they may yield different shaped curves as is shown in Fig. 6.1. The individual curves are commonly referred to as *isotherms*, and to differentiate between the two processes it is common to refer to a *desorption therm* (desorption isotherm) and an *adsorption therm* (adsorption isotherm). The isotherms for many ingredients that might be used in the bakery have been studied using solutions of known strength (i.e. known moisture and solids contents) and measuring the water activity of these solutions. By making a series of different strength solutions, it is possible to plot a curve and so derive the ingredient isotherm of interest. However, it should be appreciated that in the complex processes that are involved in the preparation of bakery foods, it is likely that many of the ingredients used undergo both of these

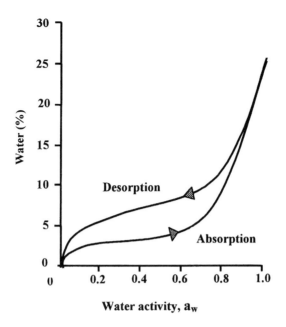

Fig. 6.1 Stylised absorption and desorption curves.

changes, perhaps more than once. It is also difficult to be sure that the ingredient interactions that typically occur in bakery processes have not influenced the nature of a particular ingredient isotherm. Consequently it can be particularly difficult to prepare the 'true' isotherm that would be the most relevant for practical use. In such cases other, less precise but more practical techniques may be of greater value. Some of these techniques are considered below and in more detail in Chapter 8.

The relationship between product moisture content and water activity depends on the nature and composition of the ingredients and the processing that has been carried out to convert the ingredients to a baked product. This is what makes the particular relationship unique. Many workers have determined the moisture–humidity relationship for bakery-related foods. Some examples for biscuits, cake and Christmas puddings published previously by Cooper *et al.* (1968) are given in Fig. 6.2, while other recorded examples include soda crackers, dried chocolate syrup, gelatine-based desserts, powdered molasses (Landrock & Proctor, 1951), wheat and potato starch, radish and figs (Yanniotis, 1994), and savoury pie pastry (Butcher & Hodge, 1984). It should be noted that individual ingredient and product isotherms are temperature-specific, and the temperature at which the isotherm was established should always be quoted. Once an isotherm has been established for a given food, changes in moisture level can be used to predict changes in product water activity.

The stability of a baked product is dependent on both its moisture content and its water activity. Only in pure water are the water activity and moisture content identical, i.e. 1.0 and 100% respectively. Once ingredients and their concentrations within a product are taken into account, along with their effects on the water availability, the moisture content and the water activity values will differ. Generally

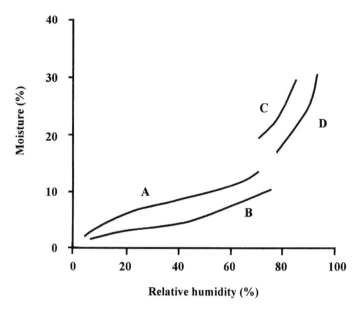

Fig. 6.2 Moisture–humidity relationship for bakery-related foods. A, water biscuits at 27°C (80°F); B, short sweet biscuits at 27°C (80°F); C, Christmas puddings at 21°C (70°F); D, plain cakes at 21°C (70°F).

for a given product as the moisture content increases or decreases, the water activity increases or decreases accordingly. Many products with high moisture contents also have high water activities, while those with low moisture contents have low water activities. However, it must be noted that although two bakery product recipes might have the same moisture content, their water activities can be quite different. Similarly, for a given product it is possible for its moisture content to change without making a major change to its water activity. This can occur when previously undissolved materials in the product, such as sugars, go into solution in the extra water associated with the higher moisture content.

An example of two product recipes that have the same moisture content but different water activities is given in Table 6.4. It is also possible for two recipes to have the same water activity with differing levels of moisture. This leads to products with very different eating characteristics (as discussed in Chapter 5) and is an important consideration in achieving particular qualities both from the organoleptic and product spoilage viewpoints. This particular aspect of product formulation will be discussed in more detail in Chapter 9.

DEFINITIONS OF WATER ACTIVITY AND EQUILIBRIUM RELATIVE HUMIDITY

A number of definitions may be given for water activity (a_w) and equilibrium relative humidity (ERH), but before doing so it will be helpful to establish the relationship between them. Water activity expresses the 'availability' of the water in

Table 6.4 Recipes for comparison.

Ingredient	Quantity	Quantity
	Recipe 1	Recipe 2
flour	100.0	100.0
sucrose	117.5	125.0
fat	35.3	35.3
whole egg	30.7	30.7
baking powder	4.5	4.5
salt	0.5	1.5
glycerol	0.5	3.0
water	105.5	112.0
moisture content (%)	30.6	30.6
ERH (%)	90.1	88.7

a given solution, whereas ERH applies, strictly speaking, to the atmosphere in contact with the solution. When the atmosphere and the solution are in equilibrium, the terms a_w and ERH can be used interchangeably. The relationship under a defined set of conditions of atmospheric temperature and pressure is straightforward and described by the following equations:

$$a_w \quad = ERH/100$$
$$ERH = 100 \times a_w\%$$

Since ERH is based on the measurement of humidity, it is usual to express it as a percentage, while a_w has no units. The scale for a_w runs from 0 to 1, with 1 representing pure water; that for ERH runs from 0 to 100%, with 100% representing pure water. Thus, a cake with an a_w of 0.82 has an ERH of 82%.

As discussed in previous chapters, when soluble substances dissolve in water the resulting solution has a lower freezing point, a higher boiling point and a lower vapour pressure. It is this latter change that is most relevant to aspects of water activity because Raoult's Law states that "the relative lowering of the vapour pressure of a solvent is equal to the mole fraction of the solute". For an ideal solution the vapour pressure relative to that of water is equal to the mole fraction. Thus, if the vapour pressures are known then the relationship p/p_o gives the vapour pressure of a particular solution, where p and p_o are the vapour pressures of the solution and water, respectively. The relationship between vapour pressures, water activity and ERH is expressed as follows:

$$p/p_o = ERH/100 = a_w$$

Although the vapour pressure of water changes with temperature, the a_w of an ideal solution is independent of temperature. In practice, most solutions in bakery products are far from ideal in behaviour, and so a_w varies a little over the range of temperatures that are most relevant for food spoilage.

Water activity is a physicochemical concept first used by Scott (1957) to show that a_w rather than moisture content determined the microbial safety of food. Water activity has been described in a number of different ways. Richardson (1986) described it as "the availability of 'free' water as opposed to the total moisture which includes 'bound' water". There has been no common agreement about how much of the water present is bound and therefore unavailable in a food, or where the bound and free water is located within the food system concerned. A relatively simple example of the uncertainty that prevails would be a mixture of water and a suitable stabiliser to form a gel. Given that we have the correct concentration of stabiliser, we can bind quite large quantities of water to create a system that is stable but still susceptible to mould growth (unless we take other precautions). Clearly the water was not sufficiently bound to make it unavailable for use by microorganisms, although it is sufficiently bound to prevent it running away if the gel is not held in a container.

The concept of *'freezable'* and *'non-freezable'* water has been used as an alternative to that of free and bound. Non-freezable water would be that portion of the moisture in the food which does not freeze at $0°C$ ($32°F$). Some of the issues regarding the conversion of water in foods to ice have been discussed above. The freezable/non-freezable water concept has some attraction, but studies with differential scanning calorimetry (DSC) and low-temperature nuclear magnetic resonance have shown that non-freezable water exhibits a high degree of mobility and so is not bound in the energetic sense (Ablett and Lillford, 1991).

The concepts of bound/free and freezable/non-freezable water work well when stored foods are in thermodynamic equilibrium, but since this is not the case with most foods other more appropriate means of describing the state of water in food have been sought. In composite bakery foods, the lack of thermodynamic equilibrium may be related to the properties of the individual components, e.g. cake and jam, although even at the molecular level lack of storage equilibrium may exist (e.g. see the discussion on bread staling in Chapter 5). The current 'models' for the stability of foods during storage are based on the glassy/rubbery states and glass transition temperatures as discussed previously. Within this model, stability of the food is achieved when it is stored below its glass transition temperature. The development of these models for food storage stability owes much to the work of Slade and Levine (1987).

There is no direct link between the measurement of water activity as a measure of available water, the freezing point as a measure of freezable water, and glass transition temperature. However, there is an indirect link in that if product formulations are ranked according to their a_ws, freezing points and T_gs, the order is likely to be the same, i.e. the sample with the highest a_w will also have the highest freezing point and the highest T_g (Cauvain, 1998). Thus, the measurement of the water activity of a bakery food still has practical value for predicting its storage stability and potential changes in textural properties.

The relationship between a_w and ERH has been described above. The ERH of a product may be defined as that unique humidity at which moisture is neither lost nor gained by a product, or at which the rate of evaporation of moisture from the product equals the rate at which moisture is absorbed by the product (Cauvain & Seiler, 1992). In other words, the humidity within the product is in equilibrium with that of the atmosphere surrounding it. In practical terms, we see this if a product is wrapped in a moisture-impermeable film since, with time, a point is eventually reached where the humidity within the product is the same as that in the atmosphere surrounding the product in its package (provided none is lost through the packaging film). At this point, the rate at which the product loses water is the same as the rate at which it gains water from the atmosphere in the package.

The ERH of a product can be measured using suitable instrumentation, or it can be calculated if particular data are known for each of the ingredients present in the product formulation, along with any relevant data on the moisture losses that may have occurred during the processing, baking, cooling and storage of the product. The methods used to determine the a_w, ERH and moisture content of products are discussed in some detail in Chapter 7; *see also* Chapter 8 for the calculations.

WATER ACTIVITY AND MICROBIAL SPOILAGE

Reducing the level of available moisture has been used for many years as a way of preserving food (e.g. drying, salting, sugaring and pickling). Dehydrating ingredients (e.g. vine fruits), foods (e.g. meat) and other perishable materials (e.g. leather) so that they no longer provide a comfortable environment for spoilage to occur was used by our ancestors long before the concepts of microbial contamination and the mechanisms of microbial growth and spoilage were known. Early sailors benefited from long shelf-life products such as ship's biscuits (hard tack), which were extremely low in moisture and are probably the hard eating forerunner of the modern European semi-sweet dough biscuits and crackers.

Scientists working in the latter half of the nineteenth century began to discover that a relationship existed between the level of moisture present in a food and its tendency to spoil; in general the higher the moisture content, the faster the foods spoiled. They observed that the water vapour pressure fell during the drying of foods and later they linked the spoilage to the effects of water availability or how the water was bound in the food rather than the absolute amount of moisture present (Troller, 1989). An Australian microbiologist, W.J. Scott (1957), noted that the relative humidity of the refrigerated cabinet in which meat was stored influenced the rate of microbial growth on the meat surfaces. However, the term 'relative humidity' was deemed to be an inadequate descriptor for the condition of water in a product, and so another term was sought to better describe what was happening to the water within a product: 'water activity'.

Attack by microorganisms is one of many assaults that baked products encounter before they are consumed, and is a very important food quality and safety consideration. Some of the factors that control or determine the rate at which microbial spoilage will develop on bakery, and most other foods are listed below:

- Numbers of microorganisms contaminating a product (its microbial load)
- Types of microorganism present
- Product surface water content (providing localised high moisture/a_w conditions)
- Product water activity
- Storage temperature

- Storage relative humidity
- Product pH
- Presence of inhibitors

Microorganisms contain high levels of water within their cells. They need a supply of water to maintain their life functions, e.g. feeding, growth and reproduction, just as humans do. For some microorganisms, reproduction can result in the formation of toxins that are hazardous to human health; these are commonly referred to as pathogenic organisms. In other cases there may be the production of unsightly, coloured blemishes (mould colonies) or off-odours and flavours, e.g. yeast fermentation of jams may result in a 'winey' odour.

The availability of water in a product can be a powerful controlling mechanism on the potential for microbial growth and is often used as a predictor of which organisms may flourish on a given food and how quickly a product can be spoiled by such microbial activity. The relationship between the concentration of the liquid and its vapour pressure within the microorganisms' cells and that of its surroundings can encourage or discourage the movement of water through the cell wall membrane. As the vapour pressure (water activity) falls, the opportunities for microbial growth reduce and when a water activity of 0.6 or less is reached, growth is not normally possible. Table 6.5 shows the levels of water activity at which growth is suspended for different groups of microorganisms, but it should be recognised that the optimal growth conditions will vary for specific organisms within a given group. For example, Seiler (1977) considered the time at which mould growth became visible on the surface of cakes with different ERHs stored at 27°C (80°F) and found that *Aspergillus* species were likely to show before *Penicillium* species at ERHs below 84%. When the cake ERH was 88%, colonies of both species were equally likely to become visible at similar storage times.

Table 6.5 Minimum water activity levels for microbiological growth.

Water activity (a_w)	Organism
0.6	osmophilic yeasts
0.65	xerophilic bacteria
0.75	halophilic bacteria
0.80	most moulds
0.85	most yeasts
0.91	most bacteria
1.0	(pure water)

As a rule of thumb, bacteria need more available moisture for growth than yeasts, which in turn need more than moulds. The data given in Table 6.6 link typical water activity levels for bakery products with the types of microorganisms that are likely to grow. Some microorganisms have become especially adapted to situations of low moisture availability. These are the halophilic (salt-loving), xerophilic (dryness-loving) and osmophilic (osmotic-pressure-loving) organisms that will grow from a_ws

Table 6.6 Spoilage types for typical bakery products.

Water activity (a$_w$)	Products	Spoilage types
0.99	creams, custards	bacterial spoilage, e.g. 'rope' mould growth and 'chalk moulds'
0.90–0.97	breads, crumpets, part-baked yeasted products	bacterial spoilage, e.g. 'rope' mould growth and 'chalk moulds'
0.90–0.95	moist cakes, e.g. carrot cake	mould and yeast, bacterial spoilage, e.g. 'rope'
0.8–0.89	plain cakes	moulds and yeasts
0.7–0.79	fruited cakes	xerophilic moulds and osmophilic yeasts
0.6–0.69	some dried fruits or fruited cakes	specialised xerophilic moulds and osmophilic yeasts, sugar-tolerant yeasts
<0.6	biscuits, chocolate, some dried fruits	no microbial spoilage

of 0.75 down to 0.60 respectively. The osmophilic yeasts are often implicated when spoilage occurs in high sugar coatings and fillings, such as jams, fondants, marzipans and marshmallows. The spoilage mainly manifests itself as 'winey' (fermented) or off-odours associated with the product. It may be particularly noticeable when the product package is first opened and the gases present in the pack headspace are released.

In some cases, although growth is initially prevented by a lower ERH, the microorganism is capable of surviving – but will be inactive – and may spring back into life when conditions again become favourable for activity and growth. For example, this may occur when wrapped products are moved from a cold to a warmer environment, e.g. from chill to room temperature, which can lead to condensation on the product surface within the pack. Even though this product may have had a low initial ERH, the presence of extra water on the surface can locally raise the ERH to such a level that it is now capable of supporting greater microbial growth than before. This sort of problem is exacerbated when the products are wrapped (although it can occur with unwrapped products), and often occurs when frozen products are being defrosted.

As the storage temperature is lowered, the water present in a product becomes increasingly unavailable for use by microorganisms and their growth rate slows considerably. Low temperature storage forms the basis of controlling the growth of pathogenic organisms, and for 'high risk' foods (i.e. with high water activity) may be enshrined in suitable legislation. In the UK the Food Hygiene (Amendment) Regulations (1990) represent one such example; although their introduction did lead to reduced microbial risks they also introduced some adverse changes in bakery product eating qualities (Bailey, 1992; Bailey & Cauvain, 1994). Once water is frozen in a product, it becomes largely unavailable for microbial growth. The value of using low temperatures to prevent food spoilage has been appreciated for many hundreds of years and until the introduction of the refrigerator in the twentieth century, icehouses were used on large estates as a means of extending the supply of 'fresh' products throughout the winter (Beamon, 1987). For greater detail of how microorganisms grow under particular sets of defined conditions the reader is referred elsewhere, e.g. Troller (1989) and Walker (1996).

WATER ACTIVITY AND THE MOULD-FREE SHELF-LIFE OF A PRODUCT

Mould growth is the major microbial spoilage agent for many baked products, as shown in Table 6.6. If the bakery food has a high enough ERH, it will support the growth and reproduction of individual mould spores. As the numbers of individual mould cells increase, a time is eventually reached when the colony is large enough to be seen with the naked eye. At this point the visible blemishes on the product are sufficient for it to be considered spoiled. The length of time taken for the colony to reach a visible size depends on many factors, many of which were identified above. A key factor in determining the point at which the colony becomes visible is the product water activity, but the microbial load is also a major determinant: the greater the initial microbial load, the more rapidly the colony will become visible as individual spores form small colonies and merge.

The visibility of mould colonies is an important aspect of determining the end of product shelf-life. Mould spores are almost always present on the sterile surface of a baked product since contamination occurs the moment the product leaves the oven. Subsequent handling operations, such as cooling, finishing and wrapping, all contribute to the microbial load. The moment at which the mould colony becomes visible varies according to the type of mould contamination, which varies according to the particular mould species and the ERH of the product. Some mould colonies are readily visible because their colour contrasts with that of the surrounding product. Blue- and green-coloured colonies are readily distinguished on the golden-coloured surface of cakes and bread crusts, and the crumb (should this have been contaminated). White-coloured colonies are not readily visible on light coloured surfaces, such as bread crumb, but are particularly visible on darker surfaces, e.g. chocolate cake. In the case of chocolate cakes, brown-coloured moulds would be difficult to distinguish on the product crust or crumb. The problems associated with the visibility of mould colonies is one of the main factors giving rise to inaccuracies in determining the mould-free shelf-life of bakery products.

There is a direct relationship between the ERH of a product and the time for which it will remain free of mould growth (*see* Fig. 6.3). This relationship was established by scientists working at the Flour Milling and Baking Research Association, Chorleywood, (Cooper *et al.*, 1968) using a representative selection of baked products, which they stored at various temperatures, and observing the point in time at which mould colonies first became visible. Some variations in the timing of the onset of visible mould growth were observed consistent with the problems outlined above. However, the relationship proved robust and later the storage temperature range was extended (Cauvain & Seiler, 1992). Figure 6.3 shows the relationship between ERH and mould-free shelf-life (MFSL) for a range of storage tempera-

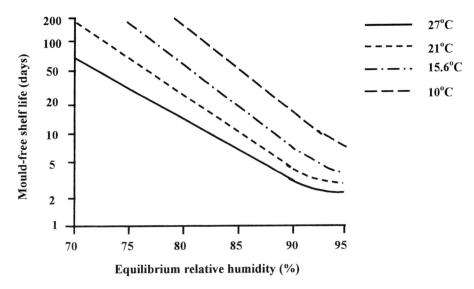

Fig. 6.3 Relationship between ERH and MFSL.

tures. In simple terms, the lower the storage temperature for a product of given ERH, the longer will be its MFSL. For products with ERHs above 93%, reducing the ERH by a relatively small amount, say 1%, causes very little change in MFSL. However in the range 85 to 70% reducing ERH by 1% causes a much greater increase in shelf-life. In practical terms this means that there is little opportunity for reducing ERH for products such as breads (*see* Table 6.7) without significantly changing the character of the product, e.g. making them sweeter by the addition of sugar. Biscuits and drier baked products with ERHs below 60% are not significantly affected by mould growth as moisture levels are usually too low. However, cakes and pastries with ERHs lying between 70 and 85% are ideal candidates for the

Table 6.7 Levels of water activity in typical bakery products.

Water activity (a_w)	Products
0.99	creams, custards
0.95–0.99	breads, fermented products
0.84	fruit pies
0.90–0.95	moist cakes, e.g. carrot cake
0.90	yeasted pastries e.g. danish, croissant
0.8–0.89	plain cakes e.g. madeira, sponge cakes
0.7–0.79	fruited cakes
0.6–0.69	some dried fruits or fruited cakes
0.3	pastries
0.6	biscuits, chocolate, some dried fruits
0.05–0.25	extruded products
0.65–0.66	bread crumbs, biscuit crumbs

approach of manipulating ingredients to maintain water content of the product whilst reducing the ERH (*see* Chapter 9).

Figure 6.4 shows how the mould-free shelf-life of a product stored at 21°C can be extended from five to nine days by reducing the ERH by 3%. This can be put to beneficial use by the bakery product developer, particularly where the product moisture content remains largely unchanged and ingredients can be manipulated without considerably changing the organoleptic or textural characteristics of the product under development, e.g. cake and pastry products. Weight loss over a period, and its effect of increasing shelf-life, is illustrated in Fig. 6.5. As the product ERH falls, so does the weight (moisture) loss because the water is less available for evaporation. However, the loss of water will extend product MFSL regardless of the product ERH.

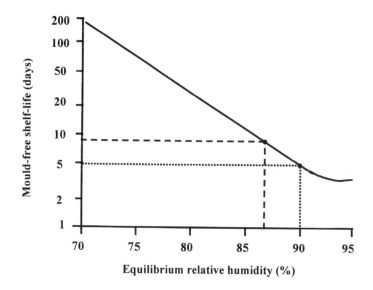

Fig. 6.4   Product ERH and MFSL at 21°C.

EFFECTS OF PACKAGING

In the final assembled state, most bakery products with shelf-lives greater than a few hours are wrapped in protective film to preserve optimum product quality and prevent further contamination by microorganisms. The permeability of the wrapping material to moisture evaporation plays an important in role maintaining the required product quality. In many bakery products, the wrapping film is largely impermeable to moisture so that product moistures and ERHs remain at the same level as that when they were wrapped. This means that it is very important to ensure that the product ERH is low enough to prevent the growth of undesirable microorganisms, such as moulds. Often the relative humidity of the air is lower than that of the product so that a small amount of water evaporates from the product in order to establish equilibrium between product and pack atmosphere (compare this with

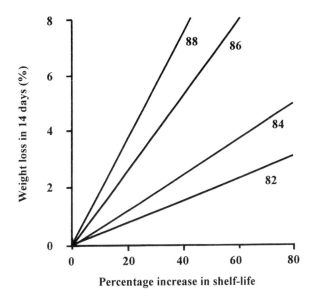

Fig. 6.5   Effect of ERH on weight loss and percentage increase in shelf-life.

the definition of ERH given above). However, when the humidity of the atmosphere is higher than that of the product there is some opportunity for moisture to migrate from atmosphere to product and raise the ERH of the product. The presence of undissolved sugars in icings and toppings confers humectant properties, which may be a particular problem for the control of ERH and mould growth.

The total quantity of moisture that may migrate from a product to a drier pack atmosphere depends in part on the product ERH and also on the ratio of the water mass in the product to the volume of air within the pack. The greater the volume of air in the pack, the greater the mass of water required to saturate that atmosphere. As discussed previously, the saturated vapour pressure depends on the temperature of the air, and so the mass of air required to achieve saturation also changes with storage temperature. When held in an impermeable pack, a point is normally reached during storage at which the product and pack atmosphere are in equilibrium; should the storage temperature change, that equilibrium will be disturbed. If the temperature falls condensation may become a problem within the pack, leading to an increase in the ERH on the product surface and increased potential for microbial growth. If the storage temperature increases, there will be an increase in the evaporation of water from the product. Changes in pack equilibrium with changes in storage temperature, especially those that lead to condensation, are often overlooked when trying to trace the cause of mould growth on wrapped products.

In some instances a wrapping material that allows some loss of water from the product may be used to control microbial growth or maintain product eating quality. A common example is the use of semi-permeable wrapping films with pastry products to assist in maintaining the required low moisture content and crisp eating quality in the pastry. Such changes do not usually lead to any increase in the potential for microbial growth. Butcher and Hodge (1984) showed how increasing the permeability of the wrapping material could be used to extend the time taken for savoury pie pastry to go soft, and Robb (1991) showed that a similar principle could be used to retain the crisp eating character of sweetened pie pastry with apple pies. The link between the type of packaging and the quality of stored foods is discussed in some detail by Stollman *et al.* (1996).

WATER ACTIVITY AND PRODUCT RANCIDITY

Bakery foods with low a_ws, such as biscuits, cookies and crackers, may be stored without supporting mould growth but are still susceptible to water-activity-related spoilage. In this case the problem is associated with the autoxidation of the lipids that are present in the baked product formulations. This problem usually occurs relatively rapidly in products with a_ws of less than 0.3. As the a_w increases towards 0.5, oxidation decreases but increases again thereafter (Troller, 1989).

The processes that develop rancidity in products are complex but involve any free radicals present in the product. These come potentially from a number of sources, most obviously the addition of fats to product formulations, including most biscuits and cakes. In the case of cakes, rancidity is not commonly noticed because the higher water activity will support mould growth, which causes product rejection before levels of rancidity are high enough to be detected and to become the cause for rejection. Other sources of free radicals are ingredients that have a naturally high fat content, including soya flour and oat products, both of which are used in bakery products. The use of oat products is common in some speciality biscuits, and with their low a_w they are particularly susceptible to the development of rancidity.

Lipases (fat-splitting enzymes), if present, can react with the fat component of cookies and biscuits, causing off-flavours such as soapiness. Lipases are most active at higher water activities, but will continue to react at water activities down to 0.25 and so can be a problem in biscuits, crackers and cookies. The lipases exist in soya flour, oats, spices and cocoa powder, and should be destroyed by heat processing before or during production. However, in some cases the heat processing of baking may be insufficient to ensure that full inactivation occurs and they may contribute to product spoilage.

THE INFLUENCE OF INGREDIENTS ON WATER ACTIVITY

The majority of ingredients used in the manufacture of bakery products have an effect on final product water activity. This comes from both the moisture content of the ingredient, as discussed above, and the analytical composition of the individual food ingredient, e.g. the starch, protein and fibre components. In their undissolved or dry state, ingredients do not have any effect on water activity, but once in solution or hydrated they exert an influence on water activity because of their ability to hold or lock up moisture molecules. This ability depends on the type of solute, its molecular weight, degree of ionisation and the quantity present with respect to the moisture content of the product.

The quantities and nature of ingredients in a given formulation govern the way water is held in a product. There are a number of mechanisms by which intramolecular bonds are formed, some of which have been introduced in the discussion above. There is a rule of thumb for the order in which water is held by an ingredient: the greater the energy that is required to break the bonds holding the water to other molecules in the ingredient, the better its water-holding ability and therefore the greater its effect on water activity will be.

The ionic molecular bond has the greatest influence on the water-holding power of ingredients. Common salt (sodium chloride) is an example of an ingredient that exhibits a powerful hold on water through the ionic effect, and the salting of meat has been used for centuries as a means of preservation. In baked products however, the amount of salt that can be used is limited because of its strong effect on flavour and its inhibitory effect on some of the other ingredients, e.g. high levels of salt inhibit the activity of yeast in fermented doughs (Williams & Pullen, 1998). In its solid form, salt comprises positively charged sodium ions and negatively charged chlorine ions held in a crystalline matrix. When salt crystals come into contact with water molecules, the affinity between them allows the salt crystals to dissociate into the sodium and chloride ions and salt goes into solution. Consequently this increases the number of dissolved particles in the solution which tie up more water molecules, thus lowering the vapour pressure (*see* Fig. 6.6). The bonding between these two substances is so strong that the water molecules are held or bound and are unavailable for other purposes, such as mould growth. The ionic effect on water activity is a more powerful effect than would be expected from the molecular weight of salt. The same sort of effect is observed for some buffer salts, such as calcium carbonate (the chalk addition in UK flours), sodium phosphate (used to control the pH of water in fish tanks), and some flavouring acids, e.g. citric acid.

Some food ingredients have the ability to exploit the fact that water has two hydrogen atoms and one oxygen atom and are able to form hydrogen bonds which bind the water, molecules to the ingredients. Other ingredients utilise covalent effects to bind water, but this bonding is not as strong as the ionic or hydrogen bonding effects. Covalency describes bonding between carbon atoms. Sugars are

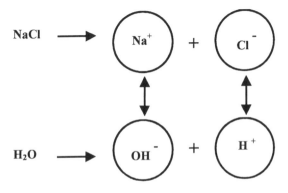

Fig. 6.6 Simplified representation of molecular conditions in salt solutions.

one form of carbohydrates which dissolve readily in water to form solutions. In its amorphous glassy state, there is a higher internal area available within the sucrose molecule, making it easier for the water to penetrate into the hydrogen-bonded structure. The large number of hydroxyl groups in sugar molecules tie up water very efficiently. The solubility of sucrose changes little within the temperature ranges normally encountered with bakery product storage, and in the absence of other solutes a saturated solution of sucrose will contain about 2 g sucrose/g of water. The ERH of a saturated sugar solution will be between 85 and 86% (Cooper *et al.*, 1968).

When different types of sugar dissolve, they lower the vapour pressure of the solution to different degrees and therefore lower product ERH to different degrees. Thus saturated solutions of different sugars will have different ERHs. As discussed above, the ERH of a saturated sucrose solution will be around 86% and therefore it is susceptible to mould growth and yeast fermentation. In order to prevent such microbial activity, it would be necessary to add other types of sugar to lower the ERH. However, when a mixture of sugars is dissolved, the solubility of one sugar will affect the solubility of another. For example, when a mixture of equal quantities of sucrose and dextrose is dissolved, the lower molecular weight of the dextrose (180) means that there will be more particles present in the dextrose solution than in the sucrose solution (the molecular weight of sucrose is 342). The result is that more water molecules will be held by the dextrose molecules and the water activity of the mixture will be lower.

If the quantity of the dextrose in the dextrose–sucrose mixture is increased so that the overall level of solutes is increased, sucrose would precipitate from the solution. If this happens in a bakery product the undissolved sucrose would try to absorb water from the surrounding atmosphere. This is the effect seen when icing and toppings become sticky after exposure to humid atmospheres, or when moisture migration occurs in composite products (*see* Chapter 7). This effect should not be confused with humectancy. The term 'humectant' is usually applied to materials that are more effective at lowering solution vapour pressure than would be suggested from molecular weight considerations, for example, sodium chloride and glycerol (glycerine).

Other higher molecular weight food components, such as proteins, or complex polysaccharides like pectins, starches and gums, will, under certain conditions of hydration, form high molecular weight colloidal solutions that reduce the water activity of the solution. They also exert some influence on the water activity in the finished product, although this may be smaller than that seen in a relatively simple solution. Even fibres have a water-binding capacity (WBC). Labuza (1989) provided a list of water binding capacities for fibres from different sources and compared their WBCs by three different methods.

SUCROSE EQUIVALENCE

As a result of their ability to bind water, sugars are used to preserve the shelf-life of many sweet goods products. In fact, because of the popularity of sucrose in this context, it is commonly used as a 'yardstick' by which other ingredients are judged for their ability to extend the mould-free shelf-life in a product. Grover (1947) studied the influence of different strengths of different sugar solutions on water vapour pressure and devised a method to calculate the effect of formulation changes on the water activity of sugar confectionery. In this scheme the sucrose equivalence (se) of an ingredient could be defined as 'the effect that the ingredient has on water activity compared to the effect an equal quantity of sucrose would have'. Cooper *et al.* (1968) adapted Grover's concept of sucrose equivalence to devise a method by which the ERH or water activity could be determined from ingredients in a product formulation. This method relies on determining the sucrose equivalence of each of the ingredients in a recipe and their individual contributions to the sucrose concentration in the product. Some examples of sucrose equivalences for bakery ingredients are given in Table 6.8. The application of this method for calculating product ERH is described in detail in Chapter 8. It was first used in the baking industry to allow the prediction of the mould-free shelf-life of cakes (Jones, 1996), but its application has been successfully extended to many more bakery products and to non-microbial aspects of product shelf-life and storage stability.

Table 6.8 Sucrose equivalence of typical bakery ingredients.

Ingredient	Sucrose equivalence
flour	0.2
fat	0
yeast	0.5
sucrose	1.0
salt	11.0
sultanas	0.9

CONCLUSIONS

The concepts of water activity and the related property ERH have been used for some considerable time as measures of food safety and quality. While they may explain many of the changes that occur during product storage they cannot be used to account for all aspects of quality losses. The concept of the glassy and rubbery states, and the measurement of glass transition temperatures, are being used increasingly to understand the factors that underlie the lack of product storage stability, especially those attributes which are major contributors to physical quality changes during storage, e.g. staling. While a_w and ERH are less effective as indicators of quality loss, they still provide a relatively simple, low cost and practical way in which to assess the potential for product quality changes during storage. An understanding of the factors that determine the product a_w and ERH, and their measurement, still remain very important when considering the microbial aspects of product storage stability, especially in the current marketing environment which seeks ever longer product shelf-lives and reduced microbial risks for the consumer.

REFERENCES

Ablett, S. & Lillford, P. (1991) Water in foods. *Chemistry in Britain*, November, 1024–6.

Bailey, C. (1992) Refrigeration in baked goods – facts, fallacies and legislation. *FMBRA Chorleywood Digest*, **122**, 124–7.

Bailey, C. & Cauvain, S.P. (1994) Refrigeration of baked foodstuffs. *Proceedings Institute of Refrigeration*, **6**, 1–8.

Beamon, S. (1987) Ice-houses. *Current Archaeology*, **105**, 294–6.

Butcher, G.J. & Hodge, D.G. (1984) Pastry technology: The softening of pork pie pastry during storage. *FMBRA Report No. 116*, CCFRA, Chipping Campden, UK.

Cauvain, S.P. (1995) Putting pastry under the microscope. *Baking Industry Europe*, 68–9.

Cauvain, S.P. (1998) Improving the control of staling in frozen bakery products. *Trends in Food Science and Technology*, **9**, 56–61.

Cauvain, S.P. & Seiler, D.A. (1992) Equilibrium relative humidity and the shelf life of cakes. *FMBRA Report No. 150*, CCFRA, Chipping Campden, UK.

Cooper, R.M., Knight, R.A., Robb, J. & Seiler, D.A.L. (1968) The equilibrium relative humidity of baked products with particular reference to the shelf life of cakes. *FMBRA Report No. 19*, CCFRA, Chipping Campden, UK.

Food Hygiene (Amendment) Regulations (1990) *SI 1990 No. 1431*. Ministry of Agriculture, Fisheries and Food, London, UK.

Franks, F. (1991) Water activity: a credible measure of food safety and quality? *Trends in Food Science and Technology*, March, 68–72.

Grover, D.W. (1947) The keeping properties of confectionery as influenced by its water vapour pressure. *Journal of the Society of Chemistry and Industry*, **66**, 201–5.

Jones, H.P. (1996) Ambient packaged cakes, in *Shelf Life Evaluation of Foods* (eds C.M.D. Man & A.A. Jones), Blackie Academic & Professional, London, UK, pp. 179–201.

Labuzza, T.P. (1989) Fiber's water binding capacity. *Cereal Foods World*, **34**, 566–7.

Landrock, A.H. & Proctor, B.E. (1951) A new graphical interpolation method for obtaining humidity equilibria data, with special reference to its role in food packaging studies. *Food Technology*, **5**, 332–7.

Podmore, J. (1997) Baking fats, in *The Technology of Cake Making*, 6th edn (Ed. A.J. Bent), Blackie Academic & Professional, London, UK, pp. 25–47.

Richardson, T. (1986) ERH of confectionery food products. *The Manufacturing Confectioner*, December, 85–9.

Robb, J. (1991) Moisture migration in apple pies. *FMBRA Report No. 145*, CCFRA, Chipping Campden, UK.

Scott, W.J. (1957) Water relation of food spoilage microorganisms. *Advances in Food Research*, **7**, 83–127.

Seiler, D. (1977) Problems estimating the mould-free shelf life of baked products. *FMBRA Bulletin No. 4*, CCFRA, Chipping Campden, UK, pp. 112–21.

Slade, L. & Levine, H. (1987) Structural stability of intermediate foods – a new understanding, in *Food Structure – Its Creation and Evaluation* (eds J.R. Mitchell & J.M.V. Blanshard), Butterworth, London, UK, pp. 115–47.

Stollman, U., Johansson, F. & Leufven, A. (1996) Packaging and food quality, in *Shelf Life Evaluation of Foods* (eds C.M.D. Man & A.A. Jones), Blackie Academic & Professional, London, UK, pp. 52–71.

Troller, J.A. (1989) Water activity and food quality, in *Water and Food Quality* (ed. T.M. Hardman), Elsevier Applied Science, London, UK, pp. 1–32.

Walker, S.J., (1996) The principles and practice of shelf life prediction for microorganisms, in *Shelf Life Evaluation of Foods* (eds C.M.D. Man & A.A. Jones), Blackie Academic & Professional, London, UK, pp. 40–51.

Williams, T. & Pullen, G. (1998) Functional ingredients, in *Technology of Breadmaking* (eds S.P. Cauvain & L.S. Young), Blackie Academic & Professional, London, UK, pp. 45–80.

Yanniotis, S. (1994) A new method for interpolating and extrapolating water activity data. *Journal of Food Engineering*, **21**, 81–96.

Young, L.S. (1997) Water activity in flour confectionery product development, in *The Technology of Cakemaking*, 6th edn (ed. A.J. Bent), Blackie Academic & Professional, London, UK, pp. 386–97.

7 Moisture migration and its control in composite products

Composite bakery products having two or more components, each with very different appearances, textures and eating characteristics, have been developed for a number of reasons. They include a desire on the part of manufacturers to present a mixture of different sensory characteristics in a single product, for example a cream-filled cake where the soft, moist cream contrasts with a soft, sweet jam and firmer, drier-eating cake. Another reason for the development of composite foods was to use one material as an edible package for another. A good example of this in the UK is a pork pie, which can be eaten cold and held in the hand.

Some products appear to be single-component products, but the single component contains large particulate materials. These should be considered as a 'multi-component' within a single product. Examples are fruited cakes or breads, and are discussed later in this chapter. The rules of moisture migration are as applicable to these products as composite products that are built from separately prepared components and assembled after baking.

When two components with different moisture contents and water activities are placed in contact with one another, nature perceives the system to be unbalanced and tries to achieve equilibrium by moving moisture from the wetter to the drier component. This transfer of moisture from one component to another may have disastrous consequences for one or all of the components in a multi-component system. Sometimes the manufacturer may seek to create this imbalance immediately after baking in order to preserve the eating characteristics of the product during its expected shelf-life. For example, with apple pies it is advantageous for moisture to move from the pastry to the filling over the life of the pie in order to maintain the crisp-eating pastry and the soft-eating filling.

Thermodynamics and the dynamics of mass transfer largely control the way that moisture moves in composite products. Labuza and Hyman (1998) provided a comprehensive review of the fundamental mathematical models that may be applied to the moisture migration processes in multicomponent (multidomain) foods. Aspects of their review will be considered in later chapters, which deal with methods of determining the availability of water in bakery foods and the application of strategies for the extension of product shelf-life. In this chapter, we shall look at the moisture migration mechanisms from a practical viewpoint and consider their application to the optimisation of composite bakery foods.

MECHANISMS OF MOISTURE MIGRATION

Moisture migrates in bakery foods in one of three ways, summarised as follows:

(1) By direct diffusion from the component with the higher moisture content to the one with the lower moisture content.
(2) By vapour phase transfer, where the moisture migrates from the component with the higher ERH to the one with the lower ERH.
(3) By the formation of surface water through syneresis within a gel as a result of crystallisation or aggregation of polymers.

Diffusion

Direct diffusion of moisture arises when two or more components with differing water activities are in direct contact with one another (*see* Fig. 7.1). The diffusion of moisture may occur at the macroscopic level and is aided by factors such as capillary action, or it may occur at the molecular level as described by Labuza and Hyman (1998). The moisture diffusion rate between the components depends for the most part on the water activity levels of each of the components. The greater the difference in water activity, the faster the rate of diffusion of the moisture will be. For example, in a sponge cake with an a_w of 0.85 which is in contact with a cream filling of a_w 0.95, moisture will move out of the cream and into the sponge. The difference of 0.1 a_w between components is not excessively large, so moisture will move at a relatively moderate pace and it may take several days for complete equilibration to occur (provided no moisture is lost from the total system). In products such as quiches or flans where the filling may well have a water activity of 0.95 and the pastry 0.4, the differential (0.55) is much greater and moisture moves more rapidly from the filling causing the base to become soggy quickly. This can happen over a matter of hours rather than days. Very slow moisture migration occurs in products where component a_ws are very close together. For example, jaffa cakes with their outer dry chocolate coating encasing a jam filling sitting on a sponge base may take several months for complete moisture equilibration to be achieved.

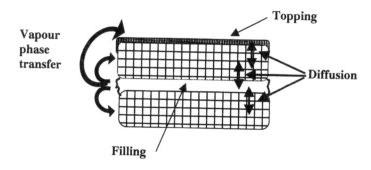

Fig. 7.1 Mechanisms of moisture migration in composite products.

In such products, the dry sponge has a lower a_w than the filling and so pulls moisture from the jam causing it to shrink away and become toffee-like with a chewy instead of soft-eating character.

Gravity assists in the movement of water in the above examples, with the base component (cake or pastry) generally receiving moisture ahead of the side or upper components. While the latter also have low a_ws they must wait for capillary action to diffuse some of the moisture from the base up through the sides. The rate of moisture migration also depends, to a lesser extent, on the physical nature of the materials in contact with one another. The structures of many baked products, with their macroscopically broken cells, act like many small capillary tubes and moisture is drawn into them. However, the rate at which moisture may diffuse through the network is influenced by the porosity of the material. If the material has a largely closed network, i.e. a dense, un-aerated structure, rates of moisture migration will be low. As the structure becomes more aerated, diffusion rates increase, but as the openness of the structure continues to increase, diffusion rates may well stop increasing as capillary forces become less dominant and vapour transfer takes over. Robb (1991) used baking powder additions to increase the porosity of sweetened pastry, and showed that moisture diffusion rates increased causing the pastry to soften more rapidly during storage.

Other aspects of product formulation may influence diffusion of moisture. One example is the presence of fat filling the voids in the baked component and impeding the diffusion or gravitational movement of water. This effect may be seen in savoury, short pastry products such as the UK pork pie. During the baking of the pie, the solid fat turns to liquid oil under the influence of heat and becomes mobile. The effects of gravity mean that the oil will try to move downwards and fill the voids in the lower levels of the pastry (e.g. the base) where it resolidifies when the product cools. This action typically results in a base pastry with a higher fat content, which becomes less permeable and more resistant to diffusion of moisture from the filling that is in contact with it.

Vapour phase transfer

Moisture migration by vapour transfer is most evident with wrapped products, athough it does occur with all composite products. In this mechanism, moisture leaves a product component through surface evaporation to enter the surrounding atmosphere from where it can then be absorbed by another component. Vapour phase moisture transfer is not normally evident with unwrapped products because the water vapour that may evaporate from the product surface is usually swept away by any air movement over the product. Verification of this latter influence is shown by the effect of the wrapper permeability on moisture migration: the more moisture-permeable the wrapping material, the more moisture is lost by vapour phase transfer. This was shown for savoury short pastry by Butcher and Hodge (1984) and for sweetened short pastry by Robb (1991). The major driving forces behind vapour phase moisture transfer come from the differences in component ERHs and the relative humidity (RH) of the atmosphere in the package (*see below*) and the product moisture mass to air volume ratio in the pack.

Syneresis

The shrinkage of gels due to crystallisation or aggregation of polymers can cause loss of water from the surface of components. This problem is common with some starch gels, particularly those subjected to freezing and thawing. Surface water forms because of the breakdown of the gel and subsequent release of the water, which may evaporate to be absorbed by other components by diffusion, or be lost from the product leading to drying out and shrinkage of the gel, or the moisture may be transferred to another component. This effect on moisture migration is considered in more depth later.

FRUITED CAKES AND BREADS

Fruited cakes or breads are interesting examples of a multi-component bakery product. Here the two main components – fruit and base cake or bread – are in intimate contact with each another from mixing through baking, cooling and storage to the point of consumption. Under these circumstances we might expect that moisture equilibration between the two components would be achieved either during mixing or at the very least during baking. However, the difference in sugar concentration, and therefore water activity, between the dried fruit and the dough or batter to which it is added, is sufficient to delay moisture equilibration until well after baking. When the products are cooled and stored the moisture that is present is still not equally distributed throughout the product and moves from the bread or cake crumb into the fruit. This process may take several days depending on the magnitude of the difference in component water activities and the storage conditions.

Moisture migration results obtained by Cauvain and Screen (1987) for fruited high ratio cakes are illustrated in Fig. 7.2; they show that equilibrium was reached after four days of storage. The loss of moisture from the cake crumb to the fruit during this period was sufficient to confer an overall drier eating quality to the base cake. Cauvain and Screen (1987) also showed that to overcome the loss of moisture from the crumb, it was necessary to reduce the water activity of the fruit component by raising its moisture content by soaking it before adding it to the cake batter (*see* curves in Fig. 7.3). In their example, this action restricted the loss of moisture from the crumb as well as raising the overall moisture content of the product. A similar end result could have been effected by lowering the ERH of the cake crumb. However, this would have meant a fundamental reformulation of the cake recipe, which would have changed dramatically the final product quality. Marston (1983) showed that the dry eating character of fruited fermented products (e.g. buns) also came from moisture migration from crumb to fruit and this could be overcome by increasing the fruit moisture content through soaking.

While the overall increase in product moisture content by soaking the fruit reduces moisture migration, it will give a desirable improvement in the moist eating character of the product. It also leads to an overall increase in product ERH, which will shorten its mould-free shelf-life. An example of the typical changes in moisture content that might occur in cake crumb, based on data published by Cauvain and Screen (1987), is given in Table 7.1.

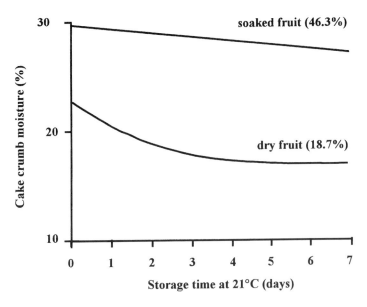

Fig. 7.2 Effect of fruit moisture content on crumb moisture.

In other cake products that are effectively multicomponent, such as carrot cake and banana cake, and some baked products containing vegetables, moisture migration from the high-water-containing ingredients, such as carrot, into the surrounding crumb provides the moist eating character commonly sought in such cakes. Many products are not at their best until the moisture has equilibrated throughout the product, e.g. rich fruit and celebration-style cakes may need to be stored for

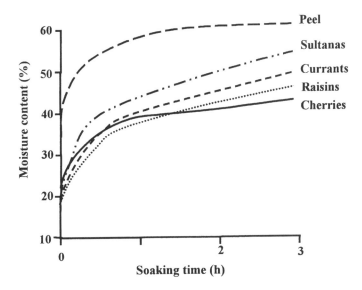

Fig. 7.3 Effect of soaking fruit.

Table 7.1　Effect of soaking fruit on cake moisture content (%).

Fruit	Dry	Soaked
sultanas	24.2	36.3
currants	25.4	35.3
raisins	26.6	37.4
mixed peel	26.9	37.9
glacé cherries	25.8	31.5

many days until moisture has fully equilibrated and thus provided the required eating character. The equilibration period can be as short as a few days or considerably longer where the moisture is more tightly held by the ingredients.

CREAM CAKES

A common example of a multicomponent cake system is the popular dairy cream cake. During whipping, air is drawn into the cream by the mechanical action of the whisk or beater. Fat chains within the cream are drawn on to the surface of the air bubbles giving strength and stability to the foam. With standing time, these bubbles progressively collapse, and eventually free water under the influence of gravity migrates to the bottom of the cream layer, which is also the interface with the cake. Here it is absorbed and the cake moisture content rises, conferring on the product an unacceptable wet or soggy texture. In addition to changes in the eating character of the cake, breakdown of the cream also occurs and manifests itself as an undesirable change in physical appearance and loss of volume. To prevent the breakdown of the cream and subsequent release of water it would be necessary to reduce the ERH of the cream and move it closer to that of the cake. However, in the case of dairy cream (certainly in the UK) there are specific regulatory requirements which limit the type of addition that can be made to it (Cream Regulations, 1970). It is common practice to use some form of stabiliser to confer water-binding properties to the macromolecules present (Labuza & Busk, 1979). Ito and Hodge (1985) studied the use of a range of stabilisers based on alginate, modified cellulose and gums with fresh cream stored at ambient temperature and subjected to freezing and thawing. They found that all were effective at controlling moisture losses at ambient temperatures, but that xanthan gum was particularly effective at controlling cream breakdown after freezing and thawing.

Seepage of liquid also occurs from non-dairy creams and has similar spoiling effects on both cake and filling. Both fat and moisture migration can occur from non-dairy creams as illustrated in Fig. 7.4 using data published by Robb (1986). The rate at which seepage occurs depends to a large extent on cream formulation and storage temperature, with rates of both moisture and fat seepage being greater as the product storage temperature increases. In the case of fat seepage, the effect of temperature is linked directly with the solid fat index of the fat being used. As the storage temperature increases, the proportion of fat existing as oil increases, as does the mobility of the system. However, the transition from solid

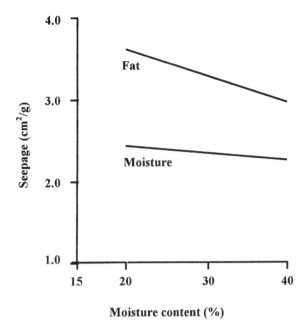

Fig. 7.4 Fat and moisture migration from non-dairy creams.

fat to oil is not linear and depends on the blend of oil fractions used in the manufacture of the fat.

Robb (1986) developed a simple but effective method for measuring fat and moisture seepage in non-dairy creams. He prepared experimental recipes in which water-soluble (Malachite green) and fat-soluble (Oil red O) dyes were dispersed. After mixing and aerating, the cream samples were packed into a cylinder (34 mm in diameter and 30 mm high) and placed on to a filter paper. With storage time, the seepage of fat and moisture were recorded as rings of colour, which spread radially across the surface of the filter paper (*see* Fig. 7.5). From this simple chromatogram, the extent of fat and moisture migration could be measured and comparisons made for different cream formulations and storage conditions.

Using the technique described above, Robb (1986) showed that storage humidity had little effect on fat migration, but seepage of moisture from typical non-dairy cream formulations was reduced as the storage humidity approached the ERH of the cream formulation (*see* Fig. 7.6). From these observations we can infer that moisture migration from non-dairy creams can be reduced by keeping cake and filling ERHs as close together as possible. However, fat seepage will not be reduced by changes in the ERH of the filling.

The fat present in non-dairy creams helps to incorporate and stabilise air bubbles in the cream in a similar manner to that described above for dairy creams. The incorporation of air increases the specific volume of the cream and makes it less firm eating. The temptation for some manufacturers is to increase the aeration of the cream as much as possible in the belief that the greater the bulk in the cream, the better its perceived value in the final product. However, both fat and moisture

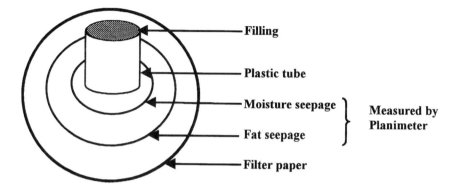

Fig. 7.5 Recording fat and moisture seepage from non-dairy creams.

migration will increase as the cream specific volume increases (*see* Fig. 7.7) and thus over-aeration of the cream should be avoided if moisture migration problems are to be kept to a minimum. Using skimmed milk powder, pregelatinised starch or marshmallow (a common constituent of filling creams because of its ability to stabilise the foam) had little effect on controlling seepage. The only emulsifiers that Robb (1986) found to prevent seepage were proprietary ones containing monoglycerides and polyglycerol esters. However, they had to be used with care and were applicable only where there was sufficient moisture present in the formulation.

To minimise the degree of seepage from non-dairy fillings a few points should be noted:

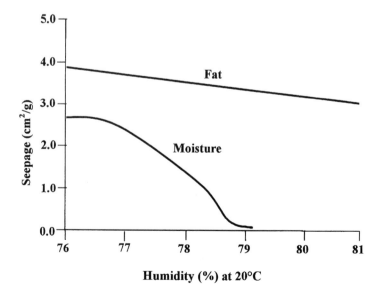

Fig. 7.6 Effect of humidity on moisture migration from non-dairy creams.

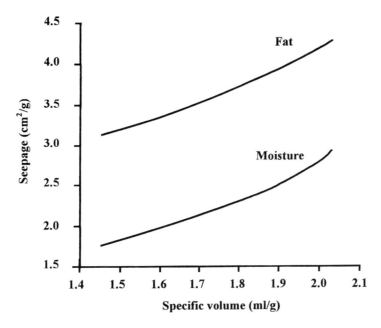

Fig. 7.7 Effect of non-dairy cream specific volume on moisture seepage.

- Use refrigeration to slow down the rate of moisture migration
- Do not overmix the filling
- Ensure that the ERH of the filling is as close as possible to those of the other components
- Reduce the fat content of the filling as far as possible while maintaining the aeration and firmness required

SUGAR-BASED TOPPINGS

As discussed earlier in Chapter 6, the water content in many bakery food systems may be too low to permit the complete dissolution of all the soluble materials present in the formulation. This is particularly true for sugars such as sucrose. The presence of crystalline material in sugar-based toppings makes them hygroscopic, i.e. likely to absorb water, especially when exposed to humid atmospheres or in contact with high-moisture-content materials. This situation often occurs within packaged bakery products when moisture evaporating from the product surface saturates the atmosphere within the pack and raises its RH above that of the topping. The topping will act hygroscopically and absorb water from the atmosphere; as the crystalline sugar goes into solution it causes the topping to become sticky. Vapour phase transfer also occurs through the structure of product components. For example, the cream-filled éclair comprises a fondant on top of a baked choux casing which holds a high water activity filling (cream or custard). Moisture evaporating from the filling can diffuse through the open cells of the casing to be absorbed by the fondant icing. A 'free' water layer may form at the interface of the casing and the fondant, until it is absorbed by the fondant. While the water remains as a liquid it may act as a lubricant and permit the fondant to flow under the influence of gravity off the top of the casing, potentially to fall to the bottom of the container in which the product is held.

A particular problem created by the absorbtion of water by sugar-based toppings occurs when they are part of frozen products, and is observed as craters or crystalline growths on the surface (*see* Fig. 7.8). This phenomenon is related to the formation of sucrose hydrate, a complex crystalline growth first studied by Young *et al.* (1951), who provided a phase diagram to relate sucrose concentration and storage temperature to the formation of the hydrate. The problem tends to be

(a)

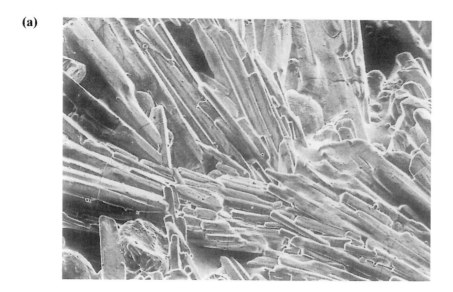

(b)

Fig. 7.8 (a) Photomicrograph of sucrose hydrate growths (full width = 0.11 mm); (b) sucrose hydrate growths on yeast-raised doughnuts.

spasmodic in production and requires the presence of seed crystals which come most often from recycling material that has been allowed to dry out during production. Reformulation of the icing to reduce the sucrose concentration often provides a practical solution to this problem.

SAVOURY PASTRY PRODUCTS

In cake products, consumers generally equate higher moisture contents with increased freshness (*see* Chapter 5). On the other hand, in many pastry products, especially those which are eaten cold, consumers expect the pastry casing to be crisp eating and are more likely to equate softening of the pastry, which occurs as its moisture content increases, with increased staleness. In the UK there is a tradition of savoury pastry products that are eaten cold. The best-known example is the pork pie, and for many consumers the ideal product is one with a crispy outer pastry surrounding a moist inner filling. A gelatine-based jelly filling the voids between the meat and the pastry may or may not be present.

It has been known for some time that the major cause of softening in pork pie pastry during storage is absorption by the crisp, outer shell of moisture from the meat filling and jelly (if used), rather than from migration of fat (Butcher & Hodge, 1984). The driving force for this moisture movement comes from the large differential in water activity between the crisp pastry layer and the moister pie contents, as shown in Table 7.2.

Table 7.2 Water activity of savoury pie components.

Component	Water activity
pastry	0.24
jelly	0.99
filling	0.98

Recent work has provided further information on the mechanism of moisture transfer in pork pies. In a project evaluating the effects of refrigerated display cabinet design (DTI, 1998) experimental work with pork pies showed, as expected, that moisture migrated from filling to the surrounding pastry and evaporated to the surrounding atmosphere. What had not been appreciated previously was that the moisture lost by the side walls of the pies came mostly from the base pastry by capillary action. The filling was in direct contact with the base pastry and diffusion of moisture in this case was probably aided by the effect of gravity in a similar manner to that seen in moisture seepage from creams.

Since the moisture that causes savoury pie pastry to soften originates from within the pie, the measures that might be taken to extend shelf-life are limited. There is little room for manoeuvre for adjusting the water activity of pie contents or the pastry because those ingredients which might be used, e.g. salt and sugar, will affect flavour adversely. Similarly, adjustment to the moisture content of the components is difficult because it is already high in the filling and increases in pastry moisture content are the prime cause of pastry softening.

There are two main courses of action that may be taken to reduce moisture migration in savoury pastries:

(1) Reduce the rate of moisture movement by lowering the storage temperature.
(2) Increase the initial firmness of the pastry so that even though it softens at the normal rate, at expiry of the increased storage period it will still be acceptably crisp.

Pastry crispness is commonly associated with the maximum force required to fracture the pastry during biting and can be measured with sensory panels or a simple mechanical puncture test. Butcher and Hodge (1984) showed that there was a strong relationship between sensory panel assessment and the puncture test (*see* Fig. 5.2). From such relationships it is possible to determine a 'neutral' crispness value, i.e. a mechanical force that equates with a panel rating defined by the term 'neither crisp, nor soft'. Neutral crispness values are useful for comparing the rates of change that might occur in moisture migration.

Butcher and Hodge (1984) confirmed that the moisture responsible for softening pastry originated from within the pie in experiments on baking pork pies with and without their meat and jelly components. Their results showed that the whole pie took about $3\frac{1}{2}$ days to reach neutral crispness, whereas pies that were not jellied did not reach that stage at all during a ten-day testing period. Pastry shells from which both meat filling and jelly had been removed did not soften significantly during storage (*see* Fig. 7.9). The rate at which moisture moves between components

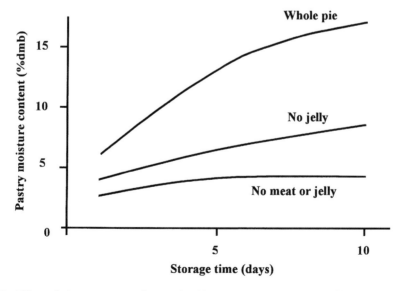

Fig. 7.9 Effect of pie contents on changes in side pastry moisture content (dmb = dry moisture basis).

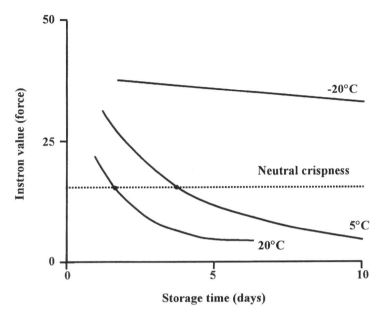

Fig. 7.10   Effect of storage temperature on moisture migration.

decreases as the storage temperature decreases. This effect is illustrated in Fig. 7.10 for savoury pies. When stored at 2°C, only 1½ days passed before pies reached the neutral crispness value, whereas those stored at 5°C reached the same point after three days. There was no loss in crispness when pies were stored in a deep freeze at –20°C.

SWEETENED PASTRY PRODUCTS

Similar moisture migration considerations to those described above apply to sweetened short pastry composite products. A typical product example for this category of product is an apple pie, which comprises a moist filling in contact with a crisp pastry. In contrast to the situation encountered with pork pies, adjustment of water activity to minimise moisture movement between the components is more feasible because changes in recipe sugar levels, for example, can be accommodated in either the paste, the filling or both.

   To understand the way in which moisture moves during the manufacture of apple pies, we must first consider the changes that take place during baking, since there is just as much potential for moisture migration during this period as there is during storage. While the time periods concerned with baking are much shorter than that experienced by the product during storage, the elevated temperatures during baking provide greater quantities of energy, which will accelerate reactions such as moisture movement.

   Typical moisture contents for unbaked and baked apple pie components are illustrated by data in Fig. 7.11 and Table 7.3.

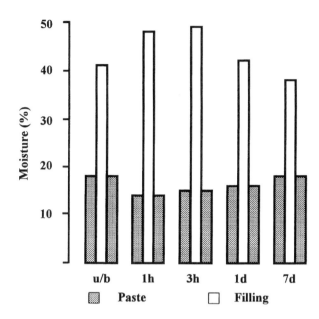

Fig. 7.11   Moisture content of unbaked and baked apple pie components.

We can see that some of the moisture lost by the paste during baking is actually absorbed by the filling and the moisture content of the latter increases to above its starting value. In the illustrated example, this process continues for about three hours after baking. Gradually, during storage, moisture is lost from the filling and is absorbed by the pastry. As storage continues, the pastry loses moisture to the atmosphere at a rate depending on the permeability of the wrapping material. In the UK, apple pies sold from ambient storage are usually wrapped in permeable or semi-permeable materials to encourage moisture loss and therefore retention of pastry crispness. During storage, moisture migration in apple pies can occur by the mechanisms of vapour phase transfer and direct diffusion as described above, and if held in a moisture permeable pack does so in roughly equal amounts (Robb, 1991).

Pastry used in the production of apple pies commonly has a lower ERH than the filling by virtue of its lower moisture content. If we lower the filling moisture content to reduce ERH and move it closer to that of the pastry, we will produce a more jam-like filling rather than the fruity one that has become widely accepted in UK ambient products. Another way to reduce filling ERH is to add more of the soluble materials, like sugar, or to add a humectant, like glycerol. Robb (1991) showed that as the ERH of the filling was lowered, pastry hardness after 21 days' storage increased.

Table 7.3   Moisture contents (%) of apple pie components.

Component	Unbaked	Baked
paste	17.5	12.1
filling	41.5	45.3

USING STABILISERS TO CONTROL MOISTURE MIGRATION

The addition of materials that form complexes with water or other ingredients in the formulation is a common method to prevent loss of water from within a bakery product matrix (Labuza & Busk, 1979). Such materials can also be used to help control moisture migration between components in multicomponent products. Most fruit pie fillings contain a stabiliser of one type or another; typically, modified (pregelatinised) starches and gums such as guar, locust bean, xanthan, sodium or carboxymethyl cellulose (CMC) are used. Robb (1991) found pregelatinised waxy maize starch, guar gum and CMC were the most effective in maintaining base pastry hardness. The effectiveness of many of these stabilisers is influenced by allowing sufficient time to elapse after the filling has been prepared and before it is deposited on to the pastry and the whole product baked. The example of a pregelatinised maize starch given by Robb (1991) is considered in Fig. 7.12. The results show clearly that the effectiveness of this particular stabiliser in reducing moisture migration from the baked filling to the surrounding pastry reached its optimum if it was mixed into the apple filling and the bulk mixture allowed to stand for about six hours before being deposited into the individual unbaked pastry cases. Other stabilisers have different hydration times before they achieve full effectiveness; some will require less and some more time than the example given.

MOISTURE MIGRATION IN COMPOSITE BISCUIT PRODUCTS

Biscuit, cookie and cracker products are sometimes combined with creams or other sweet fillings. In most cases the biscuit cream formulation is such that its water activity is very low and comparable with that of the biscuit with which it will be

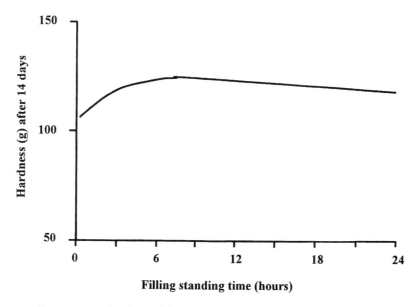

Fig. 7.12 Effect on pastry hardness of filling standing time before depositing.

combined. This requires the biscuit cream formulation to be essentially free from moisture so that many biscuit cream formulations are based on a mixture of sugars and fats. In such cases the undissolved sugars in the biscuit cream may cause it to become hygroscopic and absorb moisture from the biscuit base or the atmosphere. If the biscuits are wrapped correctly in moisture-impermeable film, there is little potential for moisture movement from the atmosphere and hence the biscuits remain crisp-eating. The lack of moisture in the biscuit cream confers a firm and fatty texture and eating quality to the product. However, if moisture is added to a biscuit cream, the resulting higher water activity will lead to a loss of water to the biscuit, which will become unacceptably soft-eating.

Moisture migration can occur within composite biscuit products such as jam rings, jaffa cakes or tartines, both by direct diffusion and vapour phase transfer. Figure 7.13 illustrates a simple piece of apparatus that may be used to determine vapour phase moisture migration. Nisbet (1987) used such an arrangement to show that vapour phase transfer cannnot be ignored when attempting to reduce moisture migration in jam biscuits. Five samples of jam, each with a different water activity, were prepared; the results showed that moisture migration, represented by jam weight loss, was rapid during the first few days of storage but slowed down thereafter. Differences in moisture migration resulting from variations in jam ERH were as expected; the higher the ERH, the faster the moisture migration, which caused greater softening of the biscuit base. Moisture migration from fruit fillings, e.g. fig rolls or fig newtons, will also cause softening of the biscuit base.

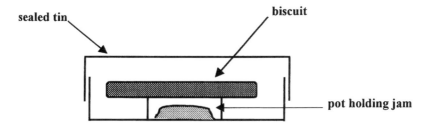

Fig. 7.13   Simple apparatus to determine vapour phase moisture migration.

THE APPLICATION OF MOISTURE BARRIERS

In composite products, we are trying to prevent moisture loss from one component to another, or the uptake of moisture by one component, or both. The simplest means of preventing loss and uptake is to place a moisture-impermeable barrier between the product components, but this is easier said than done. There have been many claims and attempts to provide barriers to moisture migration in composite products, some more successful than others. To some extent, the success of a barrier will depend on the type of product in which it is used. Any barrier used must, of course, be edible and should not adversely affect product texture or flavour.

The most obvious potential barriers are those based on fatty or oily materials. We could think of using fat to provide a 'waterproof' barrier for some unbaked products, e.g. cheese cakes, and for many baked products, e.g. cakes, pastries and biscuits. Applying a fat or oil coating to an unbaked pastry before baking will not be very successful because the fat or oil will become mobile during baking and the barrier can be broken easily by the expanding pastry and the steam that is generated during baking.

The application of fat or oil barriers to products post-baking will be more successful since there will be little movement of materials during storage. Even so, the effectiveness of such barriers may be limited depending on the product composition and configuration. As discussed above, moisture can migrate in composite products by both diffusion and vapour phase transfer. It can be relatively easy to prevent moisture diffusion between components with fat barriers, but unless one of the components is to be totally encased in fat it will be difficult to prevent vapour phase transfer since the water will simply go around the barrier. To have any effect, fat barriers normally need to be relatively thick and this may confer unacceptable eating characteristics to the final product. However, a good example of an effective barrier of this type is the cream used between a biscuit base and a jam topping. Here moisture migration is prevented by diffusion, although some will still occur though vapour phase transfer. Fat barriers have found use in some food products. The best example is the use of a chocolate coating (high in fat) on the inside of ice-cream cones to prevent moisture movement from ice-cream to wafer biscuit. In this form the fat barrier is completely acceptable to the consumer.

Cauvain (1995) provided a number of examples for effective barriers in the manufacture of apple pies based on an interpretation of the work carried out on apple pies by Robb (1991). The crispness of apple pie pastry after 21 days' storage with each of three different barriers inserted between the filling and the base pastry is compared in Fig. 7.14. The control pastry with no barrier application is on the left and the

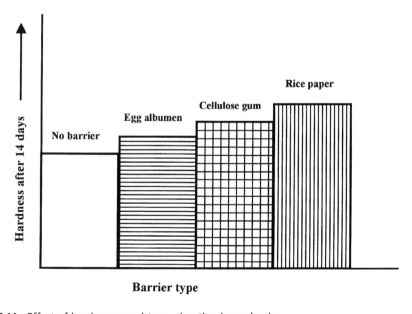

Fig. 7.14 Effect of barriers on moisture migration in apple pies.

effectiveness of barriers used increases from left to right. The egg albumen barrier was prepared as a 15% solution from dried egg white and painted or sprayed on to the pastry base before the filling was deposited on top of it and then subsequently baked as normal. Similarly, a 5% solution of methyl ethyl cellulose was painted or sprayed on to the pastry base. The final barrier illustrated in Fig. 7.14 is the use of rice paper. In this case a rice paper disc was placed on to the pastry base before the filling was deposited. After baking, the rice paper disc was no longer visible and had become part of the filling. Rice paper may be seen as an example of using a modified or pre-gelatinised starch, both of which are effective at holding on to water.

USE OF PACKAGING MATERIALS

Packaging materials can be used to assist loss of moisture by migration from fillings to casings and into the atmosphere, or to retain moisture within the product, or to prevent gain of moisture into the product from the surrounding atmosphere. In cases such as pastry or crusty bread products, where it is desirable to keep the crisp eating quality for the shelf-life of the product, a moisture-permeable film with a suitable transpiration rate should be chosen. This transpiration rate should be such that the amount of moisture lost does not render the product dry-eating too quickly. For products such as cakes and sponges, it is desirable to keep the moisture within the packaging. Here it is important to cool the product before packing and so avoid condensation on the inside of the pack falling on to the product, creating areas of high moisture content and ERH, and thus providing a suitable area for mould growth. The same precautions need to be taken for products that will be chilled after packing, and for those where temperature-controlled transport is employed to the point of sale. Where products are likely to pick up moisture from the atmosphere, e.g. biscuits, wafers or other low moisture products, moisture-impermeable films are recommended.

As discussed earlier, many bakery foods have an ERH considerably higher than the typical storage RH, so that the normal movement of moisture is from the product to the surrounding atmosphere. In the case of wrapped products, the rate at which moisture is lost is controlled by the permeability of the film that is used. The permeability of the wrapping film also plays a significant part in controlling moisture migration in composite products. Where a high moisture-permeable film is used, the escape of moisture through the film to the surrounding atmosphere may mean, for example, that the pastry case never reaches equilibrium with the air in the pack. Thus there will always be a moisture gradient from filling through the pastry, helping to maintain the perception of pastry crispness for a longer period. However, as storage time increases, loss of water from the filling to the pastry and thence to the atmosphere causes its bulk to shrink with a loss of both visual impact and moist eating character.

MOISTURE MIGRATION AND PRODUCT SHELF-LIFE

As discussed in Chapter 6, the product shelf-life can be determined from its water activity. With composite or multidomain products, the water activity and proportions (masses) that each component contributes to the full product must be considered when estimating shelf-life. This is particularly true for the mould-free shelf-life (as opposed to the organoleptic shelf-life). Where components have largely differing water activities, the transfer or migration of water from one component to another will be relatively rapid. In some cases the moisture may not move rapidly enough and so the mould-free shelf-life of the composite product will be controlled by that of the component with the highest water activity.

A geometrically averaged shelf-life can be determined as follows. A table is first created (Table 7.4) showing the water activity and proportion that each component contributes to the composite product.

Table 7.4   Product component water activity and proportion.

Component	Water activity	Proportion (%)
sponge base	0.85	70
cream filling	0.96	20
fondant topping	0.65	10

To this table is added the geometric water activity contribution from each component (a_w × proportion (%)/100), and these values are summed to give the averaged water activity (*see* Table 7.5). Using tables as described in Chapter 8, the predicted mould-free shelf-life can be determined.

Table 7.5   Water activity contribution.

Component	Water activity	Proportion (%)	Water activity contribution
sponge base	0.85	70	0.595
cream filling	0.96	20	0.192
fondant topping	0.65	10	0.065
			0.852

Note that care should always be taken in using this method, particularly if water migration is not rapid and one of the components has a shelf-life considerably less than that of the predicted averaged one.

When each of the components is baked or made up separately, this method is simple to apply once the water activity of each component is known. It can give an indication, when applied sensibly, of the composite product shelf-life. In multi-component products where a filling or a component layer is baked at the same time, i.e. together (as in an apple pie), there are several ways of determining the composite water activity. As illustrated earlier, moisture may be gained by one component and lost by another. Generally a component that gains water will have an increased water activity; the reverse will be true for a component that loses moisture. This change of component moisture level is often difficult to assess, but where it is possible one of the following methods can be used to determine shelf life:

Method 1

Using the sucrose equivalence calculation method (or appropriate route in ERH CALC™) for determining water activity as described in Chapter 8, list all of the ingredients in all components of the product and use the moisture loss of the whole product to calculate the water activity. This result will be relatively accurate if all the sugars and soluble materials in each component get into solution.

Method 2

If the moisture gain or loss is known for a filling material, calculate the quantity of water that this represents. Then using the sucrose concentration calculation method (or appropriate route in ERH CALC™) with this gain or loss of moisture added or subtracted from the water in the filling recipe, calculate the water activity with the moisture loss declared as zero. Thus a new water activity or ERH is calculated. This gives a 'worst/best' case scenario for the filling ERH and mould-free shelf-life.

Method 3

If the moisture gain or loss of each component has been worked out separately, an average moisture loss for the whole product can be calculated and applied to each component of the product. The relative proportions of each component must be known. For each component calculate:

(proportion of component in product) × (moisture gain/loss) %

Sum for all components and divide by the total number of components. This value will be the average percentage moisture loss per component. This average value can then be re-applied to each component in the product to obtain an estimate of the ERH and mould-free shelf-life.

Example

A product with three parts cake and two parts filling has a moisture loss in the cake of 10% and a filling moisture gain of 5%:

2 parts filling × 5% moisture gain	= +10% moisture
3 parts cake × 10% moisture loss	= –30% moisture
Total moisture	= –20% (loss)
Average moisture	= –20/5 (5 parts in product)
	= –4% (loss)

If the proportions of the product are expressed as percentages, the above example becomes:

A product with 60% cake and 40% filling has a moisture loss in the cake of 10% and a filling moisture gain of 5%:

40% filling × 5% moisture gain   = +200 moisture
60% cake × 10% moisture loss   = –600 moisture
     Total moisture   = – 400 (loss)
     Average moisture   = –400/100 (100 parts in product)
           = –4% (loss)

This third method should be used only where the moisture equilibration in the product is rapid (i.e. typically where the differences in component ERHs are large). For short shelf-life products where equilibration may be slow it is better to use Method 2, as a filling with a moisture gain may go mouldy before equilibration has occurred.

CONCLUSIONS

The shelf-life of all composite bakery products is influenced by the movement of moisture from one component to another, with corresponding changes to the appearance and organoleptic properties of one or more components in the system. This type of spoilage may occur before other forms of more obvious spoilage so that the product may be consumed with disappointment.

Equilibration of moisture is driven by strong natural forces and is hard to prevent. As is so often the case with natural forces, we can only delay the inevitable. There are a wide variety of ploys that can be used to slow down moisture migration in order to extend product shelf-life, but it is inevitable that moisture will move from the moister to the drier components in bakery products, from the product to the atmosphere, or *vice versa*.

REFERENCES

Butcher, G.J. & Hodge, D.G. (1984) Pastry technology: the softening of pork pie pastry during storage. *FMBRA Report No. 116.* CCFRA, Chipping Campden, UK.
Cauvain, S.P. (1995) Putting pastry under the microscope. *Baking Industry Europe*, 68–9.
Cauvain, S.P. & Screen, A.E. (1987) Fruit moisture content in cakemaking, *FMBRA Bulletin No. 6*, CCFRA, Chipping Campden, UK, pp. 258–63.
The Cream Regulations (1970) SI 1970, No. 752. HMSO, London, UK.
DTI (1998) VACR II: Refrigerated Food Display. *Final project report in Ventilation, Air Conditioning & Refrigeration Link Programme*, Department of Trade & Industry, UK.
Ito, S. & Hodge, D.G. (1985) Some proposed new cream stabilizers. *FMBRA Bulletin No. 5*, CCFRA, Chipping Campden, UK, pp. 204–9.
Labuza, T.P. & Busk, G.C. (1979) An analysis of the water binding in gels. *Journal of Food Science*, **44**, 31–7.
Labuza, T.P. & Hyman, C.R. (1998), Moisture migration and control in multi-domain foods. *Trends in Food Science and Technology*, **9**, 47–55.
Marston, P.E. (1983) Moisture content and migration in bread incorporating dried fruit. *Food Technology Australia*, **35**, 463–5.
Nisbet, E.F. (1987) Moisture migration in composite baked goods. *FMBRA Bulletin No. 6*, CCFRA, Chipping Campden, UK, pp. 241–9.
Robb, J. (1986) Control of seepage from non-dairy confectionery fillings. *FMBRA Bulletin No. 5*, CCFRA, Chipping Campden, UK, pp. 187–99.

Robb, J. (1991) Moisture migration apple pies. *FMBRA Report No. 145.* CCFRA, Chipping Campden, UK.

Young, F.E., Jones, F.T. & Lewis, H.J. (1951) Prevention of the growth of sucrose hydrates in sucrose sirups. *Food Research*, **16**, 20–9.

8 Methods of determining moisture content and water availability

When developing new products or enhancing existing ones, the technologist will, at some point, be faced with the need either to measure or calculate the moisture content and the water availability of the product. The moisture content can be used as an indication of the likely eating qualities of the product because of the important role that water plays in determining such properties (*see* Chapter 5). In general, the higher the product moisture content, the softer the eating character, which may be either desirable or undesirable depending on the product type. Moisture loss during baking can be used to create the product character. It can also be used as a quality indicator when routine production is underway. If the moisture loss varies beyond the limits defined for the product, quality control staff can be forewarned that variations in baking procedures have occurred or that quality defects are likely to develop. On occasions an erroneous moisture content in the baked product may indicate a malfunction on the plant, e.g. a faulty water valve is dispensing the wrong water level or ingredient batch weights are incorrect.

The water availability or activity can alert the developer to the potential for mould growth and therefore the likely limit to the shelf-life of the product. The higher the water activity, the shorter will be the period after baking before the product exhibits spoilage from mould growth for a given set of storage conditions. In some cases, e.g. biscuits, the products may require re-humidification to a given moisture level before they are suitable for use in composite products.

DETERMINATION OF PRODUCT MOISTURE CONTENT AND WATER ACTIVITY

Determination of product moisture content and water activity can be carried out in two ways: either by measurement with suitable methods and instrumentation, or by calculation from ingredients data using specified methods and suitable computer software. Each method has its advantages and disadvantages. Instrumentation is accurate and is sometimes linked to recording devices and software. The accuracy of the machine is usually specified so that the scope for errors in the measurement is understood. The main disadvantage is that the product has to be made before a sample can be offered to the instrument. Unless the sampling technique is well defined and executed, errors in sample preparation can lead to incorrect results. Products that are uniform, e.g. plain sponge cake, do not cause many problems. However, products containing particulate matter, e.g. fruit cakes, can pose more problems for the accuracy of the measurement pertaining to the whole product. If the sample offered to the instrument is not always representative of the whole product, variations in readings from the instrument will be inevitable. Great care is needed with clear spelling-out of the procedures for sample preparation and their implementation prior to measurement. The instrumentation should be calibrated on a regular basis and should be serviced periodically. Generally this information is given by equipment manufacturers.

The calculation of the moisture content or water activity of a product from data known about ingredients and processing can save considerable time and expense. Provided the appropriate data are known and are accurate, and the calculation method is sound, the values obtained are as accurate as those expected from measurement with appropriate instrumentation. The main advantage that the calculation methods have is that the product does not need to be made up in order to obtain useful product information. At the product development stage, many variations in formulation can be tried out before the product needs to be mixed and baked. This can lead to considerable cost savings in time and raw materials when developing new and innovative products. Once the embryonic product has the required theoretical moisture level and/or water activity, it can be taken to the test bakery, produced and its characteristics checked. The product can then be fine-tuned. The number of cycles required in order to reach the final version of the product is much reduced. The savings in developer's time and raw material and production costs in reaching this stage are not difficult to enumerate.

MEASURING MOISTURE CONTENT

There are many ways of measuring moisture content, and the choice of method to be adopted depends on its suitability to the product, the ease of use and the cost of the measurement. In some cases a practical 'rough and ready' method in order to get a ballpark figure will suffice. In others, a more accurate measurement will be required. Whatever method is used, it is vital for calibrations to be undertaken appropriate to the sample type, temperature limits and moisture content ranges so that the accuracy of the results is not compromised.

The list of methods for measuring moisture content is extensive (Christensen, 1992) and includes:

- Air oven drying
- Vacuum oven drying
- Distillation
- Chemical reaction with Karl Fischer reagent
- Electronic instruments (moisture meters)
- Nuclear magnetic resonance (NMR)
- Near infrared (NIR) spectrophotometry

Of these methods, vacuum oven drying with a dessicant and the titration method using the Karl Fischer reagent are considered to be fundamental or basic reference methods. Routine reference methods comprise distillation, vacuum oven and air oven drying methods. The Brown–Duvel distillation method involved heating the sample to be tested in a mineral oil with a flash point much above the boiling point of water, condensing the moisture that distilled off and collecting and measuring the moisture. This was once a standard method but has been largely superseded by electronic moisture meters.

OVEN DRYING METHODS

There is no single routine reference method that is applied to the measurement of the moisture content of bakery products, although there are a number of internationally recognised techniques for measuring moisture content; these have been published by a number of authoritative sources, e.g. American Association of Cereal Chemists (AACC, 1995), International Association of Cereal Scientists and Technologists (ICC, 1995) and Campden & Chorleywood Food Research Association Flour Testing Working Group (CCFRA, 1997). Brief descriptions of suitable methods are given below.

Air oven drying

Air oven drying methods can be described as single or two stage, depending on the nature of the material to be measured. Typical temperatures and times for drying bakery products are defined according to the method used. The equipment (*see* Fig. 8.1) requirements for this method are usually:

Fig. 8.1   Oven drying method.

- Ventilated electric drying oven with a fan
- Analytical balance capable of measuring to an accuracy of at least three decimal places
- Metal dishes with close-fitting but easily removable lids
- Timer capable of reading intervals of 10 seconds
- Dessicator with a thick perforated metal or porcelain plate

Common reagents used in the dessicator are phosphorous pentoxide, granular anhydrous calcium sulphate impregnated with cobaltous chloride indicator, or dry (predominantly blue) silica gel. The procedure (CCFRA, 1997) for measurement is relatively simple and easy to follow:

- The oven and fan should be switched on in adequate time to allow the oven temperature to stabilise to that set on the thermostat.
- The sample is weighed with an accuracy of ± 0.001 g into a clean dry metal dish, which has previously been dried and cooled to room temperature in the dessicator and weighed.
- The dish is covered and weighed. These operations should be carried out as quickly as possible, regardless of whether dealing with high or low moisture contents, to prevent moisture loss or gain from the atmosphere.
- The oven fan should be turned off and allowed to stop before placing the dish into the oven.
- The dish should be uncovered, the oven door closed, the fan turned on and the sample allowed to dry for the prerequisite time (approximately 2 hours for samples of about 17% moisture) from the point when the drying temperature has been reached.
- At the end of the drying period the fan should be turned off, the oven door opened, the dish with the lid replaced cooled in the dessicator to room temperature and reweighed.
- The percentage moisture content can then be calculated using the following relationship:

    Percentage moisture content $= [(M_0 - M_1) \times 100]/M_0$
    where $M_0 =$ initial weight of sample
           $M_1 =$ weight of sample after oven drying

Using this method, the repeatability between two independent single test results from the examination of identical test material in the same laboratory by the same operator using the same equipment within a short interval of time should not be greater than 0.2%. For reproducibility, the difference between two single test results from the examination of identical test material in different laboratories with different operators using different equipment should not be greater than 0.7%.

Vacuum oven drying

Vacuum oven drying methods remove water from the sample under a pressure of 0.3 to 0.5 bar and at a temperature of about 100°C. This method is intended to try and avoid losses of non-aqueous volatile ingredients, e.g. fats, which can sometimes be a problem with some products and air oven drying methods when the temperature rises above 100°C. Vacuum oven drying is also useful for products with high sugar contents (low water activities), such as cakes, when the release of water requires greater energy inputs than might be achieved with high temperature and short residence time methods.

ELECTRICAL METHODS

Practical methods using an electrical measurement of moisture with suitable meters are the ones most frequently used in association with the manufacture of baked goods. Most of the methods employed are fast, accurate, easy to use (and sometimes automated), reliable, robust for use in a factory environment and have a low cost per product sample measurement. The main electrical methods that might be used are essentially non-destructive, and some of them can be used for on-line measurements. The methods commonly used may be grouped together as electronic moisture meters, NMR, NIR and direct heating devices, e.g. using infrared bulbs.

Electronic moisture meters

These operate on the principle of electrical conductance and capacitance. They are based on the principle that the resistance of the sample to the passage of an electric current decreases as its moisture content increases. The resistance, R, of the sample is determined from Ohm's Law, $V = IR$, where $V =$ the voltage and $I =$ the current. The voltage passing through the sample is held constant and variations in the current are measured. These variations are inversely proportional to the resistance of the sample: the greater the resistance (lower current), the lower the moisture content (and *vice versa*). Electronic moisture meters must be calibrated against some standard reference method.

Electronic moisture meters are commonly used for measuring the moisture content of particulate materials, such as grain. Machines are sufficiently advanced to provide automatic sample weighing, automatic temperature correction and moisture compensation by measuring both electrical conductance and capacitive reactance for variations in surface moisture (DICKEY-john® Corporation, 1996). They are not commonly used to measure the moisture content of baked products.

Nuclear magnetic resonance

NMR can be applied to moisture measurement, but care must be taken as the results are affected by the presence of lipids in the samples. The NMR signal must be correlated against the moisture content in a set of calibration samples as determined by a standard procedure, e.g. air oven drying. A drawback with this method is that the equipment is expensive to purchase and run. However, the method is rapid and non-destructive, and the results are linear over a wide range of moisture contents (although NMR does not respond well at low moisture levels as moisture in these situations is often 'bound'). The method has been adapted successfully for measurement of moisture in doughs and dried fruit (Miller & Kaslow, 1963). NMR has found wide use in research related to the location of water in plant tissues (Ablett & Lillford, 1991; Kim *et al.*, 1998) and to study the thermal characteristics of bread (Chinachoti, 1998)

Near infrared

There are many NIR- instruments on the market capable of measuring moisture content, but not all can be used for bakery goods. Those using transmittance measurements are recommended for measurements in liquids rather than solid materials. For example, CME Telemetrix models 100 and 200 (Anon., 1998a), and those using reflectance spectroscopy are better suited to baked goods. NIR was shown to be a technique that could be applied to moisture determination in bread products (Osborne *et al.*, 1984). The samples used in the study were whole slices rather than those prepared to give consistent particle size and surface texture. The results for moisture from sample slices correlated well with results for air-dried bread samples. The instrument used was an InfraAnalyzer and the calibration constants calculated were found to be easily transferable to other similar infrared instruments.

NDC Infrared Engineering supply an instrument, the Infralab, which can rapidly provide a moisture value. The sample, which needs no special preparation, is placed in a tray, which is then inserted into the instrument for optical scanning. The manufacturer claims an accuracy of $\pm 0.1\%$ moisture. The same instrument can also measure protein and fat. Results can be saved and data manipulated using Windows based software (Anon., 1998b)

Infrared – direct heating

Infrared balances using infrared bulbs as a heat source for drying the sample are used frequently for grains, and can be used for some finished products. They mimic the oven drying method and give quick, accurate results. The instrumentation contains a precision balance. The basic procedure is as follows:

- The sample is placed on to the balance pan and its initial weight recorded.
- The sample is preheated to a set temperature and the moisture is driven off.
- The sample is weighed automatically at frequent intervals. When there is no weight change, the bulb is switched off and the moisture content calculated from the weight losses incurred. For samples of up to 30 to 35% moisture, the measurement takes less than 10 minutes. The results can be printed or downloaded to a PC.

Such instruments can also be used for batch on-line production processes where moisture measurements are needed. Care must be taken to calibrate the instrument with samples typical of the products to be measured. An 'autotest' is performed where typical samples are heated at a standard temperature for a standard time. These reference samples are then plotted against the results of similar samples using a standard reference method (oven drying) and any necessary adjustments can be made to the software. An example of an instrument of this type is shown in Fig. 8.2. These instruments have the advantage that they can measure higher moisture contents than the instruments that operate on the capacitance principle. Generally the high moisture has higher electrical capacitance and any calibration adjustments are more difficult to make since the relationship between the instrument and a reference method is complex.

Fig. 8.2 Impact FD600 electronic moisture balance (courtesy of Impact Test Equipment).

Advanced techniques for moisture measurement

New techniques are now being investigated for measurement of moisture. Recent advances in computer processing speeds, storage capacity and the low relative cost of PCs make it economically viable to create simulations of the thermodynamic changes that take place in cereal based foods using computational fluid dynamics (CFD) (Gielow, 1998). The typical output from a CFD investigation includes time-dependent distributions of average temperature and moisture content within cereal pieces (thin flakes), and good agreement was found with experimental data. This simulation technology has also been applied to cake products where the CFD modelling for water loss as a function of time agreed well with experimental results from baking trials.

Moisture contents have been measured using on-line techniques that use the absorption of infrared or ultraviolet radiation by water vapour (Scott & Pickles, 1991). In the baking industry, attempts have been made to measure on-line the moisture content of sheet cakes (Swiss roll) at the oven exit as part of a project designed to investigate automation of cake processing. One of the problems encountered was the effect of the water vapour emissions from the still hot product on the reliability of the measurement.

SUMMARY OF INSTRUMENT TYPES USED FOR MOISTURE MEASUREMENT

The suitability of the various types of instruments for measuring the moisture contents of bakery foods is summarised in Table 8.1. The costs of the instruments discussed in this chapter vary from a few hundred to several thousand pounds.

Table 8.1   Instrument types used for moisture measurement of bakery foods.

Instrument method	Suitability	Cost	Notes
oven drying	good	low	manual
conductance/capacitance	average	low	manual/automatic
infrared	good	medium	automatic
NIR	good	high	automatic
NMR	good	very high	automatic
CFD	experimental	very high	

METHODS FOR THE CALCULATION OF MOISTURE CONTENT

One of the simplest ways of calculating moisture content is shown below with the help of Table 8.2. The ingredient quantities and their moisture content are tabulated. The recipe ingredients are summed to give the total ingredient weight. The contribution that each ingredient makes in terms of moisture is tabulated and summed, e.g. for 84 g whole egg, 75% is moisture: it would contribute 84×0.75 g (i.e. 63 g) of moisture to the product moisture. This summation can be expressed by the formula:

$$\text{Total water} = W_1 M_1 + W_2 M_2 + \cdots\cdots W_n M_n$$

where W_1 = weight of ingredient 1
   M_1 = moisture content (%) of ingredient 1 divided by 100
   n = number of ingredients.

Table 8.2 Summing recipe contributions for moisture.

Ingredient	Weight (g)	Moisture (%)	Moisture weight (g)
flour	100.0	14.0	14.0
sugar	110.0	0	0.0
invert sugar syrup	10.0	20.0	2.0
egg (whole)	84.0	75.0	63.0
fat/oil	65.0	0	0.0
glycerol	10.0	0	0.0
skimmed milk powder	8.0	5.0	0.4
baking powder	4.0	0	0.0
salt	2.0	0	0.0
water	50.0	100.0	50.0
Total	443.0		129.4

The moisture loss that occurs because of baking and cooling to a certain temperature then needs to be determined. This is achieved by taking a unit weight measurement before baking and then again after baking and cooling to a specified temperature. Subtraction of the two weights will yield the moisture loss from the product when it is cooled to that temperature. The weight measurement can be made on a single unit product. However, it is advisable to take weights of several units and then to average them so that a representative weight loss is determined. In some cases there can be practical value in systematically sampling a production sequence to identify process variability. For example, sampling across an oven band may highlight uneven baking, which would have important implications when considering the product shelf-life.

For the recipe shown in Table 8.2:

Average unit weight before baking = 443.00 g
Average unit weight after baking and cooling = 395.85 g
Average moisture loss = 47.15 g

$$\text{Percentage moisture loss} = \frac{47.15 \times 100}{443.0}$$

$$= 10.64\%$$

Moisture before baking = 129.4 g
Final moisture content (moisture after baking & cooling) = total moisture − moisture loss

$$= 129.4\,\text{g} - 47.15\,\text{g}$$
$$= 82.25\,\text{g} \qquad\qquad (1)$$

$$\text{Moisture content (\%)} = \frac{\text{final moisture content}}{\text{final product weight}} \times 100$$

$$= \frac{82.25}{395.85} \times 100$$

$$= 20.78\%$$

Once the average moisture loss is determined as a percentage, this figure can be applied when modifications to the recipe are made, since most recipes changes have only a small impact on baking losses; the greatest impact on weight losses would come from changes in baking conditions. The moisture loss can also be applied for calculating the water activity or ERH of the recipe (*see below*).

METHODS FOR THE MEASUREMENT OF WATER ACTIVITY

All of the methods for measurement of water activity are linked to measurement of RH and utilise the relationship between RH and water activity discussed earlier. The accuracy of each method can vary and some methods are more appropriate or practical to apply to bakery foods than others. With today's need for rapid results, the speed of response can be an important factor when deciding which method to use for the measurement of water activity.

Psychrometry

Since the mid-eighteenth century, the principle that evaporation results in a cooling effect has been widely used for measuring RH. The rate at which water evaporates from a surface depends on the RH of the surrounding atmosphere. It is a method based on the determination of the humidity of the atmosphere in a room (Dean *et al.*, 1980) and uses two thermometers (together called a hygrometer or psychrometer), the bulb of one being covered in a constantly wet gauze. This apparatus is commonly known as a wet-and-dry-bulb hygrometer. The differences in temperatures of the two thermometers can be related (by use of standard reference tables) to the RH at the known room temperature. While this method is not used readily for measuring the ERH of baked products, it is a basic method and is worth a mention. It commonly finds use by engineers when designing bakery equipment such as provers and coolers (Wiggins, 1998).

Indicator salts

Certain inorganic salts when exposed to atmospheres of different RHs exhibit changes in colour. This has been used as a basis for methods of determining humidity. However the accuracy is usually no greater than about $\pm5\%$ over a range of 10 to 80% RH, and is not particularly suited for use with bakery products. Using the same principle, papers that have been impregnated with different salts known to change colour at different humidities can be used. Where a saturated solution of the salt used to impregnate the paper strip has an ERH higher than the atmosphere being tested, the paper strip remains dry. When the saturated solution has an ERH lower than the test atmosphere, the strip becomes translucent from the uptake of moisture. The ERH of the atmosphere under measurement will lie between the values of the last salt paper to become moist and the first to remain dry when the papers are used in ascending or descending orders of ERH values. The main disadvantage of this method for estimating bakery product ERH is the lack of suitable salts with sufficiently close ERH intervals.

The same principle has been extended to crystals of selected salts chosen to cover the range of humidities, and forms the basis of measurement used by the Novasina hygrometer type equipment described below. Such instruments are reliable and easy to use, although care must be taken to calibrate them regularly at the temperatures used for measurement to compensate for any drift that might occur (Stekelenburg & Labots, 1991).

Mechanical methods

Changes in dimensions of organic materials when exposed to humid or wet atmospheres have found practical uses throughout history. Roman soldiers building Hadrian's Wall used wooden wedges forced into man-made crevices in boulders; the wedges enlarged when soaked in water, and split the boulders into more manageable pieces. The effects of wafer sheets expanding after absorbing moisture to crack the chocolate coating have already been discussed in Chapter 5. Human hair changes length when exposed to atmospheres of different humidities and this phenomenon is used as the basis of the hair hygrometer. Basic devices based on expansion and contraction of hair or other materials can still be used, although they do not have the accuracy or speed of response of more recently developed methods.

Dew point

The temperature at which dew or moisture is deposited on a metallic surface is widely used for measurement of RH. Visual detection of the first appearance of dew requires skilled application. This method is used widely and its accuracy has been improved by the use of electrical/electronic or optical/electronic systems for the detection of the first formation of dew.

This principle is applied in the Aqualab instrument described below. In this type of instrument a sample is equilibrated with the headspace in a sealed chamber containing a mirror and a means of detecting condensation on the mirror. At equilibrium the RH of the air in the chamber is the same as the water activity of the sample. In modern devices the mirror temperature is controlled precisely by a thermoelectric (Peltier) cooler. Detection of the exact point at which condensation first occurs is observed with a photoelectric cell. A beam of light is directed on to the mirror and reflected into a photodetector cell. The photodetector senses the change in reflectance when condensation occurs on the mirror. A thermocouple attached to the mirror records the temperature at which condensation occurs. Care must be taken when using this method that the surface of the metal does not become greasy. Errors can also arise from the variations in size of the deposited moisture droplets and contaminants in the test atmosphere.

The basic principle involved in dew point determinations is that air may be cooled without change in water content until saturation (dew point) is reached. In other words, the saturated vapour pressure (SVP) at the dew point temperature is equal to the ambient vapour pressure. This can be expressed as:

$$P = P_0(T_d)$$

where P is the partial vapour pressure of the water in the air of the chamber, P_0 is the SVP for pure water, and T_d is the dew point temperature. The vapour pressure is related to the equilibrium relative humidity by the relationship:

$$ERH = P/P_0$$

To compute the SVP from the temperature, a convenient, empirical equation (with a close connection to the Clausius–Clapeyron thermodynamics equation) is the Tetens formula:

$$P_0(T) = \mathbf{a}exp[\mathbf{b}T/(T + \mathbf{c})]$$

where T is the temperature in degrees Celsius and **a**, **b** and **c** are constants chosen to optimise the fit of the equation for various ranges of data. This equation can be used in place of tables and psychrometric charts for finding the SVP. Some commercial dew point instruments measure water activity values between 0.030 and $1.000a_w$ and have a resolution of 0.001.

Electric and coulometric methods

Methods have been developed which depend on changes in electrical conductivity or capacitance of a hydroscopic sensing material. For example, Norrish (1966) used a ceramic pellet whose resistance changed as the RH of the atmosphere varied. The accuracy of the method was approximately 1 to 2% ERH over a range of 50 to 100% ERH. Mossel and van Kuijk (1955) used a cell impregnated with a saturated lithium chloride solution. Here the temperature of the cell was measured when a current passing through the cell raised its temperature until the vapour pressure of the saturated solution of lithium chloride equalled the water vapour pressure of the test atmosphere. This temperature could then be linked to the RH of the test atmosphere. The measurement of the current required to electrolyse completely the moisture in a gas stream has also been used to ascertain RH, the moisture being absorbed in a cell containing phosphorous pentoxide. The instrument using this principle relies on the calculation of RH of the atmosphere from basic electrochemical considerations (Faraday's Law).

Spectroscopic methods

The absorption of infrared or ultraviolet radiation by water vapour is another technique that has been applied to the measurement of RH. As the NIR reflectance technology of this method has become more available, the costs of instrumentation have fallen, although it is still relatively expensive compared with other techniques. It has been applied in situations where moisture measurement needs to be made on-line and be non-invasive (Scott & Pickles, 1991).

Quartz crystal oscillation

A quartz crystal oscillator coated with a moisture sensitive material gains weight when exposed to moisture (King, 1965). Its frequency of oscillation decreases as it gains moisture. This method is very sensitive and the response times are short, but it has not found application in rapid routine determination of ERH.

Thermal conductivity gas analysis

The rate at which an electrically heated wire loses heat to the surrounding atmosphere can also be used as an indication of the RH of the atmosphere, provided the only change in the composition of that atmosphere is due to the changes in the amount of water vapour present. Where there is the possibility of other changes occurring in the atmosphere, gas chromatography could be used. However, the instrumentation for this is both expensive and complicated, and so the technique is not applied routinely to evaluation of bakery products.

Weight change method

A simple method based on weight changes was suggested by Landrock and Proctor (1951) and can be used for the determination of moisture–humidity relationships of certain foods. It is, however, time-consuming. The only requirements are a balance, dishes to hold the sample, and suitable humidity chambers containing saturated salt solutions of known RH at the temperature of measurement. For the latter, dessicators, each containing a slurry of an appropriate saturated salt solution and an excess of the salt, can be used with a device enabling the air in the chamber to be stirred either occasionally or, preferably, continuously. Table 8.3 shows suitable salts for use as saturated solutions.

Table 8.3   Relative humidity of air over saturated salt solutions at various temperatures (Landrock & Proctor, 1951).

Salt	15°C	20°C	25°C
potassium sulphate	97	97	97
potassium nitrate	94	93	92
potassium chloride	87	86	85
ammonium sulphate	81	81	80
sodium chloride	76	76	75
ammonium nitrate	69	65	62

Samples of size approximately 1 g are prepared and weighed to the nearest milligram. Each sample is placed in a weighed dish, and two dishes of each sample are placed into four chambers containing saturated salt solutions covering an appropriate range of RHs. The samples should be placed in the chambers immediately after weighing to avoid any moisture loss. The chambers should preferably be kept at a constant temperature, e.g. 21°C (70°F). After a suitable time period, the samples are removed and immediately reweighed, again to the nearest milligram. Storage overnight between weighings is often a convenient and adequate time, but shorter periods can be used. If shorter storage times are used, changes in the sample weight will be small and care should be taken to reweigh the samples after exposure in the same sequence and at the same intervals as the original weighings.

The change in weight per gram of sample is calculated and plotted against RH. The line of best fit is drawn through the individual points and the point at which this curve crosses the zero weight change line gives the ERH of the sample. An example of the curves obtained by this method is illustrated in Fig. 8.3. Alternatively, the data can be entered in a PC spreadsheet program, its equation determined, and the ERH for the sample calculated. Sample preparation is very important to ensure accurate results (*see below*).

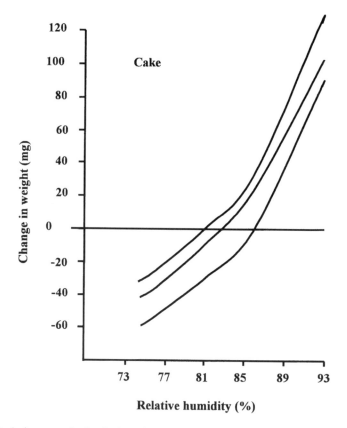

Fig. 8.3 Typical curves obtained when determining the ERH of cake using the 'weight change' method.

PREPARING SAMPLES FOR ERH MEASUREMENT

Whatever the equipment or method used to determine the product ERH, the preparation of the sample to be tested requires great care and is important for the accuracy of the results. Sample preparation will vary according to the type of baked product being assessed. Some general pointers for sample preparation include the following:

(1) Choose an appropriate test portion from the product under investigation: crumb or crust; component of product (usually tested before the final product is assembled); or whole product.
(2) Place the sample portion in a clean dry polythene bag and seal to prevent any moisture entering or leaving the sample.
(3) Reduce the sample to a uniform crumb size. This is usually done by crushing the sample by hand. If the sample is an icing or other moist component, ensure it is mixed to a homogeneous state without significant loss or gain of moisture.
(4) Remove a sub-sample from the bag and place it in a clean, dry receptacle or pot designed for the instrument being used and to the level recommended by the equipment manufacturer. In the case of the Aqualab and Novasina instruments, a 5-ml teaspoonful is usually adequate.
(5) Place the lid securely on the pot to prevent any loss or uptake of moisture during the measurement.
(6) Duplicate or triplicate samples should be used at all times in order to get representative results.
(7) Accurate measurements can be obtained only with constant humidity and temperature conditions in the measuring environment.
(8) Ensure that the internal and surface temperatures of the sample under consideration are identical and remain unchanged throughout the measurement.
(9) Ensure that the instrument is placed on a level surface and in a location where the temperature remains stable, and there is no risk of extraneous moisture entering the machine.
(10) Ensure that moisture or contaminants are not imparted to or from the sample or the receptacle by the operator's fingers (salts are perspired from pores in the skin).
(11) Ensure that the receptacles are clean by rinsing after washing in distilled water, and that they are dry before being used.

Many of these points are common sense, and if employed as good laboratory practice can yield accurate and repeatable ERH results.
   A guide to sample preparation for differing product types is considered below.

Bread, rolls, plain cakes, biscuits and cookies

A representative sample must be taken, e.g. the whole of a cross-section from a loaf or cake, or opposite quarters from a slab cake. The sample is placed in a dry, clean plastic bag (to avoid any moisture loss, gain or contamination), crumbled and mixed well.

Swiss rolls

Take thin cross-section samples, including the filling.

Fruit cakes and Christmas puddings

These are difficult products to sample satisfactorily because of their heterogeneous nature. Reasonably representative samples can be obtained by taking borings at the same position in each product using a cork borer or an apple corer. Borings of constant volume can be used as sub-samples. These should weigh about 3 to 5 g, depending on the size of the sample pots.

Filled products

Products such as cream-filled cakes and meat pies present a special problem as the ratio of crumb to filling affects the mean ERH of the composite product. In addition, the RH in the proximity of the filling may be different from that of the crust or crumb. This may be true for several days after the product has been made, and it may be necessary to allow a period of equilibration before making a meaningful measurement. With such products, it is preferable to examine the cake or casing and filling components separately to give a more accurate assessment of any risks associated with microbial growth. This is because areas of initially high ERH can provide a suitable environment for initiating mould growth, even though that particular area may change to a lower and less microbiologically favourable ERH later during storage.

INSTRUMENTAL MEASUREMENT OF ERH

Two popular instruments for measuring the water activity are those developed by Novatron Ltd (a Swiss company) and Decagon Devices Inc (a US company). The water activity instruments from both of these companies are easy to use, accurate and have fast response times. It is important to control the temperature to achieve accurate and reproduceable results.

Earlier Novasina instruments used a reference indicator salts method and the a_w was measured in the 0 to 50°C temperature range. Conductivity was measured through a reference salt. This salt was brought into equilibrium with the test sample in an enclosed chamber. The extent of electrical conduction (absence of resistance) is related to the amount of crystal hydration and hence to the a_w. The international standard laboratory practice for a_w testing is at 25°C. Instruments can be calibrated automatically at six points ranging from 0.11 to $0.98a_w$. Response times to equilibrium varying from 10 minutes for biscuits, cakes and snacks, to 15 minutes for bread, and up to 25 minutes for meat products are claimed. More recent versions of the Novasina, e.g. the TH200 (*see* Fig. 8.4), have an electrolytic substance within the sensor which absorbs or desorbs water from the air surrounding it as the RH changes. The electrical impedance varies with water content, and a temperature reference sensor is used in conjunction with the electrolyte. Such instruments employ an improved electrolyte, and equilibrium of readings within 5 to 10 minutes is claimed.

The Aqualab instruments (*see* Fig. 8.5) use the chilled mirror (condensation) hygrometer method or chilled-mirror dew point method to find the dew point

Fig. 8.4 Novasina TH200 (courtesy of Novatron Ltd.).

temperature of air which is in equilibrium with a 7-millimetre sample. The sample temperature is measured using infrared thermometry. An internal microprocessor-controlled data acquisition system converts the two measurements to vapour pressures and computes the ratio to find the water activity of the sample. The internal electronics provide an automatic self-diagnostic to tell the operator if there is any contamination in the system, since it is very important to avoid it with this type of instrument. It can be set to read at one temperature only (25°C) or, with a water bath, can read at any temperature between 4 and 40°C, with claimed response times of approximately 5 minutes. It is possible to link both the Novasina and the Aqualab to PCs for data processing.

While rapid equilibration times are claimed for both types of instrument, some products, such as those with low moisture contents and a_w, and those which contain high levels of undissolved sugars, may require longer equilibration times than may be available for a particular instrument setting. It may be advisable in some cases to link the meter with a chart recorder to more accurately determine the true equilibration point. Low moisture content non-dairy creams and buttercreams with large quantities of undissolved sugars have been known to take up to 2 hours to achieve full equilibration with the measurement atmosphere.

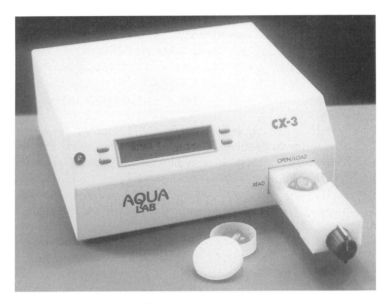

Fig. 8.5   Aqualab CX-3 (courtesy Labcell).

METHODS OF CALCULATING WATER ACTIVITY AND ERH

In Chapter 6, the concepts of water activity, water availability and ERH were discussed. As previously explained, for practical purposes the terms water activity and ERH can be used interchangeably. ERH, expressed as a percentage, is measured on a scale of 0 to 100, whereas water activity is expressed in the range 0 to 1.0. In mathematical terms the relationship between them is expressed by the equation:

$$\frac{p}{p_0} = a_w = \frac{ERH}{100}$$

where p = vapour pressure of a solution, and p_0 = vapour pressure of pure water.

As with moisture content, the ERH of a product can be determined if certain data are known about the ingredients. There are two common methods that are appropriate for use with baked products:

- Sucrose equivalence method
- Sucrose concentration method

In both cases the calculation method relies on being able to predict the ability of soluble materials to lock up water and therefore reduce the saturated vapour pressure or relative humidity within the product. All materials in a given recipe that are able to go into solution affect the ERH of the product to a greater or lesser extent. Materials that do not readily go into solution have a lesser or no effect on water availability. However, where there is competition for water in a recipe, some materials will go into solution more readily than others because of their ability to attract and hold on to the water molecules. Materials that do not go into solution during preparation and baking may attempt to do so later in the product's life during storage. These issues were discussed in Chapter 6 (in relation to ingredients contributing to product spoilage) and in Chapter 7 (in relation to moisture migration in composite products).

The method chosen for the calculation of ERH depends on whether or not there is sufficient water to dissolve all soluble materials and fully hydrate others. The sucrose equivalence method assumes that all sugars and other soluble materials have gone into solution. In cases where there are soluble materials not in solution the results given by the sucrose equivalence method will be less accurate. Great care should be taken before beginning any calculation to choose the most appropriate method. If all soluble materials do not get into solution, the sucrose concentration method should be adopted. If applied appropriately with the correct ingredient and processing data, these two methods can be as accurate as a physical measurement and can save considerable time and money to the product developer.

Bakery products where sufficient water is available to dissolve all materials in the recipe are suitable for use with the sucrose equivalence method; they include bread and fermented products, all types of cakes and many types of fillings and creams. The sucrose concentration method is more suited to those with lower moisture contents, including biscuits, cookies, many pastries, fondants, icings and some fillings. As a rule of thumb, if there is no more than twice as much sugar as water in a recipe, the sucrose equivalence method is the more appropriate.

Sucrose equivalence method

As described in Chapter 6, Grover (1947) devised a means of determining the water vapour pressure for solutions of sucrose and other sugars in sugar confectionery. The method relies on a 'sucrose factor' or 'sucrose equivalence' being given to an ingredient to express that ingredient's effect on water activity in solution compared with sucrose, on a weight for weight basis. Sucrose is given a factor of 1.0. Table 8.4 shows a list of typical ingredients used in bakery products with their relevant sucrose equivalence (se) values. These sucrose factors are mostly based on data reported by Grover (1947) and Norrish (1966) with amendments made to take into account more recently published data (Cauvain & Seiler, 1992). The sucrose factors are only approximate as they vary slightly with the concentration of the ingredients. From Table 8.4 it can be seen that salt, on an equal weight basis with sucrose, has a factor of 11 and is very effective at lowering water vapour pressure and therefore ERH. Humectants, such as glucose syrup, invert sugar, sorbitol and glycerol, will also lower the ERH of a product. The use of sugars such as invert sugar or dextrose will also lower ERH, while 64 and 42DE glucose syrups when used on a weight for weight replacement basis will raise the ERH because of the water that is present in the material. However, if only the glucose syrup solids were used, the ERH would decrease.

Table 8.4 Approximate sucrose equivalence of common bakery ingredients.

Ingredient	se
sucrose	1.0
flour	0.2
fat	0
margarine, butter[a]	0.2
egg, whole	0
skimmed milk powder	1.2
sultanas	0.9
baking powder	3.0
salt	11.0
glucose syrup 42DE	0.7
glucose syrup 64DE	0.9
invert sugar, dextrose	1.4
sorbitol	2.0
glycerol	4.0

[a] Depends on salt concentration.

Determining sucrose equivalence data values

There are three methods that can be used for determining the necessary sucrose equivalence data: one is by indirect and two by direct means.

Indirect method

If the composition of an ingredient is known, i.e. the percentages and types (e.g. sugars and starch) of carbohydrates, fat, moisture, salt, fibre, etc., and the molecular weights for each of the composition materials, it is possible to calculate an approximate se from the individual contributions that each component makes.

Direct method 1

The se of an ingredient may be determined by heating a known quantity of the ingredient with a sucrose solution similar to that existing in the baked product, under conditions where no moisture is lost. The ERH of the mixture can be compared with the ERH of a sample of the sucrose solution without the added ingredient and the se of the material calculated from any changes in the solution ERH.

For example, 2.5 g dried egg heated with 20 g of 60% w/w sucrose solution gave an ERH of 89%, equivalent to 1.57 g sucrose/1 g water (*see* Table 8.5 for relationship between ERH and aqueous sucrose solutions). Thus, 2.5 g dried egg in 8 g water, or 0.31 g in 1 g water, had the equivalent effect of 0.07 g sucrose/1 g water. A conversion factor for the dried egg would be $0.07/0.31 = 0.23$ (se).

Table 8.5 ERH of aqueous sucrose solution.

Sucrose concentration (wt. sucrose/wt. water)	ERH (%)
0.78	95
1.07	93
1.32	91
1.57	89
1.82	87
2.08	85
2.32	83
2.55	81
2.80	79
3.06	77
3.32	75
3.57	73
3.87	71

Direct method 2

By comparing the ERH of products containing the ingredient in question with that of the control product, and allowing for any differences in moisture contents between the products, the se of the ingredient can be determined by calculation. This method is not precise since the factors obtained could have been influenced by any inaccuracies in factors attributed by other ingredients. In practice, however, this method has given satisfactory and validated results for many bakery ingredients. It does have the advantage with baked products that the se determined for a given ingredient takes into account any change in its water-holding capacity as a result of thermally-induced changes, e.g. gelatinisation of starch. The factor for flour of 0.2 was determined in this way (Cooper *et al.*, 1968).

Calculating ERH using the sucrose equivalence method

The se method requires that the sucrose concentration from individual contributions is calculated for the final product. The sucrose contribution from each ingredient is summed and this total is expressed as the concentration of moisture in the product after baking and cooling. The following example is given using the same recipe as used for the moisture calculations above.

The individual sucrose contributions are summed using the following:

$$\text{Total sucrose} = W_1 se_1 + W_2 se_2 + \cdots W_n se_n$$

where W_1 = weight of ingredient 1
se_1 = sucrose contribution of ingredient 1
n = number of ingredients

For this example:

$$\begin{aligned} \text{Total 'sucrose'} &= (100 \times 0.2) + (110 \times 1.0) + (10 \times 1.1) + \cdots \text{etc.} \\ &= 20.0 + 110.0 + 11.0 + \cdots \text{etc.} \\ &= 224.6 \end{aligned}$$

Table 8.6 Summing recipe contributions for sucrose.

Ingredient	Weight (g)	Moisture (%)	Moisture weight (g)	Sucrose equivalence	Sucrose contribution
flour	100.0	14.0	14.0	0.2	20.0
sugar	110.0	0	0.0	1.0	110.0
invert sugar syrup	10.0	20.0	2.0	1.1	11.0
egg (whole)	84.0	75.0	63.0	0	0
fat/oil	65.0	0	0.0	0	0
glycerol	10.0	0	0.0	4.0	40.0
Skimmed milk powder	8.0	5.0	0.4	1.2	9.6
baking powder	4.0	0	0.0	3.0	12.0
salt	2.0	0	0.0	11.0	22.0
water	50.0	100.0	50.0	0	0
Total	443.0		129.4		224.6

To obtain the sucrose concentration in the aqueous phase of the product the total sucrose is divided by the final total moisture so that:

$$\text{Sucrose concentration} = \frac{224.6}{82.25} \qquad \text{from (1) (p. 165)}$$

$$= 2.73$$

Using Table 8.5, the ERH is derived from the sucrose concentration (Grover, 1947).

Assuming a linear relationship, for the sucrose concentration calculated, the ERH can be interpolated as follows:

sucrose concentration	ERH(%)
2.55	81
2.73	*x*
2.80	79

$$\frac{81 - 79}{2.55 - 2.80} = \frac{x - 79}{2.73 - 2.80}$$

$$\frac{(81 - 79)\,(2.73 - 2.80)}{(2.55 - 2.80)} + 79 = x$$

$$\frac{2 \times (-0.07)}{(-0.25)} + 79 = x$$

$$0.56 + 79 = x$$

Therefore ERH at *x* (when sucrose concentration is 2.73) is 79.56%.

Using graphs similar to those shown in Chapter 6, this ERH value can be used to estimate the mould-free shelf-life of the product. It is important when using these methods of calculation that the data values used are as accurate as possible. This is particularly true of the baking and cooling and storage losses. An error of 2% in determining product moisture loss in the above calculation would result in a difference of almost 1% in ERH.

Sucrose concentration method

The origins of this method lie in the candy (sugar confectionery) industry and it is a combination of methods proposed by Money and Born (1951), Norrish (1966), Grover (1947), and Cakebread (1973), and expanded by Richardson (1986). During the late 1980s, it was applied by Cauvain and Seiler (1992) to a range of flour confectionery products. With the advent of ERH CALC™ (1990), it has been used in practical environments for a much wider range of food products. The method, as for the sucrose equivalence method, is based on the substances in solution in the product. In low water products, such as candies, icings and biscuits, there is too little moisture to ensure complete dissolution of all of the soluble materials. Any undissolved or crystalline forms of substances used in the formulation play no part in determining the water activity.

The first step with the sucrose concentration method is to calculate, from the formulation, the total amount of sugars that are in solution. Other sugars present, such as invert sugar, and other soluble and water-absorbing materials such as proteins, because of their affinity for water, depress the amount of sucrose that could have been dissolved if sucrose had been the only solute present. The sucrose concentration is determined using the following equation (Grover, 1947; modified by Cakebread, 1973):

$$S = \frac{1.994}{1 + 0.1775 \, \Sigma G} \tag{2}$$

where S = number of grams of sucrose dissolved by 1 g of water
G = number of grams of soluble solids dissolved by 1 g of water

Using this equation, we can determine the composition of the solution and consequently calculate how much of the sucrose in the formulation can be dissolved in the aqueous phase.

The ERH/water activity of the solution can then be calculated using the equation (Money & Born, 1951):

$$ERH = \frac{100}{1 + 0.27N} \tag{3}$$

where N = sum of moles of solute per 100 g of water

For example, when using a recipe with 75 g sucrose, 3 g invert sugar and other soluble materials, equation (2) predicts that only 20 g of sucrose could get into solution; then a sucrose level of 20 g needs to be used in equation (3) and summed along with the calculations for the moles of other solutes.

The following equation is used to determine the moles of solute per 100 g water:

$$\text{mole}/100\,\text{g water} = \frac{\text{weight \% of soluble solid}}{\text{\% moisture}} \times 100 \times \frac{1}{\text{molecular wt solute}}$$

In this example, with 20 g of sucrose (44% of soluble solids) in a formulation containing 26% moisture, the mole contribution from sucrose (molecular weight 342) would be:

$$\text{mole sucrose}/100\,\text{g water} = \frac{44}{26} \times 100 \times \frac{1}{342}$$

$$= 0.495$$

If, after calculating the mole contributions from the other soluble solids, N is summed to be 0.82 then applying equation (3):

$$\text{ERH} = \frac{100}{(1 + 0.27\text{N})}$$

$$= 81.9\% \quad (a_w = 0.819)$$

Determining the effective molecular weights of soluble materials other than sugars can present a problem. Colloids in solution, e.g. starches, pectins and proteins, are very high molecular weight materials, and using the Money and Born (1951) equation we would expect to see an increase in the water activity when these materials get into solution. However, in practice they are seen to depress the water activity, and so it is more realistic to use an 'apparent' molecular weight which better reflects their effect on water activity. Grover (1947) suggested an apparent molecular weight of 427 for such materials. Richardson (1986) considered that, while this approach was strictly not accurate, Grover's value worked better than those of Money and Born (1951) and Norrish (1966).

OTHER METHODS FOR CALCULATING WATER ACTIVITY

One of the key problems in calculating water activities from formulations is the values that are used with individual ingredients, as well as the method used for the calculation. Ross (1975) examined the problem of predicting water activity when non-solute components were present, and derived an equation largely based on summing the contributions of single components to the composite a_w. Teng and Seow (1981) studied the water activity of multicomponent aqueous solutions using results from the Ross equation, and considered that this was a poorer predictor than the equations suggested by Ferro Fontan *et al.* (1980) or the Zdanovskii–Stokes–Robinson equations (Water Analyser Series, 1999), with the latter being considered the most reliable.

As seen previously, a problem for the bakery technologist wishing to calculate product water activities is that many of the prediction approaches use data derived from aqueous solutions or with high moisture/low solids systems, which do not necessarily provide appropriate simulations for the processes that take place during baking and product storage. Choosing the calculation method that works best for a given bakery product range is commonly influenced by familiarity with the ability of the method to predict what the technologist sees in practice, i.e. the reliability and validity of the results with actual products.

SOFTWARE TO CALCULATE WATER ACTIVITY

Whatever the calculation method used to derive the final water activity value for a bakery food, a number of assumptions have to be made, and complicated, tedious, error-prone calculations undertaken. With the dramatic increase in computing power in the 1980s and 1990s, suitable software programs have been developed which considerably reduce the time taken for calculating water activity. Each of the programs available is built on a different set of assumptions and may use a suite of calculation methods. The choice of which water activity program to access must be left to the reader, although the words of caution expressed by Peleg and Normand (1992) are worth bearing in mind: "... the reliability of the calculated values primarily depends on the reliability of the experimental data from which the isotherms have been derived, and *on whether the data are truly representative of the ingredients in question.*" Some of the problems associated with the validity of ingredient data for bakery products have been discussed above. In addition to the ability to calculate water activity, some software programs include the ability to estimate the mould-free shelf-life of bakery products (e.g. ERH CALC™, *see below*).

The sucrose equivalence and sucrose concentration methods described in this chapter yield results that are as accurate as measuring instruments, provided that the data pertaining to the ingredients used in the equations are as correct and accurate as they can be for the ingredeints and recipes in question. The sucrose equivalence method can be used easily with the aid of a calculator, and calculations using the sucrose concentration method can also be determined using a calculator. However, as the equations become more complex and the data values more difficult to determine, calculating the water activity manually by this method is prone to error and is time-consuming. Some of the calculation problems can be overcome with a suitable computer spreadsheet program. Peleg and Normand (1992) reviewed the use of microcomputer methods for estimating the moisture sorption isotherms of formulations containing ingredients with known or unknown isotherms and initial moisture contents, and gave examples of appropriate software solutions. Some software programs are now available for use through the World Wide Web. For example, WebTech and Dr. Labuza provide a series of programs (Water Analyser Series, 1999) covering many aspects of water activity isotherm determination, plotting and estimation.

ERH CALC™

Scientists and bakery technologists working at the Flour Milling and Baking Research Association based at Chorleywood, and latterly, the Campden and

Chorleywood Food Research Association, have built up a database of ingredient data values for use when determining water activity using both the sucrose equivalence and concentration methods described earlier. These values have been validated through appropriate baking trials. The same group has also developed computer software – ERH CALC™ – to take much of the tedium out of the calculations and to provide technologists with an easy-to-use, accurate means of calculating water activity values for product formulations. The software (a Windows program) applies the concepts and rules developed by a number of workers in the area of water activity, along with their own data values for ingredients determined theoretically, modified in the light of baking trials and validated by comparing calculated and measured values. The program does not determine the water activities of 'ideal solutions' but determines water activity of real, multicomponent products from their formulations.

The values calculated in ERH CALC™ are as accurate as measurement using instruments, i.e. within $\pm 1\%$ ERH. The main advantage is that the product does not need to be made up for an accurate water activity value to be determined. Values are determined very quickly and many variations of product formulation can be tried out on a PC before mixing and baking the product. The program also links the calculated ERH with the mould-free shelf-life of products, and has found particular use in the development of new cake products (Jones, 1996). Of course, when launching a new product the water activity should still be checked using a water activity meter, and the keeping trials to determine shelf-life should still be undertaken to ensure maximum food safety, but the time taken to reach the 'embryonic' short-listed product stage in the development cycle is much reduced.

A typical consultation using ERH CALC™ to determine water activity of a product is described below. Recipes can be entered from scratch or retrieved from previously saved files for further manipulation (*see* Fig. 8.6). Product details such as its name, the moisture loss during baking, storage and cooling, and the storage temperature for the product are entered (*see* Fig. 8.7). Ingredients are selected from a comprehensive list provided in the system or from a client master list built up by users for their own specific ingredient sets. The quantities for each ingredient are entered and basic statistics such as the recipe weight, moisture content, etc., are displayed as each ingredient is added (*see* Fig. 8.8). Once the recipe is complete and the calculations made, the ERH is displayed along with the moisture content of the product after baking and its predicted mould-free shelf-life (*see* Fig. 8.9). The recipe can be manipulated easily either by modifying existing ingredient quantities, by adding new ones or by varying the moisture losses. The process is rapid and enables the developer to try out many iterations before making up the recipe in the test bakery. If the final MFSL is insufficient from the ERH or water activity adjustments, the user can employ a mould inhibitor tool to calculate the amount of preservative required (*see* Fig. 8.10). There is a Help file attached with information about the ingredients, the calculation methods and operation of the program, which users can consult at any point.

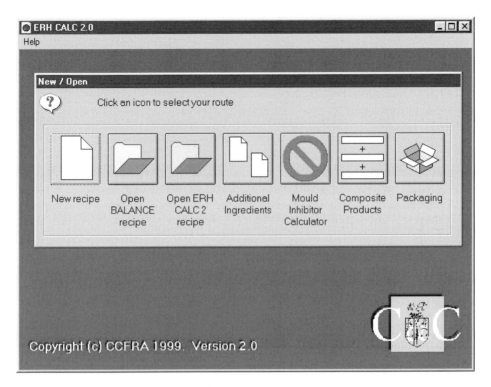

Fig. 8.6 Routes available in ERH CALC™.

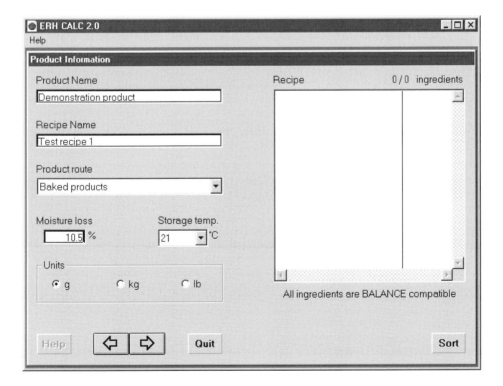

Fig. 8.7 Product detail specifications.

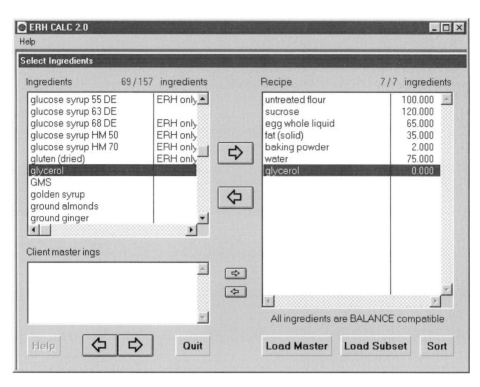

Fig. 8.8 Selection of ingredients and quantity input.

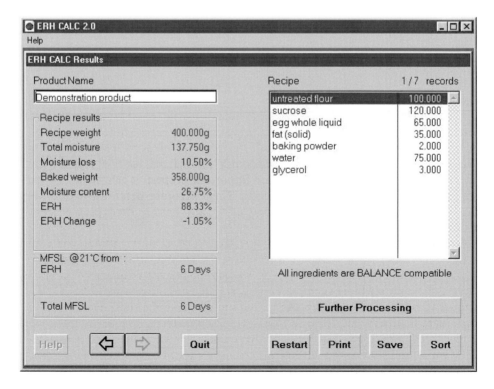

Fig. 8.9 Results screen from ERH CALC™.

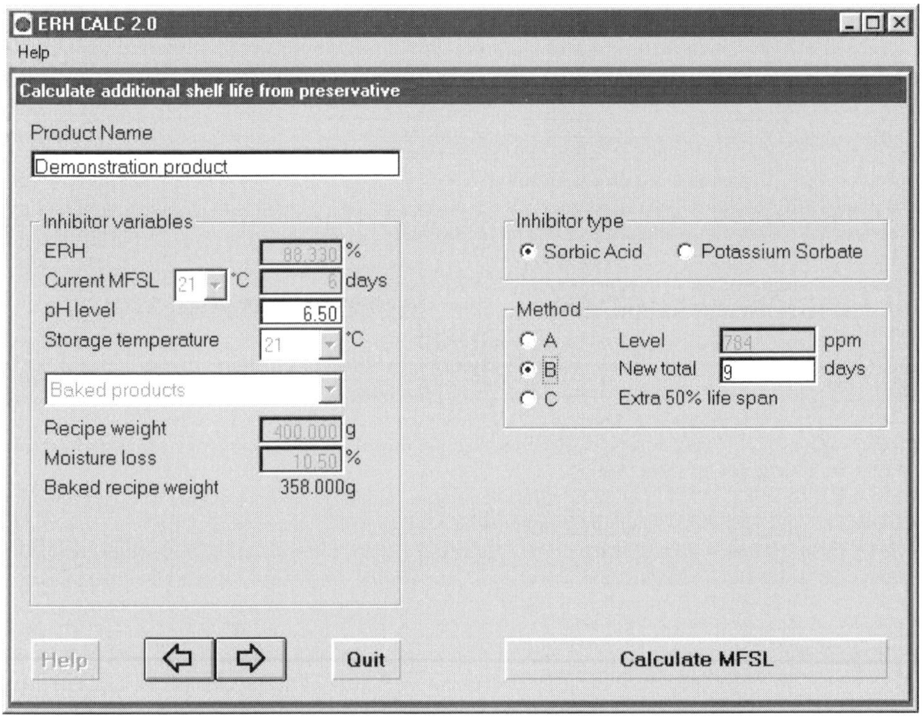

Calculate additional shelf life from preservative

Product Name

Demonstration product

Inhibitor variables

ERH   88.330 %
Current MFSL   21 ▾ °C   6 days
pH level   6.50
Storage temperature   21   ▾ °C

Baked products   ▾

Recipe weight   400.000 g
Moisture loss   10.50 %
Baked recipe weight   358.000g

Inhibitor type

⦿ Sorbic Acid   ○ Potassium Sorbate

Method

○ A   Level   784   ppm
⦿ B   New total   9   days
○ C   Extra 50% life span

Help   ⇦   ⇨   Quit   Calculate MFSL

Fig. 8.10 Mould inhibitor calculator.

CONCLUSIONS

The moisture content of bakery foods has a profound influence on the perception of product quality, especially organoleptic qualities and perceived freshness. A knowledge of bakery product moisture contents is therefore important for quality control and assurance, and product development. Product moisture content and water activity/ERH are strongly related but require separate consideration. Water activity and ERH are important properties related to the storage stability and safety of bakery foods. Their accurate determination is very important for quality assurance and food safety, and once again in product development.

A range of methods exists for the determination of moisture content and water activty/ERH, and these often form the basis for quality control and assurance. During product development, however, measurements are often time-consuming and require that a product sample be available for measurements to be made. A number of methods exist which can be used to calculate the required information from ingredient data and thus reduce development times without compromising product quality or safety. Computer software programs with reliable databases now exist, which can be used to further reduce development times and allow bakery technologists to be more innovative in product development.

REFERENCES

AACC (1995) *Approved methods, Vol. II*, AACC, Minneapolis, USA.
  Method 44–01 Calculation of percent moisture
  Method 44–10 Moisture – electrical methods
  Method 44–11 Moisture – dielectric meter method (grain)
  Method 44–15A Moisture – air-oven methods
  Method 44–16 Moisture – air-oven (aluminum plate) method
  Method 44–19 Moisture – air-oven drying at 135°C
  Method 44–40 Moisture – modified vacuum-oven method
Ablett, S. & Lillford, P. (1991) Water in foods. *Chemistry in Britain*, November, 1024–6.
Anon. (1998a) New food quantifier instrument. *Food Marketing & Technology*, December, 39.
Anon. (1998b) A speedy window into moisture measurement. *British Baker*, October, 19.
Cakebread, S. (1973) Confectionary ingredients: osmotic properties of carbohydrate solutions IV. *Confectionery Production*, August, 424–7.
Cauvain, S.P. & Seiler, D.A.L. (1992) Equilibrium relative humidity and the shelf life of cakes. *FMBRA Report No. 150*, CCFRA, Chipping Campden, UK.
CCFRA Flour Testing Working Group. (1997) Method No. 0008, Determination of moisture content by oven drying. *Manual of Methods for Wheat and Flour Testing*. CCFRA, Chipping Campden, UK.
Chinachoti, P. (1998) NMR dynamics of water in relation to thermal characteristics in bread, in *The Properties of Water in Foods ISOPOW 6* (ed. D.S. Reid), Blackie Academic & Professional, London, UK, pp. 139–59.
Christensen, C.M. (1992) Moisture and its measurement, in *Storage of Cereal Grains and their Products*, 4th edn, (ed. D.B. Sauer), AACC, St.Paul, USA, pp. 39–54.
Cooper, R.M., Knight, R.A., Robb, J. & Seiler, D.A.L. (1968) The equilibrium relative humidity of baked products with particular reference to the shelf life of cakes. *FMBRA Report No. 19*, CCFRA, Chipping Campden, UK.
Dean, K.J., Edwards, N.E. & Russell, C.A. (1980) *Physics and Chemistry of Baking*, 3rd edn, Applied Science Publishers, London, UK, pp. 54–5.
DICKEY-john® Corporation (1996) GAC 2100 Advanced Automated Analysis. Auburn, Illinois, USA.
ERH CALC™ (1990). Software package, CCFRA, Chipping Campden, UK.
Ferro Fontan, C., Benmergui, E.A. & Chifre, J. (1980) The prediction of water activity of aqueous solutions in connection with intermediate moisture foods. III a_w prediction in multicomponent strong electrolytic aqueous solutions. *Journal of Food Technology*, **15**, 47–58.
Gielow, R.L. (1998) The emerging role of computational fluid dynamics in the cereal processing industry. *Cereal Foods World*, **43**, 618–20.
Grover, D.W. (1947) The keeping properties of confectionery as influenced by its vapour pressure. *Journal of the Society of Chemistry and Industry*, **66**, 201–5.
ICC (1995) *Standard Methods, 5th Supplement*, Vienna, Austria.
  Standard No. 109/1 – Determination of moisture content of cereals and cereal products (basic references method).
  Standard No. 110/1 – Determination of moisture content of cereals and cereal products (practical method).
Jones, H.P. (1996) Ambient packaged cakes, in *Shelf Life Evaluation of Foods* (eds C.M.D. Man & A.A. Jones), Blackie Academic & Professional, London, UK, pp. 179–201.
Kim, S-M., McCarthy, M.J., Bibbs, D. & Chen, P. (1998) Water in tissue structures by NMR and MRI, in *The Properties of Water in Foods – ISOPOW 6* (ed. D.S. Reid), Blackie Academic & Professional, London, UK, pp. 30–40.
King, W.H. (1965) Humidity and moisture, in *International Symposium on Humidity and Moisture, May, 1963* (ed. A.Wexler), Reinhold, New York, USA.
Landrock, A.H. & Proctor, B.E. (1951) A new graphical interpolation method for obtaining humidity equilibria data, with special reference to its role in food packaging studies. *Food Technology*, **5**, 332–7.
Miller & Kaslow (1963) Determination of moisture by NMR and oven methods in wheat, flour, doughs, and dried fruits. *Food Technology*, **17**, 142–5.
Money, R.W. & Born, R. (1951) Equilibrium humidity of sugar solutions. *Journal of Science Food and Agriculture*, **2**, 180–5.

Mossel, D.A.A. & van Kuijk, H.J.L. (1955) A new and simple technique for the direct determination of the equilibrium relative humidity of foods. *Food Research*, **20**, 415–3.

Norrish, R.S. (1966) An equation for the water activity coefficients and equilibrium relative humidities of water in confectionery syrups. *Journal of Food Technology*, **1**, 25–39.

Osborne, B., Barrett, G.M., Cauvain, S.P. & Fearn, T. (1984) The determination of protein, fat and moisture in bread by near infrared reflectance spectroscopy. *Journal of the Science of Food and Agriculture*, **35**, 940–5.

Peleg, M. & Normand, M.D. (1992) Estimation of the equilibrium water activity of multicomponent mixtures. *Trends in Food Science & Technology*, **3**, 157–60.

Richardson, T. (1986) ERH of confectionery food products. *Manufacturing Confectioner*, December, 85–9.

Richardson, T. (1987) ERH of confectionery food products, *Manufacturing Confectioner*, January, 65–70.

Ross, K.D. (1975) Estimation of water activity in intermediate moisture foods. *Food Technology*, **29**, 26–34.

Scott, M. & Pickles, J. (1991) Continuous measurement of moisture. *Food Manufacture*, **66**, 45–6.

Stekelenburg, F.K. & Labots, H. (1991) *International Journal of Food Science and Technology*, **26**, 111–16.

Teng, T.T. & Seow, C.C. (1981) A comparative study of methods for prediction of water activitiy of multicomponent aqueous solutions. *Journal of Food Technology*, **16**, 409–19.

Water Analyser Series (1999) http://www.users.bigpond.com/webbtech

Wiggins, C. (1998) Proving, baking and cooling, in *Technology of Breadmaking* (eds S.P. Cauvain & L.S. Young), Blackie Academic & Professional, London, UK, pp. 120–48.

9 Strategies for extending bakery product shelf-life

Manufacturers of bakery goods are challenged with the dual goals of providing a marketplace with increasing demand for new and exciting products, and of manufacturing and distributing those products as consistently, cost-effectively and safely as possible. Extending the shelf-life without radically changing the eating qualities of the product can make all the difference to the size of a production batch, and affect economies of scale. If a product has a longer shelf-life, there is less need to deliver that product as frequently to the retail chain. Longer shelf-life means there can be less product wastage from mould growth or as the result of moisture loss from, and movement within, the product. In this chapter, we shall give some practical examples of how bakery product shelf-life can be extended, how product spoilage from moisture migration can be avoided, and how other quality losses can be prevented or minimised by adjusting component ERHs.

MANIPULATING WATER ACTIVITY USING INGREDIENTS

Controlling the water activity of a product is the key to controlling its mould-free shelf-life (MFSL). As discussed in Chapter 6, water activity is linked directly to the MFSL of a product: the lower the ERH, the longer its MFSL. Water activity expresses the availability of water in a baked product, or any food product, to take part in particular processes, such as microbial spoilage. In Chapters 5 and 6, we discussed the role played by ingredients in affecting the water activity of bakery goods by comparing the staling rates of breads and cakes, and concluded that the differences were related in part to the recipe sugar level. In Chapter 8, we also considered the difference between moisture content and water activity, and noted that although related, they do not mean the same thing as far as shelf-life is concerned. For example, the cake recipes given in Table 6.4 have the same moisture content but very different water activities. Because of its lower water activity, Recipe 2 will have a longer MFSL than Recipe 1.

As discussed previously, when soluble materials like salt and sugar dissolve in water, they reduce the vapour pressure of that solution. This affects the mobility of the water in the system and its availability. This of course is the basis for traditional preservation techniques, such as the salting of meat or the preserving of fruits as jams. The potential effect on water activity of a particular ingredient depends on the individual chemistry of the ingredient in question and this concept was discussed in detail in Chapter 6. Other ingredients may not go into solution but may absorb water into their structure and hold it there; a familiar example is wheat flour, a common component of many bakery product recipes.

In Chapter 8, we gave a table of sucrose equivalents for different ingredients typically used in the manufacture of bakery products. The higher the sucrose equivalence of an ingredient, the more effective it is at 'locking up' water molecules, thus making the water less available for microbial growth. Using ingredients with high sucrose equivalents and manipulating their levels can be a valuable technique for the product developer when the extension of MFSL is required. The main ingredients that we shall discuss are:

- Water
- Sugars
- Humectants
- Salt
- Preservatives
- Other materials

We shall take the example of a high ratio cake recipe and describe the potential strategies and steps which might be used to extend the product shelf-life. A high ratio cake is one in which the levels of sugar and liquids exceed the level of flour in the recipe. The basic concepts that will be discussed can be applied to many other baked products, such as pastries, soft cookies, quiches and flan cases. However, before looking at the manipulation of a recipe's ingredients it should be mentioned that there are other means by which a product's shelf-life can be extended. Both temperature and pH can play a significant role in delaying mould growth or by providing an environment hostile to the activity of moulds.

STORAGE TEMPERATURE

It is well known that by reducing the temperature at which products are stored, mould growth will be delayed and foods preserved for longer than if they were stored at ambient temperatures (Seiler, 1977; Troller, 1989). Our ancestors used icehouses for this purpose. However, care must be taken when using low temperatures that the product is well protected since moisture losses and other quality changes can still occur with storage time, as discussed in Chapters 3, 5 and 7. In cake and most other bakery products, the lower the ERH of the product, the greater will be the effect of lowering storage temperature. Table 9.1 shows the approximate increase in the MFSL for cake products stored at temperatures of 21°C and 27°C (70°F and 80°F). With a reduction in the storage temperature of 6°C (10°F) from 27°C to 21°C, a cake with an ERH of 90% will gain an extra day's shelf-life. However, for a cake with an ERH of 84%, the gain will be five days.

Table 9.1   Approximate increase in mould-free shelf-life (MFSL) for reductions in storage temperature.

Cake ERH (%)	MFSL (days)	
	at 27°C (80°F)	at 21°C (70°F)
90	4.0	5.0
88	5.0	6.5
86	6.5	9.0
84	9.0	14.0
82	12.0	20.0

EFFECTS OF pH

The pH of a product is another means by which its shelf-life can be manipulated. Moulds have their 'comfort zones', and when the pH of a product falls outside this zone mould growth is halted or considerably slowed. Results from tests carried out at the Flour Milling and Baking Research Association (FMBRA), Chorleywood, on plain and fruited cakes have shown that in the absence of anti-mould agents, the MFSL is largely unaffected within the pH range 5.0 to 7.5 (Cauvain & Seiler, 1992). The pH of a product varies according to the recipe used, and for a typical plain cake recipe the baked product pH will usually lie between 6.0 and 7.0. There are exceptions, such as chocolate cake where the pH may be more alkaline because an excess of sodium bicarbonate in the recipe helps achieve a more chocolate colour in the baked product. When fruit is included in the recipe, the pH is reduced. The level of reduction depends on the type and level of fruit used.

It is not always possible with baked products to achieve changes in pH that will be sufficient to have a significantly inhibiting effect on microbial activities. In some cases the nature of the ingredients themselves make it difficult to achieve pH changes because they may interact with acids, e.g. sodium bicarbonate, or they may provide a buffering effect, e.g. the presence of calcium carbonate (chalk) in UK flours (as required by UK law). In other cases the required product character may be affected adversely if the final pH is too high or too low, e.g. soda scones are expected to be alkaline. Baked products that lend themselves to manipulation of pH for shelf-life extension include those where an acid flavour is an advantage, e.g. fruit fillings in pies, and where acid flavours may be masked or acceptable, e.g. Christmas puddings. If the manipulation of product pH for shelf-life extension is not an acceptable option, the addition of preservatives may provide an alternative, as discussed later in this chapter.

EXTENDING PRODUCT SHELF-LIFE BY ADJUSTING WATER CONTENT

One of the easiest ways to extend baked product MFSL is to reduce the amount of moisture left in the product. This can be done by removing added water or by reducing ingredients that have high percentages of water, e.g. milk or eggs. However, care must be taken to ensure that removing recipe water will not cause adverse changes in processing, or the product eating character or appearance. The following example illustrates the effects of reducing recipe moisture levels in a typical high ratio cake recipe. The basic recipe is given in Table 9.2. For the purposes of this example a moisture loss of 10% and a storage temperature of 21°C are assumed.

Table 9.2　High ratio style cake.

Ingredient	Weight (g)
flour	100.0
sugar	115.0
egg (whole)	85.0
fat/oil	65.0
skimmed milk powder	8.0
baking powder	4.0
salt	1.0
water	50.0

Moisture loss	= 10.0%
Moisture content	= 22.1%
ERH	= 85.5%
Mould-free shelf-life at 21°C	= 10 days

In our specimen recipe a reduction in added water of 5 g will cause the moisture content to drop but the eating and appearance characteristics to remain largely unchanged. Such a reduction will gain one extra day's shelf-life, as shown in Table 9.3.

Table 9.3　Manipulating water content.

Ingredient	Weight (g)
flour	100.0
sugar	115.0
egg (whole)	85.0
fat/oil	65.0
skimmed milk powder	8.0
baking powder	4.0
salt	1.0
water	45.0

Moisture loss	= 10.0%
Moisture content	= 21.2%
ERH	= 85.1%
Mould-free shelf-life at 21°C	= 11 days

CHANGING SALT LEVELS

Salt, as described in previous chapters, has powerful water-binding properties because of its ionic nature. With a sucrose equivalence of 11, a relatively small quantity of salt can be added to a recipe and yet have a large effect on product ERH. There is a limit, however, to the quantity that can be added to baked products because of its effects on processing, e.g. changes to the viscoelastic properties of gluten and inhibition of yeast in bread doughs (Williams & Pullen, 1998), and particularly because of its strong effect on flavour. In addition there is a move towards decreasing salt (sodium chloride) levels in all foods for potential health benefits and so salt levels should be changed with consideration to all of these aspects. As a rule of thumb, for baked products the salt level can be increased to about 2% of flour weight before any adverse flavour is detected in cake products. In some stronger flavoured cakes such as ginger or fruit cakes, the 2% flour weight ceiling may be increased slightly. Similar rules regarding salt apply to many fermented products, with higher levels of addition likely to be more tolerated in some speciality breads and fermented products, and pizza bases.

In the example high ratio cake recipe, the salt level is increased to 2%, which increases the mould-free shelf-life by two days (*see* Table 9.4).

Table 9.4   Manipulating salt content.

Ingredient	Weight (g)
flour	100.0
sugar	115.0
egg (whole)	85.0
fat/oil	65.0
skimmed milk powder	8.0
baking powder	4.0
salt	2.0
water	50.0

Moisture loss	= 10.0%
Moisture content	= 22.1%
ERH	= 84.9%
Mould-free shelf-life	= 12 days

Salt is not often seen as part of the formulation for higher water activity products like creams and sweet fillings, partly because it confers a flavour profile that does not fit that required for such products. Also, in products with ERHs greater than 92% the levels of addition as restricted on flavour grounds would be too small to have any significant effect on the product MFSL. Salt finds greatest use in savoury fillings where it complements the flavour profile but has little effect on extending product shelf-life because of the high water activities of such products.

EFFECTS OF SUGARS ON CAKE SHELF-LIFE

Sugars are another category of ingredients that can prove very useful to product developers when trying to extend product shelf-life. Sugars have multifunctional roles in cakemaking (McAughtrie & Cunningham, 1997). Sucrose in particular is important in forming the structure of the product by regulating the gelatinisation of starch, helping to incorporate air and acting as an anti-staling agent. In the context of this chapter, it is very effective at binding moisture. By increasing the sucrose level in a recipe, the amount of water available for microbial growth will be reduced. However, if the sucrose level is too high by comparison with the water (moisture) content in a cake recipe, it will be unbalanced and the resulting cake may have a coarse and open structure, possibly with structural collapse, known to bakers as an 'M' fault.

Sugar, of course, has a strong influence on the flavour of the product, and different types of sugars have different levels of relative sweetness. Different sugars also have varying levels of sucrose equivalence. A comparison of relative sweetness and sucrose equivalents for some types of sugar is given in Table 9.5.

Table 9.5 Relative sweetness and sucrose equivalents of some sugars.

Sugar	Relative sweetness	Sucrose equivalence
sucrose	1.00	1.0
dextrose monohydrate	0.80	1.3
fructose	1.40	1.4
lactose	0.16	1.2
maltose	0.33	1.0
high dextrose glucose syrup	0.65	0.9
regular glucose syrup	0.50	0.8

By considering the sucrose equivalence in combination with relative sweetness and the rules of cakemaking, one sugar can be replaced with another to achieve both additional shelf-life and the sweetness required in the product. For example, increasing the level of sucrose will inevitably increase the sweetness of the cake. If this increase is unacceptable, it is possible to compensate for this increased sweetness by using other sugars which are, weight for weight, not as sweet (*see* Other sugars *below*).

Sucrose

Table 9.6 shows the effect of increasing the sucrose level in a high ratio cake recipe by approximately 5% of the flour weight. This increase of sucrose means that there will be a small reduction of 5% in the ERH, while the MFSL is increased by one day.

The shelf-life of the cake could be extended by further increasing the sucrose level in the recipe. In the UK, sugar levels may go as high as 1.3:1, sucrose to flour, while in the USA the norm is 1.4:1. Care must be taken, however, that

Table 9.6   Manipulating sucrose level.

Ingredient	Weight (g)
flour	100.0
sugar	120.0
egg (whole)	85.0
fat/oil	65.0
skimmed milk powder	8.0
baking powder	4.0
salt	1.0
water	50.0

Moisture loss   = 10.0%
Moisture content   = 22.7%
ERH   = 85.3%
Mould-free shelf-life at 21°C = 11 days

levels are not pushed too high by comparison with recipe moisture content, as this may cause sugar spotting on the baked product. This would reduce the effectiveness that the sugar would have on the product ERH, since it would not be in solution. Another consequence of recrystallised sugar is the increased hygroscopicity of the product surface, which may lead to problems with sticky surfaces on cakes, biscuits and meringues because of the absorption of moisture from the atmosphere.

Other sugars

Sometimes, increasing the sucrose level in a cake recipe is not practical because of the excessive sweetness or a possible imbalance within the recipe. The addition or partial replacement of sucrose with simple sugars may offer an alternative means for extending product shelf-life. Unlike sucrose, which is a disaccharide, simple sugars are monosaccharides, i.e. they are smaller molecules than sucrose and as such are generally more efficient at binding moisture when used in baked products. However, the quantity that can be used in cakes is limited due to the increased Maillard browning effect that can occur in the cake crumb with their addition (Cauvain & Screen, 1994). This browning is caused by the reducing sugars reacting with the amino acids or proteins within the batter to form brown pigments, and is pH sensitive. For these reasons a maximum level of 10% based on sucrose solids is commonly recommended in cakemaking. A slightly higher level may be possible in ginger or chocolate cakes, where the browning of the crumb would be less noticeable, although care must be taken to avoid causing other problems, such as thicker top crusts on the baked product, unwanted flavour changes and alterations to the baking profile of the product.

A further advantage of some monosaccharides, such as glucose, is that they are less sweet than sucrose. Laevulose or fructose is sweeter than sucrose, whereas dextrose or glucose syrups are not as sweet as sucrose. Dextrose or glucose syrups have sucrose equivalents greater than unity, and so are often used as alternatives to sucrose. Glucose syrups are grouped according to their Dextrose Equivalent (DE). The DE value indicates the degree to which starch has been broken down and converted into glucose units by hydrolysis. The higher the DE value, the more able the syrup is to bind moisture. Unfortunately, at higher usage levels the glucose syrups cause more browning of the crumb. If a glucose syrup rather than a powder is added to a recipe, an adjustment of the recipe water level is needed to compensate for the water content of the syrup.

Table 9.7 shows the effect of replacing 10 g of the sucrose with dextrose mono-hydrate in a high ratio cake recipe. The ERH is reduced to 85.0% and the MFSL is increased to 12 days. The weight for weight replacement of sucrose with dextrose monohydrate has the same effect on product shelf-life as a 5 g increase in the sucrose level addition alone, and can be used to reduce product sweetness while maintaining shelf-life. Further increases in shelf-life can be obtained with higher levels of dex-trose monohydrate addition, but potentially at the expense of other product char-acters, for example excessive darkening of the crumb, thicker and darker crusts, and loss of volume (Cauvain & Screen, 1994).

Table 9.7 Manipulating sucrose and dextrose levels.

Ingredient	Weight (g)
flour	100.0
sugar	105.0
dextrose	10.0
egg (whole)	85.0
fat/oil	65.0
skimmed milk powder	8.0
baking powder	4.0
salt	1.0
water	50.0

Moisture loss	= 10.0%
Moisture content	= 21.7%
ERH	= 85.0%
Mould-free shelf-life at 21°C	= 12 days

Sucrose and other sugars find other uses for lowering water activity in baked products. For example, in fermented products the addition of sucrose to American breads, hamburger buns, rolls and fruited buns results in a lower product ERH and thus a longer MFSL. Relatively high levels of sugar are found in baked products in many of the warmer climates of the world; for example, in India sugar levels in breads may rise to as high as 30% flour weight. Some of the more common and effective uses of sugars in bakery products are in the production of creams and fillings. The sweet-tasting sensation is one advantage, but perhaps more important is the effect on ERH, which is lowered by their addition. This allows for the potential of producing a soft-eating cream while reducing fat levels through an increase in added water and a suitable stabilising agent.

USING HUMECTANTS

A humectant can be defined as an ingredient that is hygroscopic, i.e. has the ability to absorb a greater quantity of moisture from the surrounding environment than suggested by its molecular weight. In doing so, humectants commonly confer an increased soft-eating character to the crumb of baked products. They are more effective in this activity at lower ERH levels (Cooper *et al.*, 1968). By adding humectants to cakes, it is possible to maintain the ERH and increase the moisture content, or to reduce the ERH without reducing the moisture content. Sorbitol and glycerine are the humectants commonly employed in cakemaking and other aspects of baking. Weight for weight, glycerine is usually twice as effective in bakery products than sorbitol; at the time of going to press it is also more expensive. The level of sorbitol that can be used is restricted due to its laxative effect, and so a balance has to be reached between cost and effectiveness when using these ingredients. Baking losses may be reduced with high levels of glycerol addition, but usually the changes in product quality are unacceptable (Cauvain & Screen, 1994).

Table 9.8 shows the effect that a 10 g addition of glycerol (which has a sucrose equivalent of 4.0) has to the high ratio cake base recipe. There is a significant reduction in the cake ERH by 4% to 81.6%, and an increase in MFSL to 21 days.

Table 9.8 Effect of glycerol addition.

Ingredient	Weight (g)
flour	100.0
sugar	115.0
egg (whole)	85.0
fat/oil	65.0
skimmed milk powder	8.0
baking powder	4.0
salt	1.0
glycerol	10.0
water	50.0

Moisture loss	= 10.0%
Moisture content	= 22.3%
ERH	= 81.6%
Mould-free shelf-life at 21°C	= 21 days

Humectants may be used in many bakery products to lower ERH. Robb (1991) used glycerol to lower the ERH of apple pie fillings and thereby reduce moisture migration to the pastry, so that the pastry remained crisper for longer. Similar effects would be observed in other sweet fruit fillings. Additions of glycerol to extend the shelf-life of fermented goods are possible, although the lower vapour pressure in the dough will have an inhibitory effect on yeast activity.

SUMMARY OF THE EFFECTS OF RECIPE CHANGES TO CAKE SHELF-LIFE

The effect on the MFSL of the high ratio cake example if all of these changes to ingredients and their quantities discussed above are adopted is illustrated in Table 9.9. In this example, the product shelf-life has been extended from 10 to 31 days, with only a small and probably acceptable change in moisture content. If further reductions in ERH are required and mould inhibitors are not desired, reducing the moisture content will have to be considered. This can be achieved simply by reducing the water gradually or trying to optimise baking conditions. Ultimately such actions will give the same result, namely a drier-eating cake. As the total water content of the cake moves to below 20%, a drier-eating cake will be produced which may lack consumer appeal.

Table 9.9   Modified recipe.

Ingredient	Weight (g)
flour	100.0
sugar	105.0
dextrose	10.0
egg (whole)	85.0
fat/oil	65.0
skimmed milk powder	8.0
baking powder	4.0
salt	2.0
glycerol	10.0
water	45.0

Moisture loss	= 10.0%
Moisture content	= 20.9%
ERH	= 79.6%
Mould-free shelf-life at 21°C	= 31 days

Manipulation of ingredients to achieve the extensions in shelf-life can, if employed sensibly, be a powerful tool in the product developer's hands. The example of the modification of a high ratio cake recipe has illustrated the techniques that can be employed for cake or pastry product or sweet fermented products. In savoury or non-sugar-containing products, such as some breads, there is limited action that can be taken. In these cases, the addition of permitted preservatives or the use of specialised packaging will need to be employed to extend product MFSL (*see below*). Also, greater attention must given to the hygiene of the plant to minimise the microbial loading on the products after baking. This may require the use of positive airflow and other suitable clean-room techniques.

USING PRESERVATIVES

The use of preservatives in baked products may be limited for ethical, legal or product specific reasons. In some companies, the use of preservatives is not an option as they wish to promote a 'healthy, additive-free' product image, which is often branded and needs to be maintained. In some countries, the legislation in operation permits the use of preservatives within certain bounds. The product character and its ingredients may not lend themselves to the effective use of certain preservatives, e.g. where the product pH prevents the effectiveness of the preservative. When used at high levels, preservatives can give rise to off-odours and flavours, e.g. calcium propionate used in breads is detected easily by the human nose, especially when the product is heated (toasted). However, in some cases preservatives can give products an extra safety factor when the extension of shelf-life cannot be achieved by other means. Although preservatives do not significantly affect water activity or the way water moves in or out of products, a limited discussion for the purposes of completeness in this chapter on manipulating recipes to achieve changes in shelf-life has been included.

Preservatives must be soluble in water if they are to be effective in preventing or reducing microbial activity. The effectiveness of a particular preservative depends on the product pH, the ERH and the storage temperature being used. Table 9.10 shows some of the more common preservatives used in bakery foods. A more complete list and their levels of addition for the UK are given by Williams and Pullen (1998).

Table 9.10 Preservatives used in bakery foods (based on Williams & Pullen, 1998).

Preservative	Product category
sorbic acid	cakes, pastries
calcium sorbate	cakes, pastries
potassium sorbate	cakes, pastries
proprionic acid	breads, part-baked breads
calcium proprionate	pre-packed rolls, buns and pitta
sodium proprionate	all types of breads
acetic acid	all types of breads

Flour confectionery products

Weight for weight, sorbic acid is twice as effective as propionic acid, and therefore sorbic acid is generally used for flour confectionery products. However, sorbic acid is difficult to incorporate into a batter because of its low solubility and therefore its salts are generally used. Potassium sorbate is the most widely used in flour confectionery due to its high solubility. Calcium sorbate, similar to sorbic acid, is not very soluble; sodium sorbate is not used very often as it is not considered 'healthy', and trends are towards having lower levels of sodium in foods. The effectiveness of sorbic acid and its salts depends on the product pH and therefore very little is gained if the products to which they are added have a pH approaching 7 or higher.

The data in Table 9.11 show the effect on MFSL of the addition of 1000 ppm (finished product weight) of sorbic acid. The values show that as the pH falls (i.e. the product becomes more acidic), the preservative becomes more effective. In the case of many fruit cakes, where the pH is lowered because of the presence of the fruit, the

Table 9.11   Approximate mould-free shelf-life at 21°C of cake treated with 1000 ppm sorbic acid.

ERH (%)	Untreated cake	Mould-free shelf-life at 21°C (days)					
		pH 7.0	pH 6.6	pH 6.2	pH 5.8	pH 5.4	pH 5.0
92	4.5	5.5	6	7.25	9.5	14	21
86	10.25	13	16	20	28	41	65
80	27	44	56	78	117	187	310

addition of sorbic acid or its salts increases shelf-life. However, in chocolate cakes with higher pH (due to the alkaline nature of the cocoa powder) sorbic acid and its salts do not result in significant extensions to product MFSL.

Fermented products

The high ERH and desirable moist-eating character of most bread products leaves little opportunity for ingredient manipulation for shelf-life extension. Consequently the addition of a suitable preservative is the favoured option. Propionic acid and its salts are used widely for bread and other fermented products for two reasons: they delay mould growth and they insure against spoilage from rope (Pateras, 1998). In addition to the propionates, ethyl alcohol may be used to inhibit microbial activity because of its ability to lower vapour pressure and therefore water activity. Ethyl alcohol also has the ability to inhibit bread staling (Seiler, 1984a; Pateras, 1998).

Biscuit products

The water activity of biscuits, cookies and crackers is usually too low to support microbial activity and so the use of preservatives in such product is largely unnecessary. The so-called 'soft-eating' cookies, however, do have higher moisture contents than many other biscuit products and so may require the addition of a suitable preservative to achieve the necessary shelf-life. Some fruited biscuits, e.g. fig rolls and fig Newtons, have fillings with relatively high water activities and may also require the addition of suitable preservatives to avoid problems with microbial activity.

REDUCING MOISTURE MIGRATION

As discussed in previous chapters, the major driving force for moisture migration is the differential in water activity between product and storage atmosphere, both within the product and between components in multicomponent bakery products. In the case of the latter, moisture migration can be reduced by minimising the difference in component ERH (a_w) by adjusting component formulations (*see* Chapter 7). In some cases it may not be possible to make sufficient adjustment to component formulations to reduce moisture migration without compromising the quality of one or all components, and so the application of other techniques to restrict moisture migration, e.g. through the use of barriers (Koelsch, 1994; Cauvain, 1995), may be required.

In general, large differences between individual component ERHs result in the faster migration of water between components, whether by diffusion, vapour phase transfer, or both. Thus in multicomponent products there can be more than one strategy for reducing moisture migration. In principle, it is possible to reduce moisture migration by lowering the high component ERH, raising the low component ERH, or both. In practice, the degree to which the component ERH may be changed is limited by significant changes to the intrinsic character of any individual component, the most common one being the acceptable level of moisture and its contribution to the eating qualities of the product.

In many bakery products, the levels of added salt will be limited by unacceptable flavour changes, as discussed in the example of a high ratio cake above. In multicomponent savoury products such as meat pie and pizza, there are two opportunities for adjusting salt level: one is associated with the base pastry and the other with the fillings (meat pies) or topping (pizza). Salt levels may go up or down to reduce moisture migration according to individual preference. In sweetened pastry products, sugars largely play the same potential role as salt in savoury products for changing component ERH and reducing moisture migration (Robb, 1991). Sugars are not normally used in savoury products, although the potential for using non-sweet alternative sugars should not be ignored.

Packaging materials can affect moisture migration in composite products. In particular, the permeability of the wrapping material will influence the moisture migration rate by affecting the relative humidity of the atmosphere surrounding the product. For example, packaging materials with a low moisture vapour transmission rate tend to create a high relative humidity in the pack atmosphere; this lowers the rate of moisture loss from individual components as the whole system moves to an equilibrium state. Robb (1991) showed that increasing the permeability of films used to wrap apple pies affected the rate at which the pastry gained moisture from the filling. The greater the permeability, the longer the crispness of the pastry was maintained. However, since water was still being lost from the filling the physical size of the filling component decreased. Butcher and Hodge (1984) observed similar effects for wrapper permeability on pastry crispness in the storage of pork pies.

The porosity of bakery components influences the rate of moisture migration between components. In general, the less porous the product structure, the slower will be moisture migration. However, in many cases the porous cellular structure is an integral part of the product character and so may not be greatly changed without affecting quality. For example, the cell structure of choux pastry shells is extremely porous and moisture passes readily through the casing of eclairs, whether by diffusion or vapour phase, but eclairs with a more dense structure have a hard but not crisp-eating (desirable) character. Robb (1991) added baking powder to a sweetened short pastry and used it to make apple pies. He found that the increased porosity of the baked pastry increased significantly the rate at which moisture migrated to the pastry and raised the moisture content of the latter, even when wrapped in a moisture permeable film. Such results suggest that where possible moisture migration can be reduced by making less aerated components.

EXTENDING SHELF-LIFE BY OTHER MEANS

The list below gives other techniques that can be used when further increases in product shelf-life above those obtained from adjusting ERH or from the addition of preservatives are required. These are generally considered last in the development process for shelf-life extension, mainly because they add costs to the product. They include:

- Ethanol surface spraying
- Packaging with modified atmospheres
- Intelligent packaging
- Packaging directly after baking
- Packaging before baking
- Ultraviolet (UV) or infrared (IR) irradiation

Ethanol surface spraying

Ethanol is a powerful bactericide used to sterilise utensils, work surfaces and instruments in medical, laboratory and food environments. It is also an antifungal agent that can be applied to food products. Seiler (1989) evaluated the usefulness of 95% food grade ethyl alcohol for the preservation of a wide range of bakery products and showed that it acted in the vapour phase, since much of the increase in product mould-free shelf-life occurred whether the same amount of alcohol was sprayed on the surface or placed in the pack out of contact with the product. The extensions in shelf-life were found to vary according to the water activity of the product, the tightness of the wrapping, the gas permeability of the packaging material and the seal integrity. Figure 9.1 shows the typical increase in the MFSL of bread obtained with different levels of alcohol applied to product surfaces. Different commercial sources of alcohols, e.g. brandy and whisky, are used in many premium bakery products, e.g. celebration cakes and Christmas puddings, not only to gain the increase in shelf-life but to benefit from the flavour that such alcohols impart. With creams and fillings, the addition of alcohols may also be used to add flavour and extend product shelf-life, especially microbial shelf-life. However, in some parts of the world the level of alcohol that can be used with bakery products is subject to legislation and it may not be used freely as an ingredient. For example, in the UK the use of alcohol at levels above 2% of the baked product weight incurs Customs and Excise duties.

Modified atmosphere packaging

Modified atmosphere packaging (MAP) is a popular method of packaging within the baking industry and is used as a means of extending product shelf-life and improving product image. MAP is a non-invasive and additive-free way to extend the shelf-life of fresh produce. It does not taint, discolour or pollute the product, and the gas mixtures used can be taken literally from the atmosphere around us. Other methods used as alternatives to MAP are *controlled atmosphere packaging* (CAP),

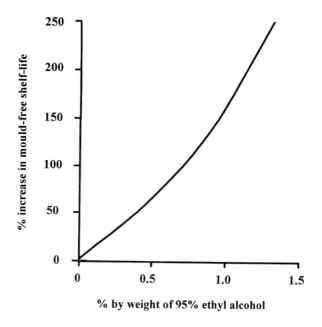

Fig. 9.1 Relationship between alcohol concentration applied and percentage increase in mould-free shelf-life.

where the proportion and type of gas mixture is controlled over the whole storage period, and *vacuum packaging*, where the product is sealed in a low-gas-permeable pack after partial or full evacuation. MAP products need to be encased, usually in a tray or robust pack, and sealed carefully to prevent escape of the pack atmosphere or entry of moisture. Such means of extending product shelf-life often appeal to the 'green' consumer as products packed in this way are regarded as being preserved by additive-free methods.

The principal method used with MAP is to replace the air in a gas-impermeable pack with a single gas such as nitrogen, oxygen or carbon dioxide, or mixtures of gases. In the absence of air (less than 1% oxygen), aerobic microbes such as moulds are unable to grow. Oxygen is seldom used for bakery products, as moulds use oxygen for growth and consequently using it would be a counterproductive means of extending shelf-life; also, in bakery products with high fat contents, oxidative rancidity would be accelerated. Nitrogen is an inert gas that has been used for many years as a gas filler to prevent pack collapse. It has a low solubility in water and fats, and only a relatively small effect on improving MFSL compared with carbon dioxide. It is used in MAP to replace oxygen, and therefore prevent rancidity and inhibit the growth of aerobic organisms. Carbon dioxide has the ability to inhibit the growth of microorganisms and so is the most popular of the gases used. The inhibitory effect has been known for many years and was demonstrated as early as 1933 (Skovholt & Bailey, 1933). Its effectiveness in inhibiting microbial growth increases with increasing concentrations (Seiler, 1989). Typical atmospheres used for MAP with bakery products are shown in Table 9.12 (Farber, 1991; Church, 1994).

Table 9.12 Typical atmospheres in modified atmosphere packaging.

Gas	Percentage
nitrogen	100
carbon dioxide	100
$CO_2 : N_2$	20–70 : 20–80

Intelligent packaging

This is defined as "an integral component or inherent property of a pack, product or pack/product configuration which confers intelligence appropriate to function and use of the product itself and has the ability to sense or be sensed and to communicate" (Summers, 1992). The method is sometimes called 'smart packaging'. It incorporates chemicals contained in a small packet, which are not in contact with the product but scavenge gases in the pack (usually oxygen) or emit a gas or anti-microbial substance into the pack. Examples include oxygen removal, carbon dioxide or ethanol release, water removal, and preservative release. Sometimes the packet external label can be the carrier for antimicrobial or antifungal agents (Seiler, 1997). Intelligent packaging is generally more expensive than conventional packaging and so is used mainly for added-value products, where the extra costs incurred can be justified.

Packaging before baking

Baked products, such as steamed or Christmas puddings, can be deposited at the batter stage into containers which are part sealed and then steamed or baked. Final sealing occurs soon after the product leaves the oven, and before the effects of increased gas pressure (because of baking) are reversed as the product cools. This approach can be used as a preventative measure so that the best shelf-life can be obtained. Another method is to bake the product in a container, e.g. a canned cake, and seal it before the product surface has cooled to 80°C (176°F). Such techniques are employed for products where the crust colour, surface condensation and staling are less important. For example, staling is commonly reversed when the product is re-heated before consumption.

Packaging directly after baking

Cooling a product quickly and packing at the correct temperature in a hygienic and clean environment can prevent contamination of the product, and therefore can be considered as controlling, or preventing a shortening of, the shelf-life. Problems are sometimes encountered where localised condensation within packaging can present good conditions for mould growth.

Infrared (IR) and ultraviolet (UV) irradiation, and microwave radiation

Seiler (1984b) showed that by irradiating the surface of wrapped breads and cakes with IR light, the product MFSL was increased. However, it is easier to apply if only one surface needs to be irradiated because there are installation difficulties for products which need multisided irradiation. Similarly, the MFSL of baked products wrapped in a clear film can be increased by exposure to UV lamps. The advantage is that the product is not heated again. The drawbacks of UV irradiation are the same as for IR, with the additional need that the safety of the operatives must be maintained. Microwave radiation for shelf-life extension has also been investigated (Seiler, 1983). The use of microwaves with bakery products is limited by the heating effect that results, since it can cause condensation problems that affect adversely the product appearance. Such heating methods are not suitable for use with composite products because different components heat at different rates and may lose their integrity, e.g. moisture migration may be increased if creams or fillings break down during heating. *Gamma* irradiation has also been demonstrated to extend MFSL but can affect adversely product odour and flavour, especially in products with high fat contents. It is not a popular technique as there is much public concern about the suitability and safety of *gamma* irradiation.

CONCLUSIONS

The strategy adopted for extending the shelf-life of a particular product depends on many factors, including local food legislation, ingredient availability and attitudes to their use, consumer acceptance and cost. Shelf-life extension may be obtained using a single ingredient or process change, or a combination of many alternative changes according to individual needs and attitudes. In this chapter, we have considered a number of the many possible approaches that might be used.

It may be helpful for bakery technologists to develop their own list of prioritised strategies that may be used in product development and shelf-life extension. The list of potential actions when manipulating ingredients and processes to extend product shelf-life as discussed in this chapter may be summarised as follows:

(1) Consider the moisture content of the product. Can this be reduced without affecting seriously the eating quality of the product?
(2) Consider increasing the salt level. Take care that the flavour of the product will not be affected adversely.
(3) Consider increasing sugar levels.
(4) Consider replacing one sugar type with another, bearing in mind the relative sweetness, sucrose equivalence and effects on product character of the replacement sugars.
(5) Consider the use of humectants.
(6) Can preservatives be used and at what levels?
(7) Can the product pH be adjusted up or down?
(8) Can the type of packaging be changed?
(9) Can the pack atmosphere by changed?

(10)   Can surface sterilisation be employed?
(11)   Is a change in storage conditions required?
(12)   Is it necessary to change process conditions?

REFERENCES

Butcher, G.J & Hodge, D.G. (1984) Pastry technology: the softening of pork pie pastry during storage. *FMBRA Report No. 116*. CCFRA, Chipping Campden, UK.

Cauvain, S.P. (1995) Putting pastry under the microscope. *Baking Industry Europe*, 68–9.

Cauvain, S.P. & Screen, A.E. (1994) The role of sugars in cakes. *FMBRA Report No. 155*. CCFRA, Chipping Campden, UK.

Cauvain, S.P. & Seiler, D.A.L. (1992) Equilibrium relative humidity and the shelf life of cakes. *FMBRA Report No. 150*. CCFRA, Chipping Campden, UK.

Church, N. (1994) Developments in modified-atmosphere packaging and related technologies. *Trends in Food Science & Technology*, **5**, 345–52.

Cooper, R.M., Knight, R.A., Robb, J. & Seiler, D.A.L. (1968) The equilibrium relative humidity of baked products with particular reference to cakes. *FMBRA Report No. 19*. CCFRA, Chipping Campden, UK.

Farber, J.M. (1991) Microbiological aspects of modified-atmosphere technology – a review. *Journal of Food Protection*, **54**, 58–70.

Koelsch, C. (1994) Edible water vapour barriers: properties and promise. *Trends in Food Science & Technology*, **51**, 76–81.

McAughtrie, J. & Cunningham, K. (1997) Sugars, in *Technology of Cakemaking*, 6th edn (ed. A.J. Bent), Blackie Academic & Professional, London, UK, pp. 84–99.

Pateras, I. (1998) Bread spoilage, in *Technology of Breadmaking* (eds S.P. Cauvain & L.S. Young), Blackie Academic & Professional, London,UK, pp. 240–61.

Robb, J. (1991) Moisture migration in apple pies. *FMBRA Report No. 145*. CCFRA, Chipping Campden, UK.

Seiler, D.A.L. (1977) Problems in estimating the mould-free shelf life of baked products. *FMBRA Bulletin No. 4*, CCFRA, Chipping Campden, UK, pp. 112–21.

Seiler D.A.L. (1983) Preservation of bakery products, *FMBRA Bulletin No. 4*, CCFRA, Chipping Campden, UK, pp. 166–77.

Seiler, D.A.L. (1984a) Preservation of bakery products. *Institute of Food Science and Technology Proceedings*, **17**, 31–9.

Seiler, D.A.L. (1984b) Controlled atmosphere packaging for preserving bakery products, *FMBRA Bulletin No. 2*, CCFRA, Chipping Campden, UK, pp. 46–60.

Seiler, D.A.L., (1989) Modified atmosphere packaging of bakery products, in *Controlled/Modified Atmosphere/Vacuum Packaging of Foods* (ed. A.L. Brody), Food and Nutrition Press, Turnbull, USA, pp. 119–33.

Seiler, D.A.L., (1997) Bakery products, in *Principles and Applications of MAP of Foods*, 2nd edn (ed. B.A. Blackstone), Blackie Academic & Professional, London, UK, pp. 135–57.

Skovholt, O. & Bailey, C.H. (1933) Effect of carbon dioxide on mould growth on bread. *Cereal Chemistry*, **10**, 446–51.

Summers, L. (1992) *Intelligent Packaging*. Centre for Exploitation of Science and Technology, London, UK.

Troller, J.A. (1989) Water activity and food quality, in *Water and Food Quality* (ed. T.H. Hardman), Elsevier Applied Science, New York, USA, pp. 1–32.

Williams, A. & Pullen, G. (1998) Functional ingredients, in *Technology of Breadmaking* (eds S.P. Cauvain & L.S. Young), Blackie Academic & Professional, London, UK, pp. 45–80.

Index